THE PENGUIN BOOK OF AUSTRALIAN JOKES

collected by Phillip Adams and Patrice Newell

Phillip Adams is an odd assortment of people who write things, film things, say things on wireless and appear on television. All of whom share an anthropological fascination for jokes. The Adams' hobbies are levity and levitation.

Patrice Newell has been a model, a television researcher, a newsreader and a presenter of public affairs programs on both SBS and the Nine Network. She now raises politically correct beef on a large cattle property.

THE PENGUIN BOOK OF AUSTRALIAN JOKES

collected by Phillip Adams and Patrice Newell

Penguin Books

Penguin Books Australia Ltd
487 Maroondah Highway, P.O. Box 257
Ringwood, Victoria 3134, Australia
Penguin Books Ltd
Harmondsworth, Middlesex, England
Viking Penguin, A Division of Penguin Books USA Inc.
375 Hudson Street, New York, New York 10014, USA
Penguin Books Canada Limited
10 Alcorn Avenue, Toronto, Ontario, Canada M4V 3B2
Penguin Books (N.Z.) Ltd
Cnr Rosedale & Airborne Roads, Albany, Auckland, New Zealand

First published by Penguin Books Australia, 1994
25 24 23

Cover illustration by Ned Culic

Typeset in 12/14pt Bodoni by Midland Typesetters, Maryborough, Victoria 3465
Text design George Dale
Made and printed in Australia by Australian Print Group

National Library of Australia
Cataloguing-in-Publication data:

The Penguin book of Australian jokes.

Includes index.
ISBN 0 14 016888 5.

1. Australian wit and humour. I. Adams, Phillip, 1939- .
II. Newell, Patrice, 1956- . III. Title: Book of Australian jokes.

A828.02

Acknowledgements

The Editors wish to thank the countless citizens who submitted jokes for this collection. Whilst many were not included because they were too slanderous or obscene, the main reason for rejection was an utter lack of funniness, even when read aloud in a character voice. Other jokes were rejected because they were minor variations on a familiar theme.

CONTENTS

Have You Heard the One About . . . 1

Dad 'n Dave 'n the Bush 31

A Sense of Identity 63

Social Niceties 145

Out of the Mouths of Babes 163

Animal Crackers 181

A Sporting Chance 209

Politics and Power 233

The Law is an Ass 261

The Work Ethic 283

Food for Thought 303

The Demon Drink 317

Love, Marriage and the Sex War 327

The Body in Question 357

History and the Yarts 375

Travel Tales 393

Religiously Observed 403

A Medical Condition 427

Going, Going, Gone 449

And the Last Laugh . . . 468

Index 472

The stupidest book in the world is a book of jokes.
J.C. Holland, Everyday Topics, 1876

Have You Heard the One About . . .

Why do fish shoal? That's neither riddle nor joke but a serious question that, recently, a number of piscatorially correct academics sought to answer. While the overwhelming majority of fish shoal on a full or part-time basis, the reason remained mysterious. What is shoaling's social and/or evolutionary purpose? Are we witnessing a form of fishy fascism, wherein members of submarine communities are forced into conformity, or is the impulse more democratic?

When you think about it, the shoaling of little fish seems to offer larger fish or the professional fisherman an easier target. If fish were more solitary, you'd hardly be able to spot one in the immensities of the ocean. Thus their sticking together smacks of a suicidal form of self-advertisement.

So the academics went to work with a will, as is their wont, and discovered all sorts of interesting things. First of all, we're not dealing with demagoguery in the deep as there's no leader of the pack in a fish shoal. Any fish can take on the task, a bit like the 'king for the day' notion encouraged by Kleisthenes in the Athens of 508 BC. The only thing that's rigidly enforced is the *mathematics* of the shoal – the lattice-like format that defines it. It seems that fish have little sensors on their gills that facilitate their flying in formation, and that they're required to maintain an average distance apart over the course of a day. Thus sometimes they'll shoal a little closer, sometimes further apart. When you do the calculations, however, you'll find that there's been a mathematical maintenance of the status quo.

But why bother with formation flight, particularly when it produces a larger blip on the enemy's radar? Well, it turns out to be wonderfully simple. Yes, a shoal is more visible than a fish flying solo, but when attacked by something higher on the food chain – a shark or a seal – the lattice explodes outwards, as if responding to a central detonation. The effect on the predator is highly confusing. It's rather like having dinner at a posh restaurant and being presented with an over-large menu. Cobwebs form and moss grows on the waiter whilst he waits for you, the perplexed diner, to order.

The academics were triumphant when they observed that, again and again, a fish attacking an exploding shoal could be observed flailing around trying to grab this fish or that fish only to finish up missing out entirely.

The point of this aquatic detour is to emphasise that traits and foibles, as well as a creature's design, should make evolutionary sense, which, according to a wide variety of scientists, jokes don't. Our reading of the literature on humour reveals that for decades academics have been scratching their heads. What is the evolutionary purpose of smiling, of laughter? How do jokes help the survival of the species? To what extent is the selection of a joke a part of the process of natural selection?

The fact that scientists seem flummoxed is deeply encouraging. It's painfully obvious that scholars should be kept at arm's length from any manifestation of humour. God forbid that what semiotics has done to the cinema, what deconstruction has wreaked on the novel, should find a parallel in the realm of the joke, that most democratic form of creativity.

For a glimpse of the danger posed by academic inquiry, consider the following description of the physiological process of laughter by one Norbert Dearborn:

There occur in laughter and more or less in smiling, clonic spasm of the diaphragm, in number ordinarily about eighteen perhaps, and contraction of most of the muscles of the face. The upper eyelid is elevated, as are also, to some extent, the brows, the skin over the glabella, and the upper lip, while the skin at the outer canthi of the eyes is characteristically puckered. The nostrils are moderately dilated and drawn upwards, the tongue slightly extended, and the cheeks distended and drawn somewhat upward; in persons with the pinnal muscles largely developed, the pinnae tend to incline forwards. The lower jaw vibrates or is somewhat withdrawn (doubtless to afford all possible air to the distending lungs), and the head, in extreme laughter, is thrown backward; the trunk is straightened even to the beginning of bending backward, until (and this usually happens soon), fatigue-pain in the diaphragm and accessory abdominal muscles causes a marked proper flexion of the trunk for its relief. The whole arterial vascular system is dilated, with consequent blushing from the effect on the dermal capillaries of the face and neck, and at times the scalp and hands. From the same cause, in the main, the eyes often slightly bulge forwards and the lachrymal gland becomes active, ordinarily to a degree only to cause a 'brightening' of the eyes, but often to such an extent that the tears overflow entirely their proper channels.

Or take Charles Darwin's description of a smile, quilled more than a century ago:

By drawing backwards and upwards of the corners of the mouth, through the contraction of the great zygomatic muscles, and by the raising of the upper lip, the cheeks are drawn upwards. Wrinkles are thus formed under the eyes, and, with old people, at the outer ends. As in laughing and broadly smiling the cheeks and upper lip are much raised, the nose appears to be shortened, and the skin on the bridge becomes finely wrinkled in transverse lines, with other oblique longitudinal lines on the sides. The upper front teeth are commonly exposed. A well marked naso-labial ford is formed, which runs from the wing of each nostril to the corner of the mouth.

And here's another scientific observation, worthy of inclusion in a Python sketch:

Spontaneous laughter is a motor reflex produced by the co-ordinated contraction of 15 facial muscles in a stereotyped pattern and accompanied by altered breathing. Electrical stimulation of the main lifting muscle of the upper lip, the zygomatic major, with currents of varying intensity produces facial expressions ranging from the faint smile through the broad grin to the contractions typical of explosive laughter.

Ambrose Bierce is less wanton with his words in *The Devil's Dictionary:* Laughter, n. An interior convulsion producing a distortion of the features and accompanied by inarticulate noises.

Some of the most solemn explorations of the joke came from Sigmund Freud who didn't hesitate to explore it as he had the dream, seeking its relation to the unconscious:

Anyone who has at any time had occasion to enquire from the literature of aesthetics and psychology what light can be thrown on the nature of jokes and on the position they occupy will probably have to admit that jokes have not received nearly as much philosophical consideration as they deserve in view of the part they play in our mental life, he complained. He agreed with Kuno Fischer that *if what is ugly is concealed, it must be uncovered in the light of the comic way of looking at things: if it is noticed only a little or scarcely at all, it must be brought forward and made obvious, so that it lies clear and open to the light of day... in this way caricature comes about.*

Freud then proceeds to render a number of jokes as unfunny as possible by rigorous analysis. Even a simple two-liner like: A horse dealer was recommending a saddle-horse to a customer. 'If you take this horse and get on it at four in the morning you'll be at Pressburg by half past six.' 'What should I be doing in Pressburg at half past six in the morning?'

On re-reading the sainted Sigmund's deconstruction of that snippet of text, you can't help feeling that it's the analysis that's funny rather than the joke. Because as soon as you start thinking about the construction and purpose of a joke the humour evaporates. It's like confusing sexual intercourse with gynaecology or art with criticism. Because it must be remembered that among the many things that jokes mock is reason itself. Jokes are anathema to logic and, consequently, hostile to analysis.

Nonetheless let us persist in examining the matter scientifically. It's said that tranquillising endorphins are found in tears of grief. Could tears of laughter be similarly spiked to produce a natural high? There's much speculation that something of the sort is going on in Near Death Experiences, that the brain produces a narcotic to numb the terrors. Isn't it likely, therefore, that a few million years of evolution have provided something similar for the thousands of little NDEs that flesh is heir to, the profusion and confusion of alarms, anxieties and humiliations that are our lot?

The one aspect of humour on which there seems to be scholarly agreement involves how our children learn to smile and laugh. The consensus is that both originate as expressions of fear or fright. Thus laughter begins when a baby is shocked by something – such as being lifted aloft by a playful parent. Within a nano-second it discovers that it is not, after all, being threatened, that all is well, that it's going to survive. The lungful of air that was to provide a drawn-out scream is, instead, employed in an explosive release of tension. The scream becomes the laugh, just as the gasp becomes the chuckle. And the smile, which began as a grimace of terror, softens as panic passes.

(It's said that the scientist's purpose is to achieve synthesis, whereas the artist aims at a juxtaposition of the familiar and the eternal. The humorist's game is different – to contrive a collision. This has led to another observation on the actual sound of laughter that runs along these lines. The discoverer's 'Eureka!' cry is identified as the ah ha! reaction. The delight of the aesthetic experience becomes the aaah . . . reaction. Whereas laughter is described as the ha-ha reaction.)

There was a time when anthropologists felt that humans could be identified as human by their use of tools. Their observation of other creatures showed that chimps used rocks for hammers, sticks for spoons and boughs for levers. We've long favoured the notion that humans alone contemplate their own mortality. Our dread of death undergoes a wondrous alchemy and becomes humour, so that Rabelais can say: 'Laughter is what characterises man.' Humour, sharing its place in the dictionary with humiliation, humility and human, is essentially about horror. The gift of humour is the evolutionary mechanism that allows us to cope with the great practical joke of life, with all its essential tragedy.

Faced by the horrors that assail us on all sides, faced with the abyss of death, we have the choice of screaming or laughing. Sometimes we do both at once – hence terms like 'a scream of laughter'. Nonetheless humour remains our best defence mechanism against horror.

In early western physiology humour was one of the four fluids of the body that were thought to determine a person's temperament and features. In ancient physiology still current in the Middle Ages and later, the four cardinal humours were blood, phlegm, choler (yellow bile) and melancholy (black bile). The variant mixtures of these humours in different persons determined their 'complexions' or 'temperaments', their physical and mental qualities and their dispositions. By further extension humour in the sixteenth century came to denote usually an unbalanced mental condition, a mood of unreasonable caprice, or a fixed folly or vice.

Which is why the greatest humour is born in various forms of adversity. Thus the bleakest, most self-deprecating humour has been provided by the people described by Arthur Koestler as 'the exposed nerve ends of mankind'. Over the millennia, and certainly within the century of Holocaust, a completely disproportionate number of jokes, and of comedians to tell them, have come from the Jews.

In a sense, terms like Jewish humour, gallows humour and black humour should be contradictions in terms. But as laughter begins as an abbreviation of fear, humour grows as an attempt to deal with the dread of despair.

Having fought its losing battle with death, humour mounts many a quixotic campaign against oppression, dispossession and fear. Humour gives the powerless a tiny bit of power over those who tyrannise them. Though the best jokes thumb their noses at the cosmos, many of the better ones are aimed at the authority figures, the pompous, the bigots. But first and foremost jokes are used to ward off the Grim Reaper like the crucifix does Dracula. Case in point, Woody Allen, who, not content with being Jewish, nurtures a deep fear of his own mortality, and everyone else's. Allen returns to the theme over and over again, as in: 'More than any other time in history, mankind faces a crossroad. One path leads to despair and hopelessness. The other, to total extinction. Let us pray we have the wisdom to choose correctly.' And less amusingly: 'Life is a concentration camp. You're stuck here and there's no way out and you can only rage impotently against your persecutors.'

Everything dies but only humans seem painfully aware of it. Death follows us around like Captain Hook's crocodile, the alarm clock ticking in its tummy. Death casts its dark shadow over every aspect of human life and in an attempt to cope with it, to deny it, even to defeat it, we've invented religions, philosophy, science and medicine. Nonetheless we still die and it remains a lonely and terrifying business. Our sense of humour allows us to blow a raspberry at the fates, to defy the nemesis we cannot escape.

Many people who've been revived after clinical death describe the Near Death Experience or NDE, involving coming into contact with a 'light of transcendental love'. Whilst Tony Staley remembers dying as a highly pleasurable, almost orgasmic experience, other friends who've died and returned – Robyn Williams and Kerry Packer – describe no loving luminosity. Both glumly report that they 'just died'. Game, set and match. Subsequently they've preferred to deal with their terminal dramas with irony and humour, the antidote that evolution has made available to all of us, irrespective of religious belief.

Perhaps that's why religions are, by and large, so humourless. 'The secret source of humour is not joy but sorrow,' wrote Mark Twain. 'There is no humour in heaven.'

Jules Renard agreed. 'We are in the world to laugh. In Purgatory or in Hell we shall no longer be able to do so. And in Heaven it would not be proper.'

Then there's that ingenious Italian novel, *The Name of the Rose*, wherein Umberto Eco faithfully explored the fundamental threat that humour poses to religious hierarchies. Interestingly the Old Testament contains twenty-five references to laughter, out of which thirteen are linked with scorn, derision, mocking and contempt. Only two usages relate laughter to joy.

Not only does humour subvert dogma and religious certainty but, of course, religion is in direct competition with humour as a method of ameliorating mortality's bleak implications. There is an implicit acknowledgement in humour that, finally, we're all stuffed, whereas religion tries to persuade us that life isn't meaningless and, against all the evidence, that we're cherished and protected by a deity who will allow us to survive death to rise from our graves like so many missiles from their silos. To allow people the pleasure of laughter would be to offer them another method of dealing with the darkness. And humour's method is devoid of much in the way of prohibition or dogma or ritual, and tries its best to defeat guilt.

Moreover one suspects that religion is incultured whereas humour is innate, that it is as primitive a response to the essential tragedy of life as a child's first chuckle of relief to a more immediate threat.

If it is true, as it seems to be, that we are the only creatures who apprehend our own extinction, then humour is the first line of defence. While it might fight a losing battle with the immensity of mortal dread, it never stops trying. The whole notion of absurdity, so fashionable in this century, and dazzlingly refined by the likes of Ionesco and Spike Milligan, involves using humour to protect us from cosmic gloom and general ghastliness. Humour, much more than religion, is the opium of the people.

Of course, increasingly, opium is the opium of the people. People take a wide range of recreational narcotics to dull the pain. Humour, nonetheless, remains as useful as Valium and Dettol for dealing with life's little problems, as well as the big ones. For on every level, from the macro to the micro, the joke begins with the things we do not find funny at all. It begins with the things that trouble us, disgust us, appal us.

At their best, jokes wound and heal in the same instant, just as they indict and pardon, diminish and enlarge. Whatever its origin, it is with the absurdity of the joke that we get through the larger absurdity of life.

Which is why jokes, in any quantity, are such depressing things. Please extend your sympathies to the humble editors of this compilation for we have been exposed to the most unimaginable misery and unpleasantness. A joke in isolation may be 'a thing of beauty and a joy forever'. Jokes in bulk, however, jokes in bulging mailbags, are appalling. Almost without exception they deal in bigotry, sexism, racism, ageism and all the other politically incorrect isms. They clearly help people deal with their deep distaste for their own sexuality, their excremental functions, their foreign neighbours, their political masters and an infinite variety of things that go bump in the night. Jokes are to self-hatred what hypocrisy is to salacity, what guilt is to desire. Indeed, apart from jokes involving innocent plays on words, almost every genre is fundamentally an act of verbal aggression against a fear or an enemy, be it defiantly targeted or dimly perceived.

A couple of years ago, this book would have been full of dingo jokes as people dealt with the Lindy Chamberlain case as worst they could. One typical example: They've reopened the Harold Holt case and are looking for a dingo with flippers. Here was a story blending many elemental and mythic ingredients: our suspicion of other people's religions, our fear of Australia's brooding hinterland, ancient notions of 'sacrifice in the desert' and the vengeance of animals on the humans who butcher them. Here were misogyny, allegations of murder, hints of Aboriginal mythology, blurred notions of guilt and innocence. So the slanderous jokes proliferated, as ugly and numerous as cane toads. Here we saw an entire nation trying to deal with its demons. The dingo genre of jokes has now disappeared, although the prejudices that gave it birth seem not only to endure but to intensify.

You can see some of it in the jokes [sic] about Aborigines. Almost without exception they're quintessential expressions of the hostility that accrues to blacks in our cities and country towns. They're included because it is important to understand what mainstream Australia regards as funny in the 1990s. To censor them would be to entirely distort the collection. We'd hoped to offset them with jokes told by Aborigines about white people, but found these elusive. Energetic attempts to track down examples utterly failed. But then, there's a distinction between jokes and humour and while Aboriginal communities have a sense of humour reminiscent of Jewish communities – and for much the same reason – these are not encoded in the form of the joke.

We discussed this at length with Kooris and Nugget Coombs who talked happily about the playfulness and humour he'd observed in Aboriginal life. However, structured jokes, with beginnings, middles and ends, seem to belong to our cultural convention, not to theirs.

In a final, desperate attempt to find Aboriginal jokes aimed at the white community, to balance the fairly repulsive Aboriginal jokes that are essentially anti-Aboriginal, we made an appeal on national television. The result was some hundreds of letters containing the same piece of verbal kitsch.

From black fellah to white fellah.
Dear white fellah,
Coupla tings you orta no.
Firstly
Wen I am born, I'm black.
Wen I grow up, I'm black.
Wen I get sick, I'm black.
Wen I go out in a sun, I'm black.
Wen I'm cold, I'm black.
And wen I get scared, yes, I'm black.
And wen I die, I'm still black.

But you white fellah.
Wen you born, you pink.
Wen you grow up, you white.
Wen you get sick, you green.
Wen you go out in a sun, you go red.
Wen you get cold, you go blue.
Wen you get scared, you yellow.
And wen you die, you purple.

And you got the cheek to call *me* coloured.

Hundreds of correspondents insisted that this was an authentic, 'ethnic' Aboriginal joke, some even providing spurious anthropological evidence for its authenticity, as if it were a verbal counterpart to an ancient cave painting.

Incidentally, many of the first anti-Aboriginal jokes in Australia were told by blacks. By African Americans. At the end of the Civil War, freed slaves tried to set up companies to compete with the white man's Black and White Minstrel Shows. Why shouldn't they sing their own Negro spirituals or perform the Stephen Foster medleys? Ironically it became necessary for them to copy the white man's make-up – so the blacks appeared on stage wearing the cosmetic masks of 'black face' whites. However, their intrusion on a highly successful business wasn't welcomed, and white entrepreneurs ran them out of town – and some of them ran straight to Australia where they began entertaining the citizens of Melbourne, Sydney and the goldfields. The productions were enormous and energetic, so much so that they soon drove the

English music hall entertainment to the wall. It seems that the Negro entertainers were not subjected to much in the way of prejudice, that they were both welcomed and admired. But to separate themselves from the Aborigines, they didn't hesitate to tell anti-Aboriginal jokes about 'the loobras at La Perouse'. It's a story explained in fascinating detail by Richard Waterhouse in *From Minstrel Show to Vaudeville: the Australian Popular Stage 1788 to 1914* (published by the New South Wales University Press in 1990) and marks the beginning of American influence, and finally domination of Australian popular culture.

Anti-Aboriginal jokes have been included to demonstrate a sorry truth to the reader. Namely, that we laugh at these jokes, albeit guiltily. We may strive for proper attitudes, to shun prejudice, to atone for sins of the past yet, despite our best intentions, we continue to laugh at jokes that embody old hostilities. If anything, our laughter may be intensified by our sense of shock and shame that we're laughing at all.

Increasingly, racial vilification legislation will prevent the publication of broadcasting of this sort of material, but that will not stop their informal circulation as long as people find them funny or therapeutic, even if they're simultaneously apologising for their laughter. 'I know we shouldn't laugh but . . .'

As such, jokes about racial or sexual relationships are the most honest of indicators about what we are really feeling. The opinions we express to pollsters may be muted, modified or cautious. Jokes are far more self-revelatory.

Of course the jokes of bigots can be turned against them. Or the powerless can seek protection from rampaging infections of bigotry by inoculating themselves with self-deprecating jokes. Thus Jewish jokes are not a lot different from anti-Jewish jokes. Indeed a good Jewish joke can become an anti-Semitic joke simply by being told by the wrong person. Finally it's not what the joke says but what it means that makes the difference. There are comics in Australia – like those associated with 'Wogs Out of Work' and 'Acropolis Now' – who'd argue that jokes of racial vilification are redeemed simply by the victims becoming the performers. You tell the joke against us, it's an insult. We tell the joke about us, it's okay. Similarly there are stand-up (or, more correctly, wobble-up) comics who, being disabled themselves, can get away with jokes about disability.

It's an interesting argument, but not entirely convincing. The unreconstructed bigot is unlikely to be won over. Impervious to the subtlety of the shift, the bigots laugh on, which leads to growing pressure, and well-meaning regulations, to censor jokes about/against a growing list of minority groups. Apart from the impracticality of the undertaking, many of us regard the censorship of jokes as entirely counter-productive. It may well prove to be a cure that is worse than the disease. As if 'political correctness' wasn't a sufficient downer, humour becomes a target of regulation in an era when deregulation is the driving force in public policy. Moreover the queue of pressure groups demanding protection now stretches round the block.

Recently, in America, a well-dressed man pulled a machine-gun from his attaché case and massacred a large group of lawyers. Within hours the head of the California Bar Association was trying to have anti-lawyer jokes outlawed, arguing that they'd led to widespread anti-lawyer feelings throughout the United States and, by implication, to the massacre. Fortunately other lawyers laughed him out of court.

This is not to say that there isn't a link between the unpleasant joke and the unpleasant social outcome. Good intentions may or may not pave the way to hell but anti-Semitic jokes certainly provided the mortar for the bricks of the crematoria.

Yes, there's a problem here. Many of the jokes in this book are entirely repulsive. But to deny their existence would be, in the long run, as hopeless an exercise as, for example, Tito's attempts to 'deep freeze' hatreds in the Balkans. Bottled up, resentments intensify rather than dissipate. Finally, down the track, they erupt.

Perhaps it's better to do what Richard Glover, a journalist with the *Sydney Morning Herald*, does – to invent a genre of anti-bigot jokes (some of the jokes he has created are printed on pages 141–4 and 273–5). Censorship solves nothing. The underlying human fear of difference, in all its manifestations, is unlikely to disappear. Certainly the way we use jokes makes a mockery of the famous utterance of G.K. Chesterton that Malcolm Muggeridge once told us. 'When you've got hold of a vulgar joke, you may be certain you've got hold of a subtle and spiritual idea.' It sounds marvellous, but we've never been able to imagine what it was G.K. was on about. Was it, perhaps, a joke?

This experience makes you suspect that, finally, the joke is a cultural artifact. There isn't much evidence of 'jokes' as such in previous centuries. Oh, there's word play galore and all sorts of funny stories. Yet the essential character of the joke, as distinct from the anecdote or exaggerated yarn or verbal stream from a stand-up comic, lies in its distinctive structure of set-up and punchline. And this seems very much of our time and space. We have a collection of antiquities containing ancient Islamic tiles in which talk balloons, almost identical to those employed in modern comics, are depicted emerging from the ceramic mouths of human beings. Nonetheless the joke seems as contemporary in form as the three-panel newspaper comic.

An anthropologist made an exhaustive study of the Kalahari bushmen of South West Africa.

On the way home we saw and shot a springbok, as there was no meat left in the camp. The bullet hit the springbok in the stomach and partly eviscerated him, causing him to jump and kick before he finally died. The bushmen thought this was terribly funny, and they laughed, slapping their thighs and kicking their heels to imitate the springbok, showing no pity at all, but then they regard animals with great detachment. (Elizabeth Marshall Thomas, *The Harmless People*, Knopf, New York, 1959.)

This was seen as evidence of 'pre-historic' humour, disapprovingly so. Yet the same detachment, the same enjoyment of cruelty, can be seen in white jokes about Aborigines, or about any of the other racial victims you'll find in this book. Everything is funny as long as it happens to somebody or something else.

Whilst professional comedians used to tell jokes – with beginnings, middles and ends – the stand-up comics of today tend to bombard the audience with various forms of verbal aggression. The humour derives from the same sources as the structured joke, exploiting the same ingredients of sexuality, bigotry and absurdity. The form, however, is essentially different, more flowing, less formal. Just as 'Monty Python' and 'Fast Forward' both decided to dump the punchline in their sketches (apart from any other consideration, they're so hard to write) the stand-up comic tends to leave joke-telling to the amateurs. In a sense, the joke is impersonal and authorless, something that is passed from person to person in a social ritual, whereas the stand-up comic likes to pretend that his or her material comes directly from his or her experience, and the delivery involves momentum and escalation rather than the old style 'Did you hear the one about . . . '

(Incidentally, we must remember that stand-up comics are so intensely aware of mortality that their jargon invariably reflects it. 'I killed them,' they say in triumph, after a good gig. Or, alternatively, 'I died.')

There was a time when the joke seemed to be the main mode of humorous transmission. Not any more. Television sitcoms, comedy shows like 'Full Frontal' and the D-Gen's 'Late Show' and the aggressive soliloquys of the likes of Wendy Harmer make little use of jokes as such. Just as other forms of narrative are less and less reliant on traditional plot, humour seems less reliant on the mini plots of jokes which have an increasingly traditional, even anachronistic look in a post-modernist era. Perhaps the use and distribution of jokes, previously told in groups or printed in magazines, will be replaced by these new modes in these comparatively new media.

We've certainly found much evidence of computers being used as modes of transport for the joke while one of the few known cases where the authorship of a joke was unequivocally demonstrated involves computer networking. Within a few hours of the Challenger tragedy, people around America were saying that NASA stood for 'Need Another Seven Astronauts'. (A journalist, determined to trace the new meaning of NASA, that acrimonious acronym, worked his way back through the umpteen computer contacts. Finally he found a bloke who happily confessed. And he was exhilarated to discover that his little joke had gone around the United States and the world within a few hours.)

This brings us to the question of a joke's Australianness. Sadly it must be reported that there seem to be very few genuinely Australian jokes. Even the aforementioned anti-Aboriginal jokes derive from jokes told against African Americans or Native Americans which are reworked for local conditions and consumption. This is emphatically true in the case of political jokes. Again and again what seemed to be an authentic local joke concerning, for example, former New South Wales Premier Nick Greiner, would be revealed as having originated as a Margaret Thatcher joke. But perhaps it wasn't 'originally' a Margaret Thatcher joke at all but one of more ancient origin, repeatedly recycled.

For example, the most common political jokes these days are aimed at Paul Keating. Some of the most vehement turn out to be recycled anti-Hitler jokes told in Munich clubs in the 1930s, specifically by two courageous comedians who ended up in Dachau. Over the years people have replaced Hitler's name with the name of whichever politician they sought to demonise.

One of Australia's most famous jokes in recent years – told by Andrew Denton – concerns a woman's desire to perform oral sex on David Hill in an ABC lift. The story earned Denton a considerable amount of notoriety at the time but turned out to have been recycled from a New York joke concerning Donald Trump. What is interesting about the joke is that Trump and Hill are seen as similar in personality, in vanity. If the joke fits, wear it. As Finley Peter Dunne observed in 1901: 'Th' las' man that makes a joke owns it.'

You can observe similar recycling in jokes that seek to decry the intellectual limitations of this or that race or group. Thus jokes told about the allegedly dim-witted Irish are all but identical to jokes told about Poles, many of which, with modification, are then targeted at blondes. Writers of novels, plays and feature films tell us that there are only about a dozen basic plots which are endlessly rejigged and reused – American writers of top television dramas have told us how script editors have asked them to 'Lear-up' an episode, or have required yet another variation on the Romeo and Juliet theme. If that is true of drama it seems trebly, painfully true of jokes.

Classic Irish jokes are frequently retold as indigenous Dad 'n Dave jokes. Moreover, no two people tell the same joke exactly the same way, so that you get a spectrum of stories based on the same core joke, with variations on names, places and punchline.

Our book contains a great many jokes that were collected at considerable personal risk by editors whose senses of humour may never recover. We have not attempted to censor the stories. To soften the words, to mute the essential nastiness would have been to mislead the reader, and to confuse the archaeologists who will try to make sense of this text in a thousand years' time. Virtually the only jokes that have been eliminated are those entirely dependent on quality of performance, involving vocal devices for which there are no typographic equivalents. Moreover, most of the jokes have been reprinted in much the form we heard them or received them, in the hope of preserving something of their spirit. So spare us pedantic letters complaining about syntax and the splitting of infinitives.

Virginia Woolf observed that humour is the first of the gifts to perish in a foreign tongue. Jokes, verbal devices in their essence, a part of oral culture, don't necessarily survive translation to the page. Believe it or not, some of the jokes you'll read in this book were once very funny indeed. But it was in the telling. In the facial expression, the gesture, the quality of performance. We can only hope that some of the better jokes that lie flat on the Penguin's pages are destined to be recycled and revived by talented joke tellers.

Nonetheless we confess, we emphasise that, at the end of the day, this collection of jokes is not particularly Australian. This is not the collection that would have been gathered twenty or thirty years ago when the idiom had been less subjected to the bombardment of global media. There may still be jokes of local origin but they would be all but impossible to identify. We must accept that, overwhelmingly, jokes are a global, floating currency subject to instant conversion. Finally the definition of 'jokes currently circulating in Australia'. What follows are the most often told jokes of recent vintage. Thus the joke of 'Pierre, the bridge builder' was recently transmogrified into 'Spiro, the boat builder', an inevitable outcome given the comparative populations of French and Greek migrants.

Yet if the hypothesis about humour holds – that it's strengthened by adversity – then Australians should have at least a great sense of irony. And jokes aside, examples abound of a highly advanced sense of the absurd. When life plays such immense practical jokes as afflicting you with drought, followed by fire which is immediately drenched by flood, you have to be laconic to survive.

So there's Ned Kelly, standing on the gallows, the noose around his neck, the knot being tightened at his ear by a bureaucratic butcher. And what does he say? What are his last words as the trapdoor opens? 'Such is life.'

Those words should be the motto on our coat of arms, emblazoned on the shield between those big-bummed, small-brained creatures that so eloquently signify Australia: the kangaroo and the emu.

Perhaps we should replace the animals with the heraldic device of that famous *Bulletin* cartoon showing a couple of builders' labourers dangling over an abyss. One clings to a girder, the other to his mate's trousers which are slowly slipping from his hips. 'Stop laughing,' says one to the other, 'this is serious.'

It's a toss up which of those two contributions would be the most apt. But both of them celebrate something about our national character that we'd like to believe in. We escape the gravitational pull of disaster – whether tumbling from a girder or falling through the gallows' trapdoor – by being flippant, courageous. Our humour, at its best, meets the definition of death defiance.

If this was a collection of Australian cartoons, it would be easy to present hundreds of marvellous examples of the laconic, the tough, the ironic, the magnificently bleak. Ever since the *Bulletin* days, the era of Bruce Petty and Mike Leunig, Australia's black and white artists have been as tough in their commentary as Samuel Beckett in Godot. But in the spoken or written joke, we are less original, less distinctive.

Yet there's one that has some of the ingredients. It is politically incorrect and distinctly chauvinist. Yet in its austerity, brevity and basic decency it speaks of an ethos that links us to the time of Lawson.

A couple of farmers with neighbouring properties were working together repairing a buggered fence. One says to the other: 'I reckon I might have a bit of a problem now the shearin's done. Head down to Synny.'

'Yeah? I hear Synny's pretty interesting. What route will you take?'

'Oh, I reckon I'll take the missus. After all she stuck by me through the drought.'

Few and far between, like gum trees on the Hay plain. But memorable in their ruggedness, a handful of such jokes survive. For the rest, they are the world's jokes, dressed up in Akubras and Drizabones.

The only serious, academic attempt to analyse Australian humour that we can identify is a contribution to *National Styles of Humour*, edited by someone with the jokey name of Avner Ziv and published by Greenwood in New York in 1988 as a part of a series on the study of popular culture. Heading essays on humour in Belgium, France, Great Britain, Israel, Italy, the United States and what used to be Yugoslavia, Hyram Davies and Peter Crofts (the former an actor and writer, the latter a stand-up comedian) tell the world about everything from *Coles Funny Picture Book* to Steele

Rudd. They cover humour in Australian film, radio, television, theatre and the visual arts and provide a comprehensive bibliography from Afferback Lauder to A.J. Wilkes' *Dictionary of Australian Colloquialisms*. But though their wide net captures everyone from Roy Rene to Barry Humphries, from Wally and the Major to Norman Gunston, their essay is more an inventory than an explanation.

It's a Who's Who and What's What of Australian humour, embracing Lawson, Banjo Paterson, Norman Lindsay, George Wallace, Ed Dyson, C.J. Dennis, John O'Grady, Stan Cross, Pat Oliphant, Bill Wannan and Ross Campbell. 'Mavis Bramston' and 'The Aunty Jack Show' are explained to scholars of humour around the world. But a definition, a differentiation of Australian humour remains elusive.

But that's not to say they don't try very hard, restating our mythology of mirth. There's talk about our 'tortured beginnings' and they argue that

the whole tradition of humour was spawned in those first fledgling years. Apart from a small birth of ethnic influence, it is the same sardonic irreverence and lack of respect for authority which characterises the mainstream of indigenous humour to this day ... The underdog battling to survive in a hostile environment, and the realisation that things are so lousy that you can only laugh, that you can't win, is a constant text in Australian humour. The harsh and mysterious land, with its inhabitants of convicts and free settlers and law and judiciary, soon imprinted its character on the people. The

Cockney twang and soft lilt of Ireland and gentle vowels of English counties and Scottish inflections, all flattened together and became the laconic Australian accent ... The ribald aggressiveness of the humour finds expression in the mateship of segregation and does not include women in its aura.

They describe the Australian pub as

the home of the country's true-blue, dinky-di humourous expression ... without the tradition of many touring professional shows, no repertory or provisional theatre, the pub became the stage for many amateur comedians, practical jokers, and raconteurs, locally known as wits, wags, and whackers. They would spin one another yarns, tell traditional stories and tall tales about tricksters, heroes, and hoaxsters, all the time holding their small territory around a hotel bar in an ambience of mateship, eulogised in Australia as perhaps the single most important virtue that the Australian male can possess.

The Australian joke is very much like those told by Australians in pubs: always masculine, at times cruel, uncouth, disrespectful, and often racist. Australians rarely came into contact with the butt of their jokes, so there was little of the strident venom of the true racist; and more often than not, the jokes were dirty and quite often directed at themselves.

Fair enough. But the sad truth remains that very, very few jokes are pristine in their ocker ethnicity. Show us an Australian joke and we'll show you an

English, an American or a German joke that has been on a long journey. Thus the 'what route are you taking?' yarn may well have had its origins elsewhere, where the culture allows route and root to be confused.

This collection also excludes the exaggerated yarns beloved of the late Frank Hardy. All but endless anecdotes whose Australianness teeters between the triumphant and the tedious are still being told around the country – indeed some communities organise competitions and Yarn Fests. But a few examples would all but have filled this volume. Also judged to be outside our terms of reference were political anecdotes which arrived in their hundreds from MPs in every State and Territory. There were enough Whitlam stories alone – both true and apocryphal – to justify a separate volume. But anecdotes are no more 'jokes' than yarns.

There may have been a time when the Australian joke, evolving in isolation, produced something of distinct comicality, analogous to the oddity of the kangaroo or platypus. But it's a long time since cultural influences arrived by sail, blown by the trade winds. Now jokes blow in on electronic winds, at the speed of light, though their internal circulation is achieved by more traditional means. The pub, however, is losing its cultural dominance and flesh and blood friendships are replaced by cathode substitutes. The dynamics of suburbia have been extensively modified, with neighbours replaced by 'Neighbours'. Our researches indicate that, these days, jokes are as likely to be communicated by fax (we received any number of Faxyarns from a service of that name) or by computer, just as the traditional 'rubbing' of rice paper and charcoal has been replaced by people putting their bums on photocopiers.

Similarly, the rich world of Australian colloquialism lives on in the works of Bill Wannan, is parodied in the glossaries of Barry Humphries and is preserved in the Macquarie Dictionary. But unless you have a copy of Lenny Lower or C.J. Dennis or Steele Rudd you'll find the words are being replaced by international jargon. Thus drongo is rarely heard. Dickhead prevails. The words like battler and wowser that gave the language such potency are now anachronisms, while phrases like 'not much chop' and 'she'll be right' seem doomed to die. Whilst there was a neo-classic period following the film version of Barry Humphries, '*The Adventures of Barry McKenzie*', it's important to recognise that many of McKenzie's colloquial efforts were pastiche. Yet people around Australia and the world started 'pointing Percy at the porcelain' or equating dryness with 'a dead dingo's donger'.

As the global culture intensifies, as the all-at-onceness of electronic communication triumphs over separate cultures, perhaps there'll be a last stand. Perhaps a few Australians, like Ned at Glenrowan, will plate themselves in thick idiom and blaze away at the cultural imperialists. Even so, such heroic figures are doomed to fall in the dust, as cultures hybridise.

DAD 'N DAVE 'N THE BUSH

31

The Australian hayseeds, Dad 'n Dave, first appeared as characters in *On Our Selection* by Steele Rudd. The Rudd stories were turned into films by the veteran Australian director, Ken Hall, with a very young Peter Finch playing Dave. The sexual escapades of Dave and Mabel have been a staple of Australian humour ever since, with most jokes focusing on the two innocents dealing with the wickedness of the big city. A familiar theme in Australian popular culture, it was recently recycled for the *Crocodile Dundee* films.

Dad and Dave were standing watching a dingo licking its privates. Dave said to Dad, 'Just between you and me, I wanted to do that all my life.'

Dad said, 'Go ahead, but I'd pat him a bit first. He looks pretty vicious to me.'

Dave was going to marry Mabel, so he went down to Melbourne to book a room for the wedding night. He found a pub he liked, in he went, in high spirits, very jaunty. 'Gidday. I'd like to book a room for me honeymoon night, luv.'

'Yes,' said the female receptionist, 'bridal suite?'

'Ahh, no thanks dear, I'll just hang onto her ears.'

Dave returned to Snake Gully after a brief trip to Europe. Dad said, 'Reckon you saw a lot of mighty fine things in that Europe.'

'Sure did, Dad. Cathedrals, palaces, mansions. But what impressed me most were the dunnies. They sure have got terrific dunnies. And they all flush.'

'Well, son,' said Dad, 'reckon you ought to build yourself one of those posh dunnies. But you'll have to get rid of the old shithouse first.'

'Nothing to it, Dad.' Dave took out a hand grenade that he happened to have on him, pulled out the pin and threw it at the shithouse.

Dad's a slow thinker and a slow mover. After a while he said, 'I don't reckon you should have done that, son.'

Out of the debris staggered Mum. She lurched up to Dad and said, 'Reckon it must have been something I ate.'

Mum sends Dave off to the market to buy a few things and Mabel tags along, as usual. After investing in a new bucket, a straw broom, a couple of live chickens and a poddy calf, Dave is struggling home, with the calf baulking and the chickens flapping and the bucket clanking – all in different directions. As they pass through a bit of bush Mabel says, 'Aw gee, Dave, I'm scared!'

Dave yanks the calf and recovers a chicken and says, 'Yeah! What of, Mabel?'

'Aw gee, you might take advantage of me in this lonely bush!' says Mabel.

'Come off it, Mabel,' says Dave, grabbing the bucket. 'Look how busy I am with this lot!'

Quick as a flash, Mabel says, 'But couldn't you put the chickens down on the ground with the bucket on top of them, and push the broom into the ground and tie the calf to it?'

Dave rode back from the Melbourne Show with a jar of liquid. Dad was curious to know what the sideshow shysters had sold Dave this time, and followed him to the old cow shed, whereupon Dave pulled a worm out of the cowyard's mud and dipped it into the little jar. Immediately the worm became rigid. Dave then used it as a nail to fix a wobbly weatherboard on the shed.

That arvo, Dad said to Dave, 'How much was that concoction?'

Dave replied, '$10 for 100 mls.'

Dad said, 'If you get me a litre of it, I'll buy you a new Porsche.'

So Dave raced off to Melbourne on his horse and returned two days later with the litre pack. He spent the next day fixing fences in the bottom paddock. When he got back to the homestead, Dad was taking it easy on the verandah, alongside of which was a nice new sporty Mazda. 'D'ya like the car, Dave?' Dad asked.

Dave exploded with rage. 'You old coot! You promised me a Porsche!'

'I did, I did,' said Dad. 'It's in the garage. The Mazda's a present from Mum!'

Dad and Dave go to town but, because of their divergent interests, decide to take separate cars. So Dad takes the Holden ute and Dave takes the Falcon. They arrange to meet in a fortnight's time at a pub near Centennial Park that they remember from the Royal Show.

When Dad turns up, he's really pissed off. 'I'm glad we're going back home. I couldn't park anywhere without some bastard giving me a ticket.'

To which Dave replies, 'You think you had troubles! I parked the Falcon outside a Catholic church and the bastards raffled it!'

When Dave goes to Ashton's Circus, he sees an elephant for the first time. A spieler exploits his innocence and sells him a pair of coconuts as elephants' eggs. 'Think of all the work elephants could do around your farm,' he's told. 'But you'll have to hatch them by taking them to bed for a week.'

Mabel wonders why Dave is spending so much time in bed. He explains that he's incubating the elephant eggs. She puts her hand under the blankets and feels Dave's genitalia. 'Ugghh . . .' she says, pulling her hand out quickly. 'It's gruesome.'

Dave says, 'Mabel, you'd better put yer 'and back . . . it's grew some more.'

Mum is working in the kitchen when Dad enters with his first erection in years. 'Mum . . . get into bed,' he says. She takes off her apron, puts all the ingredients and utensils away, washes her hands, gets into bed . . . but too late. Dad has withered away.

'Ya know . . . we can't 'ave this 'appen agin,' says Dad. 'Next time I git one of these, I'll ring the firebell so you start gittin' ready when youse hears it. When I git to the house, we'll be right.'

A year goes by. Mum's in the kitchen. She hears the firebell. She goes through all the preparations. Dad comes pounding into the house, through the kitchen, into the bedroom where Mum lies waiting for him. He looks at her and says, 'Get up, yer oversexed fool . . . the barn's on fire!'

Dad and Dave are in Paris, walking down the Champs Élysées. They are intrigued by the most beautiful marble building. There's absolutely nothing like it back in Snake Gully. What could it be? They decide to go inside and ask. They discover an extremely courteous Frenchwoman sitting at a Louis XV desk.

'*Messieurs*, is there anything I can do for you?' she enquires.

Dave leers at her and says, 'How about a blonde?'

'*Mais oui*,' says the Mademoiselle. 'Go up to the *cinquième* floor, room *vingt-six*.'

Dave goes up and finds a beautiful blonde lying sprawled over an elegant divan. There is an energetic cultural exchange. He retreats to the marble foyer and asks the Mademoiselle if there's a bill.

'*Mais* no, *monsieur*. This is *pour vous*,' and she hands him 500 francs. Dad is astonished. He decides to try his luck. As he's in the process of lighting his pipe with a box of Australian matches, he asks for a redhead.

'*Mais oui, monsieur*. Go to room *trois* on the *huitième* floor.'

He does so and, lo and behold, there's a redhead straight from a Degas painting. They have truck.

Dad returns to the foyer, slightly wobbly on his legs. Like Dave, he asks for the bill but once again, the Mademoiselle insists on giving him some francs. This time it's an even thicker wad – 5000. Dad puts the money in his pocket and says to the Mademoiselle, 'Look, I don't like to grizzle, but my son didn't get as much of this Frog money as me.'

To which the Mademoiselle replies, 'But he was only on the local Parisienne news, whereas you, *mon cher monsieur*, were seen over the entire network.'

'Dad, there's a new pub in Snake Gully. And for a dollar you get one of those new light beers, then they take you out the back and you get a root.'

'Really,' says Dad, 'are you sure about this, Dave?'

'Yep.'

'Have you been in there?'

'No, Dad, but Mabel has.'

Dad and Dave, having made some money with booming wool prices, decided to spend a bit of the proceeds down in the Big Smoke. They booked into their hotel, a commodious Edwardian pile not far from the CBD. They repaired to the saloon bar for a couple of jugs but continued their wassail well into the evening. Finally they retired to their room with its huge four-poster. Soon snores filled the room. Suddenly Dad woke up, shook his recumbent son and shouted, 'Dave, I'm as thirsty as buggery. Nip down to the bathroom and bring me back a glass of water.'

Dave did as he was bidden and came back with a brimming tumbler. Dad gulped it in one swallow and said, 'That's better – now for a bit more shut-eye.'

After half an hour he woke again and made the same request of Dave. And the procedure was repeated over and over again. But on the last occasion Dave returned without the water.

'Where's me drink, son?'

'Gee Dad, I'm sorry,' Dave replied, 'but when I went down to the bathroom, I couldn't get any. Some silly bastard was sitting on the well.'

During the rural recession, Dave got a job working a signal post on the Cairns to Townsville line. After a couple of weeks, there was a spot inspection by the local boss. 'What would you do if you had two trains coming at each other on the same line?'

Dave replied, 'I'd put all the lights on red and stop them.'

'Your lights are out of action,' says the inspector, 'what now?'

'I'd fire the flares,' said Dave.

'They're damp and won't work,' snarls the inspector, 'and by this time the trains are really close.'

'Well,' says Dave, 'as a last resort I'd go and get Mabel.'

'What could she do?' growls the inspector.

'Nothing,' replies Dave, 'but she's never seen a train crash before.'

Dad and Dave were watching a documentary on television, showing a rabbit plague in Victoria. The narrator explained that rabbits had been introduced to Australia by an Englishman. He'd imported four or five pairs for his favourite sport of shooting.

Looking at all the millions of bunnies hopping around, Dave said, 'He must have been a crook shot.'

Because he and Mabel were going to live with Dad and Mum when they got married, Dave wanted Dad to build a new dunny to replace the existing dilapidated one. Dad resisted the idea strongly.

'It's been good enough for Mum and me for all these years, so it's good enough for you and Mabel.'

Dave was determined, so he fitted a fuse and a cap to a plug of gelignite, dropped it into the dunny and retreated behind a stump to watch. He had just made it to the stump, when Dad came out of the kitchen and headed for the dunny. He rushed from behind the stump and yelled at Dad to save him from a disaster. But Dad thought he was trying to beat him to the dunny and put his head down and ran faster.

'You young blokes ain't as good as yer think you are,' he yelled. Dad got there first and had barely entered the building, when up it went. Ka-boom. Dave rushed to Dad's aid and extricated him from the wreckage.

'Are you all right, Dad?' he asked.

'I'm all right son, but stone the crows yer mother would have been annoyed if I'd let that one go in the kitchen.'

Dave and Mabel were out walking along the river bank one Sunday afternoon when they came across Herb Wilson sitting by a large tree with a fishing line in the river.

'Are yer catchin' any?' asked Dave.

'Just a few,' said Herb.

'How big?'

'Just tiddlers,' said Herb, 'about the size of your diddle.'

Dave and Mabel retreated to the other side of the tree and started to have a cuddle. Shortly after, Mabel called out to Herb. 'Eh! Herb,' she called.

'Yes, Mabel.'

'I'll bet yer catchin' some woppers, now.'

Dad and Dave went to the Royal Easter Show and were very interested in the new tractors that were on display. One salesman demonstrated his machine and then offered them a deal.

'You can have this model for $10 000 and I'll take off 10 per cent for cash.' They went away to discuss the deal.

'What's he mean by take off 10 per cent cash?' asked Dad. 'How much would he take orf?'

'I dunno,' replied Dave.

'Listen Dave, you're in pretty good with that barmaid at the pub and she looks like a pretty intelligent sort of girl, how about you ask her?' So Dave approached the barmaid.

'Tell me, Mary, if I gave you $10 000 less 10 per cent, how much would you take orf?'

'Dave,' she said, 'if you gave me $10 000 less 10 per cent, I'd take off everything bar me garters and you could use them for stirrups.'

Dave and Mabel became parents and Dave met Herb Wilson in town.

'Gee! Mabel and me 'ave got a baby. I bet yer can't guess what it is.'

'A boy?' says Herb.

'No,' says Dave, 'have another guess.'

The taxi driver took Dave to the railway station to catch a train to Sydney.

'You want to watch them wild wimmen down there,' warned the taxi driver.

'Don't worry about me,' says Dave, 'I'm as smart as them, any day.'

A fortnight later Dave gets off the train and hails the taxi.

'I want yer to take me an' the wife out to the farm,' says Dave.

The taxi driver looks at the woman standing on the station and couldn't help but notice that she was about six months pregnant. 'Is this yer wife?' he asks.

'Yeah,' says Dave, with a big grin on his face.

'But she's gonna have a baby.'

'That's right,' grins Dave.

'But it won't be your baby?'

'Course it's my baby,' protested Dave.

'How do yer make out it's your baby?'

'Well,' says Dave, 'if you buy a cow and it has a calf, the calf's yours, ain't it?'

In the days before TV and quiz shows, spelling bees were all the rage on the radio. Dave was the champion speller of Snake Gully and the whole team was involved when Dave went down to Sydney for a spelling contest. But just as Dave's turn came, a violent electrical storm cut off Snake Gully from the outside world. The whole town turned up the next morning to meet the train bringing Dave back from the Big Smoke.

'How did you go, Dave, how did you go?' boomed the Mayor as soon as Dave set foot to ground.

'No bloody good,' drawled Dave. 'Do you know what them silly buggers reckon in Sydney. They reckon you spell horse piss a-u-s-p-i-c-e.'

Dave decided to take Mabel to the Snake Gully café for lunch. Dave looked at the menu and said, 'They've got sheep tongues on the menu, Mabel. I think I'll have that. What about you?'

Mabel said, 'No, Dave, I couldn't eat anything that came out of an animal's mouth.'

'What would you like then, Mabel?' said Dave.

Mabel said, 'I think I'll have an egg.'

Dave and Mabel decided to raise pigs, but not knowing much about the facts of life, thought all they needed was a sow which could be served by a boar, and piglets would be there next morning. They approached farmer Brown down the road who informed them he charged $5, $10 or $20 per serve, depending on which boar was chosen.

'I think as we are just starting we should try the $5 boar,' said Mabel.

'Okay,' said Dave.

So they put the old sow in the wheelbarrow and wheeled it down to farmer Brown's boar. Dave got up early next morning expecting a litter of piglets.

'Gee, Mabel, I think we should have gone for the $10 boar.'

Mabel agreed so they put the old sow in the wheelbarrow and wheeled it down to farmer Brown's $10 boar. The next morning they were disappointed to find no piglets again. So Mabel said to Dave, 'Gee, Dave, we should have gone for the $20 boar in the first place.' Dave agrees, so back into the barrow goes the old sow, down to farmer Brown's for the $20 serve.

The next morning Mabel got up early because she was sure there would be piglets this time.

'Any piglets there this morning?' called Dave.

'No, Dave, but the old sow is sitting in the wheelbarrow!'

'What's the meaning of indecent?' the shearer asked his mate.

'Well,' replied his companion, 'I'd say if it was long enough, thick enough, hard enough and in far enough, it'd be in decent.'

Thirty years ago, one of the most famous and fast shearers in Australia was a bloke called Charlie Gibbs. Charlie shore all the 'long runs' between Queensland and NSW, shearing 200 a day, day after day, week after week, month after month. It was said of him that he was one of the very few shearers to have shorn 50 000 in a year. Well, this story relates to an incident that occurred after Charlie arrived back in Bourke after a very long run. As he walked into the hotel, the publican caught his eye and said, 'Charlie, there's a cocky just out of town who wants to know if you'll shear his sheep. Can you give him a ring?' Charlie sauntered off to the telephone and rang the cocky.

'Oh, Mr Gibbs,' (cockies always call shearers 'Mister' before they shear the sheep), 'I heard your shed had cut out and was wondering if it would be possible for you to come and shear my sheep.'

'Oh, I suppose so,' said Charlie. 'How many have you got?'

'Three hundred and twelve,' replied the cocky.

There was a silence and Charlie said, 'What are their names?'

The gun shearer had been invited to the very aristocratic squatter's for an end-of-season evening meal. The squatter's wife, a very distinguished matron, enquired, 'Would you care to wash your hands before dinner?'

He replied, 'No thanks, Mam. I already washed them over against that fence.'

An old swaggie turned up at the shearing shed and it was painfully obvious that he hadn't washed in years. So the shearers manhandled him into a bath and, after stripping off several layers of never-before-removed clothing, they noticed a peculiar bulge on his upper back. After a few more old flannels and singlets were peeled off, they found . . . a schoolbag.

A swagman who had tramped many kilometres along a rough outback track came to a small pub named 'George and the Dragon' and made his way around to the back in search of a handout. Before he had time to ask, the publican's wife came on the scene and gave the tramp the greatest verbal thrashing of his life. She called him a lazy good-for-nothing loafer and added if he was hoping to get even a crust of bread he could forget it. The tramp heard her out in silence, then just stood there.

'Well,' she snapped, 'now what is it you want?'

'I was wonderin',' said the man, 'if I could have a word with George?'

In 1919 a stockman was taking a mob of cattle to the Gulf country when he camped out one night with the rabbit-proof fence man. This lonely bloke hadn't seen anyone for years, so they sat around the campfire catching up with the news. After a lull in the conversation, the stockman said, 'By the way, we won the war.'

'That's good,' said the rabbit-proof fence man. 'I never could stand them Boers.'

These two rabbit trappers had been around the traps and were busy gutting the rabbits, of which there were hundreds. One of the trappers announced that he had to go into the bush to excrete. His mate said, 'All right,' and continued to gut, flinging the rabbits' entrails well out of the way so as to keep the work area comparatively clean.

One set of entrails landed directly under the rabbiter as he answered the call of nature. He was gone a bit longer than usual and when he came out of the bush his face was deathly pale and he was barely able to walk. His mate said, 'Strike me pink, sport, what's wrong?'

'You wouldn't believe it,' said the sick and sorry rabbiter, 'but I strained so hard that I passed some of my guts on the ground.'

'Strewth,' said his mate, 'we'll have to get you to a doctor.'

'No, I'll be all right soon,' said the reeling

rabbiter. 'With the help of God and a little stick I got 'em all back in again.'

Two men in a small country town shared a sizeable lottery prize. A reporter from the local newspaper interviewed them and asked each what they would do with their money. The first, a businessman, said that he would buy a new motor car, take an overseas trip and invest the remainder. The other, a farmer, said, 'I dunno, I think I will just keep farming until it's all gone.'

An old farmer was worried about his favourite bull. It was ignoring the cows. So he went to the vet and got some medicine. Next day he was telling a neighbour about it. 'I gave that Brahmin of mine one dose and within half an hour he'd serviced eight cows.'

'Blimey,' said the neighbour, 'what's the stuff called?'

'Well, the label's come off the bottle,' said the farmer, 'but it tastes like peppermint.'

A city boy was sent to the country to spend a holiday on his bushwhacker uncle's farm. When he returned home he was bubbling over with news of everything he'd seen. His mum asked him to name all his uncle's animals. 'Well, I saw horses and pigs and some bulls and cows and some fuckers.'

'Some fuckers?'

'Well, Uncle Harry called them 'eifers but I knew what he meant.'

A couple of farmers with neighbouring properties were working together repairing a buggered fence. One says to the other, 'I reckon I might have a bit of a problem now the shearin's done. Head down to Synny.'

'Yeah? I hear Synny's pretty interesting. What route will you take?'

'Oh, I reckon I'll take the missus. After all she stuck by me through the drought.'

Two old bushies were sitting on the verandah of the pub, chatting over a couple of beers. They were discussing 'the new metric system' which meant they had to talk metres instead of yards, kilos instead of pounds and hectares instead of acres. They shook their heads sorrowfully. 'What next? I suppose we'll have to drive on the right-hand side of the road.'

'Well, that'd be all right provided they brought it in gradual.'

A farmer returned from a holiday in Bali. 'Christ, those coconuts are beaut. You can get milk out of them without having to get up at 3 o'clock in the morning and risk being kicked in the balls.'

A young city bloke inherited a cattle station. On taking up residence he soon discovered that cattle were being stolen in considerable numbers. Moreover, it was obvious that the cattle duffer was his neighbour. He discussed the matter with another local who said, 'Be careful. He's a tough bastard and he's just as likely to shoot you if you accuse him of pinching your steers.'

So the young bloke had a good think and sent off a letter ending with ' . . . and I would appreciate it if you would refrain from leaving your hot branding iron lying around where my foolish cattle can sit down on it.'

A newly graduated geologist got a job with a mining company and was posted to a very remote region of far west Queensland. After he'd been there a month, and being young and fit, he started to need a woman, so he asked the resident engineer where he could find a bit of female company.

'Nothing round here, son,' said the engineer. 'The nearest town is two hours' drive away and it's been empty for years, except for a fettlers' camp and the sergeant of the Stock Squad who stops there once a month.'

'Well,' said the young bloke, 'where do all the rest of our blokes go, all clean and dressed up on a Friday night?'

'Didn't you know?' asked the engineer. 'They've got your problem, so they go out after the sheep.'

'The sheep? Dirty bastards. I won't be in that!' exclaimed the young man.

'Well, suit yourself,' said the older man easily, 'I'm only telling you what's available.'

But after another month, the young geologist was desperate and, Friday night, he spruced himself up, had a couple of stubbies at the canteen and dashed off with the rest of the men. The next morning, he woke up with a splitting headache and realised he was in a cell. Standing next to him was the engineer.

'You're awake, then. Come on, I've bailed you out.'

'What happened, why am I in a cell? I didn't have much to drink, but I've got an awful headache. What's going on?'

'You've got a headache because the sergeant

sconed you with his rifle and, if you don't go quietly, he'll charge you with bestiality.'

'Why me, for Christ's sake? What about the others – they've been doing it for bloody months!'

'Maybe, but you had to pick the Sergeant's girlfriend, didn't you!'

Two boundary riders were camped for the night by a windmill. Having finished their meal they were sitting around the fire enjoying a 'makins'. One got up and walked into the darkness to answer a call of nature. After a minute or so he called out to his cobber, 'Say, Bert, have you ever smoked a cigarette that's been pissed on?'

Bert pondered this hypothesis for a while and answered, 'No, Alf, I can't say 'as I 'ave.'

There was a studied silence till the reply came. 'Well, you 'aven't bloody missed much.'

A motorist was driving quietly along the road when, suddenly, his eyes goggled as, believe it or not, he espied a three-legged chook running beside him. It suddenly made a right hand turn, heading up a side track towards a nearby farm house. Intrigued, the motorist decided to follow the chook. At the end of the track, he met a farmer leaning on a gate.

The motorist said, 'You probably won't believe this, but I reckon I saw a three-legged chook running this way.'

The farmer was nonchalant in response. 'Yep, we breed them here.'

'But why?' asked the motorist.

'Well, you see, I like a leg, my wife likes a leg, and me son likes a leg.'

'And what do they taste like?'

'Dunno,' replied the farmer, 'no one can catch the little bastards.'

Out for a Sunday drive, a bloke passed a gate to a property where a three-legged pig was standing near the fence. He stopped, backed up for a better look, became aware of the cocky standing nearby. 'Strange pig that . . . three legs . . . how did it happen?'

'Wonderful pig, that. Dived into the dam last Christmas and saved me youngest from drowning. Pulled him out like a lifesaver. Marvellous animal.'

'Is that how it lost the leg?'

'No. Then there was the bushfire. We'd all have been burned in our beds if that pig hadn't battered down the door and woken us up.'

'Leg injured in the fire, was it?'

'Oh, no. Then I remember the time that pig fought off those three dingos in the lambing paddock. Covered with blood 'e was. Killed two of the sods.'

'So the dingos got his leg?'

'No . . .'

'Then, how?'

'Well, mate, a pig like that, such a bloody marvellous animal, almost a member of the family, you might say. A pig like that – you couldn't eat him all at once now, could you?'

Bert was the station master on a rather large property out west. One day he needed some fencing work done on one of the farm boundaries, so he called in Bill, one of his stockmen. 'Bill, I want you to go out to Bennett's boundary and fix the fence there. You can take the four-wheel drive and if you have any trouble give me a call on the two-way radio.' So Bill set off. About ten hours later Bert got a call on the two-way. 'Boss, this is Bill. I've got a bit of a problem.'

'Yes, mate, what is it?'

'Well, I was driving along in the four-wheel drive and I ran into a pig.'

'So, what's the problem?'

'Well, he got stuck in the bullbars and he's still alive and kicking and squealing so much that I can't get him free.'

'Okay mate. In the back of the four-wheel drive you'll find a .303. Take it out. Put the muzzle close to the pig's head and shoot it. It'll go all limp, and you'll be able to get it off the bullbar. Then drag it into the bush and leave it there.'

'Okay boss, I'll do that. Thanks for your help.'

About a quarter of an hour later, there was another call. 'Yes, Bill what is it?'

'Well, I took out the .303, shot the pig in the head and he went limp just like you said. And I got him off the bullbar and dumped him in the bush but I still can't go on.'

'Why not, mate?'

'Well, it's his motorbike. It's still stuck under the four-wheel drive.'

Once upon a time there was a farmer who had a very randy rooster. The rooster wasn't so bad when he was sober but in the cold evenings the farmer often had a brandy before he went to bed and would also give the rooster a cup. The only trouble was that the rooster would then charge off to the henhouse, full of brandied libido and screw the hens half to death. The farmer was getting a bit worried about this because in the morning he'd go to the henhouse and find feathers all over the place and all his hens looking totally plucked. So he told the rooster that he's going to have to lay off the booze for a while because otherwise the hens are going to be plucked to death. For a few weeks he doesn't give the rooster any brandy and all is okay.

Eventually the farmer has to go away for a week so he tells the rooster that while he's away there's to be no brandy because if he gets back and finds any of his hens plucked to death he's going to cut the rooster's crest off. This is the worst fate to befall a rooster, to be crestless, so the rooster is appropriately chastised. So the farmer goes away and, after a couple of nights, the rooster is sitting on the windowsill of the farmhouse when he notices a bottle of brandy sitting on the table inside and that the window is slightly ajar. Well the rooster is sorely tempted and even though he takes himself all the way to the other side of the farmyard he can't get the sight of this brandy out of his mind. Eventually he thinks to himself 'just a sip will be okay', so he goes back to the farmhouse, gets in through the window and has a sip of brandy. This goes down really well and he gets the taste for it. So he thinks 'well, just one glass will be all right,' and pours himself a glass. After drinking this he's well on the way, so he has another and then another and eventually staggers out of the farmhouse with the bottle under his arm off to the henhouse.

When the farmer gets back he goes to the henhouse and finds a total disaster area. There are feathers all over the place, and nearly all the hens are lying on their backs, feet in the air, dead as doornails. 'That's it,' he decides, 'I've had enough of this horny drunken rooster.' So he grabs the rooster and cuts his crest off. For the next couple of weeks the rooster mopes around the farmyard totally dejected, holding his head, looking about as crestfallen as a crestless rooster can look.

The farmer starts to feel sorry for him and decides he'll try to do something to cheer him up. He's going to his sister's wedding at the weekend so he takes the rooster with him thinking they'll have a good time at the reception and this will cheer him up. When they get to the reception, the ladies and gents have to enter through different doors, ladies to the left, gents to the right. There is a piano in between the doors so the farmer sits the rooster on the piano and asks him to tell the guests which door to go through. The rooster is doing this just fine until a waiter comes past with a tray of drinks. The rooster asks for and gets a brandy and is sitting happily on the piano drinking his brandy telling the guests 'ladies to the left, gents to the right,' when the farmer's bald uncle walks in with his wife. Whereupon the rooster says 'ladies to the left, gents to the right. And you, you baldheaded chicken fucker, up on the piano with me!'

Two kangaroo shooters, way out the back of Bourke. Their ute breaks down. They do the right thing – stay with it. But no one comes along. So they decide to walk out. The temperature is 40 plus. After two days, they're on their last drop of radiator water when they climb a rise and find, nailed to a tree, a sign saying MERCY, POPULATION 12. In the distance, a collection of ramshackle tin huts. They arrive. One hut is identified as a café. They enter. A lady appears, very proper. 'Yis,' she says.

'Bring us a drink, luv. Make it long and quick.'

'We only serve one thing here.'

'What's that?'

'Koala tea.'

'Well, bring it love, only make it quick!'

She brings it, and she is not kidding. Pathetic little paws grip the edge of the billy and little furry ears poke through the murky surface. Well, kangaroo shooters are pretty tough but they're not this tough. They look at each other and beg the woman to 'take it away please, and strain it'.

'What?' she says, 'The Koala Tea of Mercy is not strained!'

Once upon a time, way out past the back of Bourke, two grizzled old drovers were leaning on the bar of the local pub, discussing the relative merits of various dogs. 'Now, I reckon my Blue Heeler's the smartest dog in the country,' said one, '... do anything that it's told.'

'Nah,' said the other, 'me Kelpie's master. 'e thinks for 'imself.' They argued back and forth across the mounting pile of empty glasses, the yarns about what each dog could do getting wilder and more far-fetched. But neither could agree with the other. 'Tell you what,' one said, 'let's put it to the test. Meet you out by the chicken run termorrer mornin'.'

Morning rose bright and early. The two old codgers rose bluff and bleary, and went out to the chicken run with their dogs.

'Right, Bluey,' said the bloke with the Heeler.

'Now you listen here and you listen good, coz I'm only gonna tell yer once.' The dog sat and watched him, eyes bright and ears erect. 'Now Blue, I want yer to go down that road for about a kilometre and yer'll come ter a gate. Go through the gate, up over the hill, ter yer left and yer'll come ter a brick wall with another gate. Open the gate, go through and yer'll find three poddy calves. Round up the calves, bring 'em through the gate, close it, bring 'em back over the hill, through the second gate and back here. Yer got that?' The dog barked, wheeled, scampered off down the road, through the gate, over the hill, got the calves, closed the gate, over the hill, through the gate, closed it, and brought the calves back to his master.

'Geez, that's pretty smart,' said the bloke with the kelpie, 'but that's nothing. You watch this ... Oi, Kelly! Breakfast!' The dog looked around, dashed off down the road, came back, with a billy of water, collected some sticks, begged a match off his master, lit the fire, put the billy on to boil, scrabbled his way under the wire of the chicken coop, collected an egg, put it in the water, sat and watched it for three and a half minutes, took the billy off the fire, gently tipped the egg out at the bloke's feet, then stood on its head.

'Geez, that's bloody clever,' said the bloke with the Heeler, 'but what's the silly bugger doing standing on 'is 'ead?'

'Ah!' said the other bloke, "e's not so silly. 'e knows I haven't got an eggcup.'

It appeared that a bullocky with his team hooked up and hitched to a large log, was snigging it to the loading ramp for cartage to the mill. The team had been mooching along fairly well, when suddenly they stopped. The bullocky, in a few well-chosen words, told the team what was expected of them – but they wouldn't budge. So he went up the front to check on the track. And there, right across the road in front of the leaders, was a dirty great goanna. So the bullocky got a strong piece of rope and tied it round the goanna's tail. He then unhooked two of the bullocks, and tied the rope to them, but these two bullocks couldn't move the goanna. So then he unhooked the whole team from the jinker and hooked them onto the goanna. He gave the bullocks explicit instructions as to what to do, but they couldn't move the goanna. To his horror, the next thing that happened was that the goanna took off! The last thing the bullocky saw was the goanna pulling the bullocks down the hill, through the bush to the gully below.

A SENSE OF IDENTITY

An Australian tour guide was showing a group of American tourists the Top End. On their way to Kakadu he was describing the abilities of the Australian Aborigine to track man or beast over land, through the air, under the sea. The Americans were incredulous.

Then, later in the day, the tour rounded a bend on the highway and discovered, lying in the middle of the road, an Aborigine. He had one ear pressed to the white line whilst his left leg was held high in the air. The tour stopped and the guide and the tourists gathered around the prostrate Aborigine.

'Jacky,' said the tour guide, 'what are you tracking and what are you listening for?'

The Aborigine replied, 'Down the road about 25 miles is a 1971 Valiant ute. It's red. The left front tyre is bald. The front end is out of whack and it has dents in every panel. There are nine black fellows in the back, all drinking warm sherry. There are three kangaroos on the roof rack and six dogs on the front seat.'

The American tourists moved forward,

astounded by this precise and detailed knowledge.

'Goddammit man, how do you know all that?' asked one.

The Aborigine replied, 'I fell out of the bloody thing about half an hour ago.'

Botha to Evans: Do your blacks have the vote?

Evans to Botha: Only if they live to be 18.

Two Aboriginal men were talking. 'How's your brother?'

'He passed away,' his friend replied.

'I'm sorry,' said the first man, 'I didn't know he'd been arrested.'

A young Aboriginal lad observed that there seemed to be some advantages in being white, so he went off and painted himself white all over. He went and showed his mother who roused on him, and told him to go and show his father. This he did, and his father not only roared at him for being so silly, but cuffed him over the ears and sent him on his way. The boy went on and sat on his favourite log pondering his position and feeling very glum. His mate came along and asked him what was wrong.

'I've only been a white kid for half an hour,' he replied, 'and I hate those black bastards already.'

A university researcher goes up to a blackfella and says, 'I'm researching people's religious beliefs. Tell me, do you believe in reincarnation?'

'Dunno, mate. What's it mean?'

'It means that, after death, you return to the earth in another form – a snake, or a brolga, whatever. Anyway, suppose there was reincarnation, what would you like to come back as?'

'I reckon I'd come back as a dog's turd.'

'A dog's turd? What on earth for?'

'Look at it this way, mate. Nobody'd stand on you, nobody'd drive over you and, after three days in the sun, you'd be white.'

An Aborigine walked into an enormous pig farm looking for work. He met the foreman who told him with a smirk that he had the perfect job for him. All he had to do was arrive at 5 a.m. and load a truckload of pigs by 9 a.m. The foreman knew that it usually took a couple of experienced blokes all day to get the buggers on board. The following day the Aborigine turned up at 5 and the foreman left him to it. By 6 a.m. he bowled up to his boss and said that the job was done.

'Who are you kidding?' said the astonished foreman.

But it was true. The truck was loaded with all the pigs.

'How the hell did you do that?' the foreman asked. 'It must have been beginner's luck.'

The Aborigine smiled and the foreman fumed.

The next two mornings the same thing happened. The Aborigine got the job done in a fraction of the usual time. On the fourth day the foreman decided to spy on him and hid in the bushes.

The Aborigine let the pigs out of the yard, stood on the back of the truck and starting singing, 'Come on, Aussie, come on!'

Whitey was walking along the road and saw an Aborigine. 'Hey Jacky, how far is Ayers Rock?'

The Aborigine asked, 'How do you know my name's Jacky?'

Whitey replied, 'I guessed it.'

To which the Aborigine said, 'Well, bloody well guess how far is Ayers Rock.'

An Aborigine walks into a bar with one thong on. The barman asks, 'Did ya lose a thong, mate?'

'Nah, I found one.'

Feeling generous, the publican in an outback pub invited the Aboriginal yardman to have a glass of beer. The yardman drank it appreciatively and the publican then asked him, 'How was the beer, Jacky?' The yardman answered, 'Just right boss, just right.'

The publican said, 'What do you mean, just right?'

The yardman answered, 'Any worse and I couldn't have drunk it; any better and you'd have sold it.'

Two white men and an Aborigine were in prison together. One of the whites said he was in for ten years for attempted rape, but thought himself lucky he hadn't actually done the rape or he would be in for twenty years.

The other white said he was in for fifteen years for attempted murder, but was lucky his victim had lived, or he would be doing life.

The Aborigine then said he was in for twenty-five years for riding his bike without a light, but reckoned he was lucky it wasn't night time.

A man in Canberra decides the way to make a fortune is to open a ten-pin bowling alley. He builds the ultimate bowling alley with twenty lanes, two restaurants and various bars. On the afternoon before the official opening he is standing around admiring his creation when he realises he's forgotten to order bowling balls. He rings the manufacturer in Sydney and orders 1000 balls. The supplier advises that he has them in stock and all he has to do is drill and polish them and then he can air-freight them to Canberra. The bowling alley proprietor says this will cost too much in freight and asks that they be sent by road in a 22-wheeler semitrailer.

The supplier works into the night and the balls are loaded and despatched. Travelling at great speed and in the middle of nowhere the truck driver sees two blokes standing on the side of the road. He stops to offer assistance and the two guys, who he sees are Aborigines, say that their bike has broken down on the way to Canberra and they are stranded. He offers them a lift, but says they must travel in the back because company policy prevents passengers in the cabin. They climb in with their bike and he speeds off.

Shortly after he's pulled up by the police. One policeman says to his mate, 'You book him while I check his load.' He opens the back but quickly slams and locks the door. And he runs to his mate and says, 'Forget booking him. Let's just get him across the border and out of New South Wales.' Despite his mate's protests, they head off at great speed to the Canberra border, escorting the truck.

At the border they stop and the truck hurtles on.

The policeman then says to his mate, 'Will you tell me why I couldn't book him and we had to escort him here?'

He replies, 'When I opened the back I could see it was full of Abo eggs. We had to get them out of the state because two had already hatched and one of them had stolen a bike!'

Jacky was sitting on the stoop in an inner-suburban street. It was garbage day, and the council garbage truck stopped right by him.

'Where's ya bin?' demanded the garbo.

'I bin away,' answered Jacky.

'No—where's ya wheely bin?' asked the garbo impatiently.

'Oh,' said Jacky, 'I *weely* bin in prison, but I tell me friends I've bin on holidays in Mullumbimby!'.

What does an Aborigine call a boomerang that doesn't come back?

A stick.

A lot of new Australians live in Fortitude Valley, Brisbane. A Chinaman had a fruit and vegie shop. Every Friday his neighbour, a Greek bloke with a snack bar, used to pass his shop on the way to bank his takings and he always called out, 'What day is it, Chinaman?'

The Chinaman always replied, 'Flyday, you Gleek plick.'

'Not "Flyday", you dozey bastard, "F-r-r-ri-day". Why don't you learn to talk English proper?'

So, the Chinaman practised all week. The next Friday, the Greek called out, as usual, 'What day is it, Chinaman?'

'F-r-r-ri-day, you Gleek plick.'

A young Chinese student was travelling in a train compartment with a ferocious Red Guard, an old lady and a pretty young girl. The train went through a tunnel. In the darkness they heard a kiss followed by a resounding smack. When they came out of the tunnel the Red Guard was rubbing a very swollen face, and they each contemplated what must have happened.

The old lady thought, 'What a proper young lady that is to chastise the Red Guard for his unwelcome advances.'

The young lady thought, 'Why should the Red Guard want to kiss the old lady instead of an attractive person like me?'

The Red Guard thought, 'That student is a lucky

chap. He kisses the young lady and I get the smack.'

But the student knew, 'I'm a cunning fellow. I kiss the back of my hand, smack the Red Guard, and get away with it!'

Two upper class Pommy brothers, one very hard of hearing, were having a quiet drink in a Chelsea pub where a drunken loud-mouthed Aussie was regaling the bar with his opinions. 'What a place England is. Free and open and as friendly as buggery,' spruiked the Australian.

'What did he say?' asked the hard-of-hearing brother.

'He said he likes England,' said the other.

'And Pommy women are fantastic movers,' said the Aussie very loudly. 'They're terrific sports, do anything in bed, fucking great.'

'What was that?' asked brother number 1.

'He says he likes English women.'

The Aussie continued. 'And last night I picked up a brassy old broad who took me home and fucked me stupid all night. Gee, she knew some tricks. The silly old bitch. What a fuck!'

'What did he say?' asked the deafish bastard.

'He said he'd met Mother.'

The Great Australian Dream – an Italian swimming out through Sydney Heads with a Pom under each arm.

Did you hear about the Pom who came out here, married an Australian prostitute and dragged her down to his level?

Did you hear about the Pommy taxidermist who went home because Australians kept telling him to get stuffed?

Dear Dorothy Dix,

I am shortly to become engaged to a wonderful man. My psychiatrist tells me that an open, honest relationship is the foundation of a happy marriage. But there are a few things about my family that are difficult to raise in conversation. For instance, my father is a heroin dealer and touches up little boys. My mother has always been a hooker and now runs a small brothel in the Cross. My brother ran out on bail for murder and went to England where he got married and is hiding out under a false name. My eldest sister is a lesbian.

My main question is this: should I tell my fiancé that my brother has married a Pom?'

A Pommy businessman was visiting Germany. He was alone and lonely in the lounge after work when a stunning Fräulein approached him, offering company. They dined together and his melancholy mood began to lift. He offered, she accepted, coffee and liqueur in the anteroom. He invited her to his suite for port and she came willingly. He proposed an even better remedy for loneliness and she complied. The next morning he was profusely thankful. 'You've been so kind to me,' he said, 'can I offer you some money? Perhaps 50 or 60 pounds?'

She said, 'That would be nice, but I'd prefer Marks.'

'How spiffing of you,' said the Pommy, 'I'd say about seven out of ten.'

A Pommy got a job at a cattle station. He mucked up everything he was given to do. Finally the farmer gave him a last chance. He told the Pommy to take a heifer into a paddock with a Hereford bull. Later the farmer asked the Pommy how things had gone. 'Top hole, old chap,' said the Pom. 'Christ, you stuffed it up again,' said the farmer.

Outside Bullen's Lion Park there's a notice stating the fees for driving cars and buses through. It also states that Poms on bicycles would be admitted free.

A bloke's car broke down on a country road. He walked to the nearest farm and knocked on the door. The most beautiful blonde with a perfect figure opened it, with a charming smile. He explained that he needed mechanical help and she said, 'See my husband. He's around the back.'

The bloke went to the back of the house and discovered an old Aborigine trying to make a fire with two sticks. He returned to the front of the house and said, 'How come a beautiful girl like you married an old bloke like that?'

She said, 'Oh, I haven't done so bad. My sister married a Pommy.'

An American journalist was sent to England to search for a typical English joke. After several fruitless weeks, he found himself in a country pub. He approached a group of locals and explained his problem. One of them told him this story which they all agreed was typical English humour.

'Approaching a road intersection was a man walking. On another road was a man riding a bicycle; on another a man driving a car; on another a man riding a horse. They all arrived at the corner at the same time. On the corner was a pretty girl who was greeted by one of these men. Which one?'

Naturally, the American hadn't the faintest idea, so the storyteller told him, 'The horseman knew her.'

When the journalist returned to New York, he told his boss this typical English joke. 'There's a dolly bird standing on the crossroad. Along one of these roads is a guy strolling towards the corner. On another street is a bicyclist; on another a guy in an automobile, and on the other is a guy on a horse. Which one of these guys knew the gal on the corner?'

The editor said, 'Hell, I don't know.'

'Neither do I,' said the journo, 'but the answer's "horse shit"!'

This is the story of an aviator – handsome, dashing, with big dark eyes, thick, black swept-back hair, and a bushy handlebar moustache. A Frenchman from the days when men were men, women were pleased, and the planes were built of wood, fabric, and flown on sinew.

Pierre is back from a successful mission, has wined and dined a pretty young lady and taken her back to his room. He kisses her forehead, eyelids and the tip of her nose. 'Oooo,' she thinks. Suddenly Pierre goes off, gets a bottle of red wine, sprinkles it on her lips and passionately kisses her. 'Oooo,' she says as they come up for breath. 'That's very nice – but why the red wine?'

'Aha,' he says, 'I am Pierre, the famous fighter pilot. When I 'ave red meat, I 'ave red wine!'

They continue. Clothing is gradually discarded. He kisses her chin, her neck, her cleavage. 'Oooo,' she thinks. Pierre goes and gets a bottle of white wine, sprinkles it onto her breasts and kisses them passionately. 'Oooo,' she says, 'that's very nice, but why the white wine?' 'Aha,' he says, 'I am Pierre, the famous fighter pilot. When I 'ave white meat, I 'ave white wine!'

Matters progress further. More clothing is discarded. He kisses her navel, her stomach, her mons. 'Oooo,' she thinks, 'OOOO!' Pierre then goes and gets a bottle of cognac, sprinkles it liberally over the fluffy bits and sets it alight. 'AAAAHH!' she screeches, leaping off the bed and beating out the burning bush. 'You silly fool! What did you do that for?'

'Aha,' he said, 'I am Pierre, the famous fighter pilot. When I go down ... I go down in flames!'

Quasimodo was run down and his doctor ordered him to take a complete break from his job. But he felt that Notre Dame required its bells to be rung as usual, so that he shouldn't take leave until he found a suitable replacement bellringer. He advertised the temporary vacancy in *Le Monde* but there was only one applicant. It was a funny looking bloke who had no arms.

'This is crazy,' said Quasi. 'You've got no arms. How do you expect to ring the bells?'

'I'll use my head,' said the little man and took a running leap at the nearest bell, scoring a direct hit and making quite an acceptable sound.

'Not too bad at all,' said Quasi. 'Try the one on the left!'

The little man took another running leap, but his timing was out and he went over the parapet, falling 100 metres to the pavement below. Quasi limped his way down to the street. A gendarme was standing next to the shapeless remains.

'Do you know this man?' interrogated the policeman.

'Not really, but his face rings a bell.'

The next day another applicant appeared. Obviously he was the identical twin brother, also minus arms. Same deal. A demo of ringing the bells. Same outcome. Squished. Same gendarme standing over gruesome remains down on the footpath.

'Did you know this man?' asks the gendarme.

'No,' said Quasimodo,' but he's a dead ringer for his brother.'

Bruce arrives in Paris and is gazing around at the sights in wonderment. As he walks beneath the Eiffel Tower, gazing up, he bumps into a little

Frenchman and sends him sprawling. 'Sorry, mate,' says Bruce, dusting him down and picking him up. 'Look, let me buy you a beer.' The Frenchman introduces himself as Pierre, and, rather mournfully, agrees.

'What's the trouble, cobber?' asks Bruce, observing that Pierre is still looking very sorry for himself, even after a few beers.

'*Mon ami,*' says Pierre, 'do you see that cathedral over there by the river Seine? I, Pierre, I built that cathedral. But do they call me Pierre the Cathedral Builder? And do you see the bridge by the cathedral? I, Pierre, I built that bridge. But do they call me Pierre the Bridge Builder? And do you see that magnificent sculpture standing in the middle of that park? I, Pierre, I created that sculpture. But do they call me Pierre the Great Sculptor? But suck just *one* cock . . .!'

How do French women hold their liquor?

By the ears.

An aristocratic family in Delhi sent their favourite son to Harvard, whence he returned with that most desirable of degrees, an MBA. Determined to demonstrate his managerial brilliance, he approached the government with a brilliant idea. To raise money for the Indian Treasury he will conduct, on their behalf, the biggest lottery in the history of the world. The entire population of India will be encouraged to buy tickets. Although each will pay only a few rupees, the amount of money raised will be immense.

The ticket sales go very well. Finally comes the day of the draw. The young man with the MBA has arranged for all the ticket stubs to be deposited in a vast wooden barrel which is positioned high above the swelling crowds, on an elaborately carved platform. And on the platform, many of India's most famous political and cultural celebrities. A magnificently painted elephant has been trained to turn the barrel, so that the stubs are properly mixed, and India's most beauteous film star is on hand to call out the winning numbers. The entire event is compered by the young MBA, whilst the actual prize will be read out by India's Treasurer.

At the appointed time, the crowd has grown to immense proportions, stretching from one end of India to the other. The elephant churns the barrel and the movie star is asked to pull out the number of the third prize winner. The MBA proclaims the number through his microphone, his voice echoing through thousands and thousands of loudspeakers strung up lamp posts, trees and minarets. Finally there is a response from far, far away in the crowd and a thin figure in a *dhoti* is seen weaving his way through the multitude crying, 'It's me, it's me!' At last he arrives breathless on the platform. The Treasurer announces the third prize. You have won two first-class airline tickets from Air India to take you anywhere you wish around the world, along with 1000 English pounds spending money. The crowd goes wild.

Now the elephant churns the mighty barrel and the sequence is repeated for the second prize. This time the winner has to run even further, almost all the way from Jaipur.

'Congratulations,' says the Treasurer, 'you have won second prize. Here it is, this beautiful fruit cake.' The little Indian chap is very upset. 'A fruit cake? But the third prize was airline tickets and lots of money.'

Attempting to soothe the indignant prizewinner the MBA explains, 'But this is no ordinary fruit cake ... this fruit cake was baked ...' and he takes a deep breath as he makes the proud announcement ' ... by Madam Gandhi!'

To which the prizewinner responds, 'Fuck Madam Gandhi!'

'Ah no no no,' says the MBA, with a characteristically Indian shake of the head, 'that is first prize!'

One of Madam Gandhi's nephews wanted to become a fully-fledged Brahmin. He was told there was an initiation ceremony. He had to do three things within an hour. Firstly, drink a full bottle of scotch. Then make love to a woman, and thirdly, shoot a man-eating tiger. After forty-seven minutes he'd downed the whisky. He returned from the jungle torn to pieces with three minutes to go, pulled out his gun and said, 'Now where's this bloody sheila I'm suppose to shoot?'

Two blokes are walking down Lygon Street in Carlton. One of them is notorious for his prejudice against Italians. Yet when he sees an Italian organ grinder with a monkey, he throws $5 into the monkey's hat. The friend is surprised. 'But people have been telling me for years how much you hated Italians, and here you do that.' To which the bloke replies, 'Well, they're so cute when they're little.'

Maria went to Luigi's fruit and vegetable shop every week. She walked in on this particular day and said, 'Hello, Luigi. I woulda lika two kilos of tomatoes pleasa.'

'Ah, Maria, so sorry, I have no tomatoes today.'

'Luigi, don'ta you joka with me. You know that I always buy my tomatoes from you. Just give me my tomatoes, Luigi.'

'Maria, I told you, I have no tomatoes today.'

'Luigi, I'm in a hurry, please give me two kilos of tomatoes.'

'Maria, it's lika this. How you say "carrots", without the "c"?'

'Arrots.'
'How you say "potatoes" without the "p"?'
'Otatoes.'
'How you say "tomatoes" without the "f"?'
'There's no "f" in tomatoes.'
'That's whata I been trying to tell you, Maria. There's no effing tomatoes!'

Luigi, the fisherman, is out on Port Phillip Bay when his boat springs a leak and starts sinking. He frantically starts radioing for help.

'This is-a Luigi. Send-a me *plane*, and-a quick!'

Search and Rescue radios back. 'We hear you Luigi, and we're sending you a Fokker Friendship.'

To which Luigi replies, 'I don't want-a you fokker friendship! I want a fokker *plane*!'

It's necessary to register the birth of the twins (a boy and a girl) at the Almoner's office section of Births, Deaths and Marriages. As Dad speaks poor English, he asks his proud brother to do the registration. The woman on the counter asks, 'And what is the little girl called?'

'Denise.'

'A lovely name. And the boy?'

'Denephew.'

An American oil-drilling company was erecting new offshore platforms in total isolation. Their industrial psychologist was concerned about the effect this might have on the crew. It was therefore decided to test the reactions of three men. An Englishman, an American and the inevitable Irishman were selected and told to pick out their favourite leisure gear to help them cope with the next three months completely on their own in the middle of the ocean.

The American turned up with a suitcase, the Englishman with five huge plastic bags and the Irishman with only his hands in his pockets.

The industrial psychologist was, naturally, very curious. The American explained that he was taking his Linguaphone records and books to learn languages. The Englishman said he had 5000 golf balls to improve his game. Then they quizzed the Irishman who produced a packet of tampons from his pocket, reading aloud from the label. 'With this you can go swimming, scuba diving, aerogliding, dancing and do aerobics.'

Mary, a strictly brought up Catholic girl, wanted to marry Richard Todd, a Protestant. Their families were horrified, but when they could see she was determined, asked if she would first have a talk with Father O'Toole. Father O'Toole pointed out the pitfalls of mixed marriages, but he was a wise priest and could see Mary was not convinced. He therefore suggested she kneel before the statue of the Blessed Virgin, ask permission and abide by her words.

Mary thought about this, eventually agreed and, kneeling reverently before the statue said, 'Holy Mary, Mother of God, may I marry Dickie Todd?'

The priest, who'd nipped around behind the statue, replied in a rather deep voice, 'No!'

'Shut up, God,' said Mary, 'I'm talking to yer mother.'

An Irishman collected a large insurance settlement after an auto accident by pretending that his injuries had put him in a wheelchair for life. When the inspector from the insurance company warned him that he would be pursued by them for the rest of his life until they established the fraudulence of his claim, he responded by telling him that they would be following him to the Catholic religious shrine at Lourdes and 'there you're going to see the greatest miracle in your life'.

Needing to conduct a pathology test, a doctor asked a simple Irish washerwoman for a specimen. Not wishing to confess her ignorance, she returned home and went next door to ask her neighbour the meaning of the doctor's request. She came back bruised and dishevelled. When her husband asked her what had happened, she said, 'I asked her what a specimen was and she told me to go and pee in a bottle. So I said, "Go shit in your hat," and the fight was on.'

Two Irishmen rented a boat at Williamstown, rowed out into Port Phillip Bay and caught a couple of snapper. 'We should mark the spot,' one said, so they painted a big black 'X' on the bottom of the boat. 'That's no good,' said one of them, on careful re-evaluation. 'Next time we mightn't get the same boat.'

An Irishman visited Australia. When he got back to Dublin they asked him about the place. He said it was a wonderful country, that the Australians were marvellous. But he couldn't stand the white bastards.

A gridiron football match in Boston. A vociferous lady with a strong Irish accent on the fence, giving her views. As the opposing scrums inclined together for battle, she shouted, 'Give the ball to Muldoon!'

A wild scuffle, the ball emerged and was slung to a player. He was borne down by a pride of opponents and carried off on a stretcher. His replacement ran on. Still the lady shouted, 'Give the ball to Muldoon!' Another scrum. Again the ball passed to a player who was promptly flung heavily to the ground and was assisted, limping, from the arena. As his substitute ran on, the lady still shouted, 'This time, give the ball to Muldoon!'

A figure stood up in the scrum, cupped his hands and shouted back, 'Muldoon say he don't want the ball!'

When I was flying to Singapore I asked the man sitting next to me where he was going. His reply was, 'DDDDDDDDUUUUUUBBBBBBBBLLLLLLIIIINNNN.' I then asked what he was going to do in Dublin. His reply was that he was going to Dublin 'TTTTTOOOOO BBBBBEEEE AAAAAAA RRRRRAAAACCCCIIIINNNNGGGGG BBBRRRRRROOOAAADDDDCCCAAAASSSTTEEERRRR.'

I asked him if he really expected to get the job. 'NNNNNNOOOOO. They'll probably give it to a bloody Catholic.'

Two IRA men planted some explosives and were sheltering behind another building. After the detonation, a human head rolled along and stopped at their feet. After a minute, one of the IRA men said, 'You know, that looked like Father McGillicuddy.' The other said, 'It couldn't be. We gave him plenty of warning!'

So they decided to see the priest's housekeeper, Mrs O'Flaherty. Holding the head by the hair, they knocked on the door. She opened it and asked, 'Well, boys, what's the trouble?' When they explained, she said, 'Hold it up!' The fellow with the head lifted it up above his own, so she could have a good look.

'No, that's not him,' said Mrs O'Flaherty, 'he's too tall.'

Paddy was an Irishman with some experience in the building trade. But when he arrived in Melbourne he found that the recession and the troubles of the BLF made it very, very hard to get a job. He kept trying and trying. 'Oid loik a job, sir,' Paddy would say. 'Well, now,' said a foreman who wasn't too enthusiastic about the Irish. 'Before we employ anyone on this site, we always have a quick intelligence test.'

'That's or'right, sir,' said Paddy, 'you just foir away.'

'Well,' said the foreman, 'can you tell me what's the difference between a girder and a joist?'

'Well now sir, just off the top of me head, oid say Goethe wrote *Faust* and Joyce wrote *Ulysses*.'

An Irishman goes on 'Sale of the Century' and chooses Irish history as his category.

'In what year was the Easter rising?'

'Pass,' he replies.

'Who was Parnell?'

'Pass,' he replies.

'What's the difference between the Orange and the Green?'

'Pass,' he replies.

'Good man, Seamus!' comes a voice from the audience, 'tell them nothing!'

Kerry Packer had a set of dominoes with huge diamonds instead of spots. An Irishman broke into his house and stole the double blank.

'What have you got in your pocket?' one Irishman asks another.

'I'll give you a clue. It begins with "N".'

'A napple,' said the first Irishman.

'No, I told you it begins with "N".'

'A norange!'

'No, I'm telling you for the last time that it begins with an "N".'

'Would it be a nonion?'

'You've got it at last.'

There's a riot in an Irish prison and the Governor tells the guards to evict the troublemakers.

'What's that on your leg, Seamus?'

'A birthmark.'

'How long have you had it?'

A boss decides to sack his lazy Irish cleaning lady.

'Look, Bridget, I can write my name in the dust on this desk.'

'Can you now, sir?' she replied. 'Isn't education a wonderful thing!'

Have you heard about the Irishmen who waited outside a brothel for hours because the red light wouldn't turn green?

Judge: Do you want to challenge any member of the jury?

Paddy: I reckon I could fight that little bloke on the end.

There's a court case in Dublin. A German sailor's been charged with being drunk and disorderly. 'I can't understand a word he's saying,' complains the judge. 'Is there anyone in court who can translate German?'

'I'll do it,' said an Irishman.

'Good,' said the Judge, 'ask him what his name is?' 'Vot iss your name?' said the Irishman.

Seamus had BO so his girlfriend told him to go home and have a bath. 'And afterwards, use some deodorant and toilet water.'

Next day he reappeared swathed in bandages. 'Holy Virgin!' she asked, 'what happened?'

'The toilet seat hit me on the head.'

An Irishman is taking an IQ test. 'What's black and is worn on the left foot in wet weather?' The Irishman didn't know.

'It's a Wellington boot! Now, think carefully before you answer the next question. What's black and worn on the right foot in wet weather?' The Irishman shook his head in bewilderment.

'A pair of Wellington boots. Now, here's the final question. Who lives in the White House and rules over millions of Americans?'

'I know that one,' shouted the Irishman. 'Three Wellington boots!'

When an Irishman couldn't get a dance his friend decided to tell him the truth. 'Look, it's the smell from your socks. Go home and change them and you'll have no trouble.' Later in the evening the Irishman complained that he still couldn't get a dance.

'Did you change your socks?'

'Of course I did,' said the Irishman, pulling them from his pocket.

An Irishman joined the Army and was being assessed by an officer to see what regiment he should join.

'Can you shoot a gun?'

'No.'

'Well, what can you do?'

'I can take messages, sir.'

'Good. We'll assign you to the pigeon corps in charge of vital messages being carried from the front by pigeons.'

After a week's intensive training the Irishman was given his first job – to intercept a pigeon from the front bearing a message. He returned after an hour, covered in feathers and pigeon poop.

'Well,' said the officer, 'what's the message?'

'Coo, coo,' said the Irishman.

A bloke went into a pub. Seated at the bar beside an Irishman was a huge dog. 'Does your dog bite?' he asked the Irishman.

'No,' said the Irishman, 'he's as gentle as a lamb.'

So the bloke patted him and the dog just about tore his arm off.

'You told me your dog didn't bite,' he screamed.

'Yes,' said the Irishman, 'but that's not my dog.'

An Irishman, a very good Catholic, was hanging off a cliff by one arm praying for God to save him. A fishing boat passed by, and the fisherman shouted for the Irishman to let go and be rescued.

'No,' said the Irishman, 'God will save me.'

Then a helicopter came and dangled a rope over the cliff.

'Grab the rope,' shouted the pilot.

'No,' said the Irishman, 'God will save me.'

Then a submarine surfaced and the captain called out to the Irishman to jump.

'No,' said the Irishman, 'God will save me.'

A few hours later he fell off the cliff and drowned. When he arrived in Heaven he said, 'God, why didn't you save me?'

'Look,' said God, 'I sent a boat, a helicopter and a submarine. What else could I bloody well do?'

An Irishman had been missing for weeks. His wife told the police. Next day the police arrived to say that her husband's body had been found floating in the Yarra. 'Sure, that couldn't be him,' she said, 'because he couldn't swim.'

Two Irishmen escaped from Pentridge and hid up separate gum trees. Some cops arrived with tracker dogs and surrounded the first tree. 'Who's up there?'

'Miaow,' said the first Irishman.

'Let's try the other tree,' said the policeman, 'there's only a cat up that one.' So they went to the second tree and a policeman yelled, 'Who's up there?'

'Another cat,' said the second Irishman.

Did you hear about the Irishman who tried to kill himself by taking a hundred painkillers.

After two he began to feel better.

Seamus and Brendan had been on the piss. When they woke up in the morning the blinds were drawn. 'Is it day or night?' asked Seamus.

'I'll go and have a look,' said Brendan. So he lifted the blind and looked out.

'Well,' said Seamus, 'is it day or night?'

'I can't remember,' said Brendan.

What events did the Irish win at Barcelona?

Heading the shot and catching the javelin.

A wealthy Dublin woman comes into the undertakers and identifies a corpse as her father. She orders a very expensive funeral. But just as she's leaving, the corpse's jaw opens and exposes a set of false teeth.

'My father didn't have false teeth! Cancel the funeral!'

When she left, Seamus hauled the body out of the coffin and said, 'You fool, you'd have gone first class if only you'd kept your damn mouth shut.'

Seamus and Paddy were out driving together.

'Are we getting near a town?' asked Seamus.

'We must be,' said Paddy, 'we seem to be knocking more people down.'

'Well, drive slower then,' said Seamus.

'What do you mean drive slower?' said Paddy. 'I thought you were driving!'

Dear Patrick,

I have not written to you for a long time. I know that you are not a very fast reader, so I am writing this letter very slowly. You might be interested to know that your Uncle Seamus has got a new and important job. He has 500 people under him. He's in charge of a cemetery ...

Paddy had been working for an Australian company for awhile when the management called in some efficiency experts. They required all the employees to have an IQ test. Thoroughly alarmed, Paddy asked his mate, Bob, about it.

'Hey Bob, what's this IQ test?'

'Don't worry, Paddy. They just go around and ask a lot of questions and, depending on how you answer them, they give you a certain score.'

'What's the score for?' asked Paddy.

'Well, the higher you get,' explained Bob, 'the better job you'll get.'

Even more alarmed, Paddy asked, 'What's a good score?'

'Well, suppose you get 100,' said Bob, 'they'd give you a job up in the office somewhere, in the main building.'

'But suppose I only got 80?' asked Paddy.

'Well, you'd probably keep the job you've got now, out here in the yard stacking timber.'

'But suppose I only got 60 or 40 or 30?' wailed Paddy.

'Look, if you only got 30 or 40, you wouldn't have enough intelligence to do up your shoelaces.'

Whereupon Paddy burst out laughing. 'Now I know why all Australians wear thongs.'

Paddy charged into the newspaper office to insert a funeral notice following the death of his father.

'How much is it ye charge?' he asked the man at the counter.

'Two dollars per inch,' he replied.

'Holy Nellie,' said Paddy, 'and my old Dad was six foot foive!'

Two young Irish lads apply to their nearest police station for jobs as police constables. Mick Murphy is given an interview first while his mate Paddy waits in the anteroom.

Inspector to Murphy, 'I'll ask you three questions. Question one, where's the River Liffey?'

Murphy (a Dublin resident) looks stunned and says, 'Pass.'

Inspector, 'I'll ask you an easier one this time. What's the capital of Ireland?'

Murphy, 'Pass.'

Inspector (becoming exasperated), 'Well, can you at least answer this question . . . who killed Jesus Christ our Lord?'

Murphy, 'Pass.'

Inspector, 'I suggest you go away and don't come back until you find out who did.'

Murphy rejoins his mate Paddy who asks, 'Did you get the job?'

Murphy, 'To be sure, and they've put me on a murder case already.'

Two Irish travellers returning home became lost. One said, 'We must be in a cemetery. Look, here's a headstone.'

The other lit a match and peered at the stone. 'Well, he was a grand old age – ninety-five!'

'What was his name?' asked his friend.

'Oh, some fellow called Miles from Dublin.'

Old Pat Muldoon was dying of a terrible contagious disease. As he lay gasping in his bed, he felt he was truly at his end.

'Maggie,' he wheezed to his beloved wife, 'go quick and send for the rabbi. I'm dying.'

'What!' exclaimed his wife, 'all your life you've been such a good Catholic and now you want a rabbi!'

Pat opened one eye, 'What, you want a priest to catch this?' he asked.

The police pulled Paddy in for suspected rape. They put him in line with ten other fellows and the accusing woman was brought in. Paddy jumped forward, 'That's her,' he screamed, 'that's her! I'd recognise her anywhere.'

The old Cork couple had not had a holiday for fifty years and they decided to take a fortnight off. They went to the Glens of Antrim and had a splendid time. But unluckily, no sooner had they arrived home than the husband sickened and died. At the wake a friend went to pay her respects to the dead man. 'How tanned he is looking,' she said to the widow. 'Yes,' she said, 'the two weeks in the Glen did him the world of good!'

An Irishman had a very bad start to the duck season. Everyone else was getting ducks and he wasn't. He finally realised his mistake. He wasn't throwing the dog high enough.

Did you hear about the Irishman who built a bridge over the Nullarbor? They had to tear it down because too many Australians were fishing from it.

Did you hear about the Irishman who immigrated from Ireland to Australia and raised the IQ level in both countries?

An Englishman asked an Irishman, 'Has the Irish language got any equivalent to "*Mañana*" in Spanish? The Irishman thought for a moment, then replied, 'Yes, but it hasn't got quite the same sense of urgency about it.'

The scene is a court room. Patrick is being charged with causing an affray. He looks very much the worse for wear with cuts and bruises. The other contender in the brawl is in court. He is Michael O'Toole. The judge questions Patrick.

'Tell me, Patrick, what happened, in your own words?'

'Well, your honour, I was in the bar minding my own business when Michael there entered it. He had a long bit of four-by-two in his hand and he came at me and began beating me. Oi didn't stand a chance. He's entirely the injuring party.'

'But Patrick,' said the judge, 'will you tell me what you had in your hand?'

'Ah, your honour – all I had in my hand was Mrs Molly O'Toole's right breast. 'Twas a lovely thing in itself, your honour, but no earthly use in a fight.'

An Irishman was walking down town when he felt hungry. Up ahead he saw Joe's Pizza Parlor. He went in and ordered a pizza. When it came out of the oven, Joe asked the Irishman whether he wanted it cut into six or eight pieces. The Irishman said, 'You'd better cut it into six pieces. I couldn't eat eight!'

Pat and Mick were camping in the bush, but the mosquitoes were so bad they decided to pack up and move a few hundred yards. But they'd do so in total darkness, so that the mosquitoes wouldn't know where they'd gone.

They stumbled around in the dark, striking the tent by feel and groping their way through the thick scrub. Somehow they managed to repitch their tent in total darkness and, finally, fell inside exhausted. Whereupon a firefly came through the flap of their tent.

'It's no use,' moaned Pat, 'they're looking for us with hurricane lamps!'

A Pommy bloke had a prang on one of those fancy motorways and was taken to hospital. When he was off the critical list, a surgeon visited him and said, 'This news is good and bad. The good news is that you're out of danger, the bad news is that there is some damage to the brain which is not immediately life-threatening but could cause trouble later on. I strongly recommend that you authorise us to operate and remove the damaged cells.'

'I say, old boy, doesn't sound very nice. How much would have to be removed?'

'About 18 per cent, we estimate,' replied the surgeon.

'And what would be the significance of that, in layman's terms?'

'Well, it would have the effect of lowering your IQ to the level of the average Irish peasant.'

'I say, that doesn't sound at all nice. Still, I suppose you'd better do what has to be done.'

The operation was performed, and the surgeon came in to see the patient. 'The news is good and bad,' he said. 'The good news is that the operation was a complete success. The bad news is that the damage was more extensive than we thought and we had to remove 80 per cent of your brain cells.'

'Fair dinkum?'

An Irishman arrived in Australia and went into a pub in the Outback where he asked for a glass and, having pissed in it, drank it. He then walked out the door, into the chook house and proceeded to knock the hens off their perches prior to going to the paddock, where he lifted the tail of a cow and put his ear to its anus. When he returned to the bar a few minutes later, the publican asked him to explain his strange conduct.

'Before I left Dublin,' he said, 'I met an Aussie who said there are three things I had to do to be a real Australian. Drink the piss. Knock off the birds. And listen to the bullshit.'

Paddy and the priest were walking down the lane. Paddy was putting his hand in his coat pocket, looking for his cigarettes, when a packet of condoms fell on the cobbles. The priest picked up the packet and said, 'What do you use these for?'

Paddy said, 'Well, you can use them for lots of things. Like when it rains. You can put one over your cigarette to keep it dry.' As it was raining lightly at the time, the priest said, 'Then I'll get some.'

Next day he went to the chemist and asked the girl behind the counter for some condoms. She said, 'What size, Father?'

And the priest said, 'To fit a Camel.'

Paddy and Mick emigrate to Australia. Before they leave home, Paddy's dad, an old salt, gives them a bit of advice, 'You watch them Aussie cab drivers, they'll rob you blind. Don't you go paying them what they ask. You haggle.'

At Sydney airport they catch a cab to their hotel. When they reach their destination the cabbie says, 'That'll be twenty dollars, lads.'

'Oh no you don't! My dad warned me about you.

You'll only be getting fifteen dollars from me,' says Paddy.

'And you'll only get fifteen from me too,' adds Mick.

Paddy and Mick walk into the CES looking for work.

'Oh look, it's a pity Seamus wasn't with us.'

'And why would that be?' asks Mick.

'Well, there's a vacancy here for tree fellers and we could have gone for it.'

Paddy finally got the job and went along on his first day. He was given his chainsaw and told he must cut down twenty trees to earn his wages. He returned in the evening tired out.

'How many did you cut today, Paddy?'

'Five.'

'Sorry, no wages today.'

Next day, 'How many today, Paddy?'

'Ten.'

'Sorry Paddy, not enough.'

On the third day, Paddy crawls into the office.

'How many today, Paddy?'

'Fifteen, sir, and it's the best I can do.'

The foreman shook his head. 'I don't understand it. The others all reach their quota. Perhaps there's something wrong with your saw.' He took the chainsaw, started it up.

Paddy leapt back in horror. 'What's that noise?'

A doctor was doing his hospital rounds with an Irish nurse. When he came to one bed he pronounced, 'Nurse, this patient has died.'

The old fellow in the bed said, 'I'm all right. I'm not dead!'

The nurse responded, 'Will you be quiet. The doctor knows best.'

An Irish lady was given a parrot, but when she took it home it started to yell, 'My name's Sally. I'm a hooker and a goodtime girl.' So the lady went to the priest for advice.

'I have the solution,' said the priest. 'My two parrots are god-fearing, say the rosary daily and study the Bible. Put together they will make Sally forget her wicked past.'

When Sally was put in the cage with the other two, one was heard to remark, 'Put away your beads and Bible, Charlie. Our prayers have been answered!'

The ventriloquist was in sparkling form. The audience was in stitches. He'd told how the Jews got the Commandments. ('Free, already? *oi vey*! We'll take ten!'). The English-tourist-in-Wales-gag brought the house down. He'd explained why Scotsmen have thin penises. (They're such tight-fisted wankers.) 'Now,' he announced, 'I have a great Irish joke for you.' Whereupon, to his consternation, a huge man wearing a MacAlpine's jacket, jumped up. 'Listen, boyo,' he said in ominous tones, 'oim not goin' to stand for any o' them stories makin' out that us Oirish is t'ick.' The ventriloquist was somewhat alarmed. 'Now, now my good man,' he stammered, 'it's only a bit of harmless fun. No offence intended.'

'Oim not talkin' to you, mate,' replied the Irishman. 'Oim talkin' to that cheeky little bastard sittin' on yer knee.'

It was wake time in the Rafferty household. When Mulligan called to pay his last respects he found Mrs Rafferty more than usually upset. 'Sure it's his wig, Mick. You know how self-conscious he was about his baldness and how he always liked to look his best. We just can't get the wig to stay on properly.' 'Give me a minute or two wit' the carpse,' volunteered Mick, 'and oil see what oi kin do.' When Mick called Mrs Rafferty back into the room the wig was sitting perfectly on the corpse's head. 'Ah, Mick,' she cried, 'shure'n he's lovely. If only he could see himself. You must let me reward you.'

'Faith, 'twas nuthin',' the modest Mick protested.

'At least let me square up for your expenses,' Mrs Rafferty insisted.

'Well, all roight then,' Mick conceded, 'just give me a couple o' bob for the nails.'

At the height of the trouble in Northern Ireland, one of the most profitable businesses was the glazier trade. Most glaziers were so busy that stopgap measures had to be employed while waiting for new glass. Thus suppliers of plywood also prospered. But imagine the surprise of the person who broke his spectacles one Friday and was informed by the optometrist, 'We can't fit new lenses until next Monday, but we can board them up for you over the weekend.'

The young Irish lass was distraught. No one had ever explained to her the possible consquences of doing 'that'. 'Oh Mammy, Mammy,' she lamented, 'Oim pregnant. Oim goin' to have a baby.' Her mother liked to be clear on these things. 'Holy Mother,' she exclaimed, 'are ye sure it's yours?'

The Irish paratroop sergeant was explaining the technique.

'These 'chutes are army surplus,' he pointed out. 'To avoid strain, don't pull the rip cord until you're about 10 feet off the ground.'

'What if it doesn't open?' asked a worried recruit.

'Jeezus,' the sergeant bellowed, 'ye can jump 10 feet can't ye!'

Two young, teenage, Irish Catholic girls were walking home from a lecture given by the local priest on premarital sex. One said, 'Bridget, did you understand everything that Father said?'

'Oh yes,' replied Bridget, 'I know all about that stuff he was talkin' about.'

'Well, if you do,' said the first lass, 'are you one of them virgins Father was talkin' about?'

'No,' said Bridget, 'not yet!'

Did you hear about the Irishman who had a greyhound?

He had a bus painted on the side of it.

Pat and Mick decided it's time to confess. Mick goes into see the priest and says, 'I've been having a relationship with a young woman.' The priest is aghast. 'Was it Mary Houlihan?'

'No,' says Mick.

'Was it Brenda O'Shaughnessy?'

'No,' says Mick.

'Was it Maureen O'Hara?'

'No,' says Mick.

'Well, say fifty Hail Marys and don't do it again,' says the priest.

Pat is waiting for Mick outside the church. 'How did you go?'

'Marvellous. I got three new names.'

Why do the Irish call their currency a punt?

Because it rhymes with bank manager.

An Australian and an Irishman opened a Beer House in London, which failed badly. 'I know what we'll do,' said the Australian. 'Let's open a brothel on the first floor.'

'What a silly idea,' replied the Irishman. 'If you can't sell beer, how are you going to sell broth?'

A 10 p.m. curfew was imposed in Belfast. Everybody had to be off the streets by 8 p.m. However one citizen was shot at 7.45 p.m.

'Why did you do that?' the soldier was asked.

'I know where he lives,' he replied, 'and he wouldn't have made it.'

The judge in a criminal case in Dublin was shocked when the accused pleaded guilty to the charge but was acquitted by the jury.

'How did you arrive at that verdict?' he asked the foreman of the jury.

'Well, Your Honour,' was the reply, 'everybody except you knows him to be the biggest liar in Ireland.'

A Japanese businessman arrives at the Melbourne airport from Tokyo and goes straight to the airport bank. In return for a 1000 yen, the teller gives him 1260 Australian dollars. A few days later he's flying to Sydney and goes to the same counter for some extra cash. This time the teller hands him 1185 dollars for his 1000 yen. The Japanese complains, saying, 'One thousand yen, one thousand two hundred and sixty dollars, not right, not right.'

The teller calmly explains that the rates change

daily. But the Japanese, by now holding up a number of other customers, continues to demand his 'one thousand two hundred and sixty dollars.'

The teller tries patiently to explain, 'Please understand, it's the world money rate, the differences in currency.' Failing to communicate, he then said loudly, 'It's the fluctuations, the fluctuations!'

To which the angry Japanese replied, 'Well fluck you Aussies too.'

During a goodwill mission to Japan, a high-ranking Australian senator was shown over a factory manufacturing televisions. Pleasantly surprised at the number of employees who spoke English he stopped behind a young girl who was soldering.

'And what do you use for flux?' he asked.

The girl looked at him in surprise. 'Plicks, of course,' she said.

A sadistic captain in the First Fleet discovered that there were two Jews among the convicts. He had them brought before him. 'Jacob Levy and Isaac Cohen, I'm going to make an example of you. You will receive thirty lashes and be put on bread and water until we reach Sydney in three months. If you are still alive when we arrive you will be put in prison until you rot, if we don't hang you first. What do you say to that, you miserable convict Jews?'

The pathetic pair in manacles and tatters looked at each other. Jacob hobbled towards the captain and kicked him in the shin. Isaac looked at Jacob and out of the corner of his mouth said, 'For God's sake, Jacob, don't make trouble.'

A Jewish grandmother was looking after her son's children in a coffee shop in Acland Street. A friend came along and said, 'How old are the children?'

'Well,' replied the grandmother, 'the doctor is 4 and the lawyer will be 2 next week.'

The Australian Opera was halfway through the first act of *Aida* when Mrs Cohen rushed onto the stage calling out, 'Is there a doctor in the house?'

The singing stopped, the orchestra was silent, the curtains plunged and the theatre lights went on. A man in the front row stood up.

'I am a doctor,' he said.

'Would you like to meet a nice Jewish girl?' asked Mrs Cohen.

The Cohens had just married off their fourth daughter. 'That's the last one then,' said the rabbi.

'Good thing,' said Mr Cohen. 'The confetti's getting really grubby.'

Two Jewish businessmen were discussing insurance. 'You need fire insurance, burglary insurance and flood insurance.'

'The fire and theft and burglary I can understand,' said the other, 'but the flood insurance? How do you start a flood?'

A rabbi entered a delicatessen, studying the offerings in the display case very carefully. After a while he pointed to some sliced meat and said, 'Half a kilo of that corned beef please.'

The salesgirl said politely, 'I'm very sorry, sir, but that's ham.'

'And who the hell asked you?' retorted the rabbi.

Mrs Cohen sat next to a well-dressed man on the bus. She immediately peered closely at him and said, 'Pardon me, but are you Jewish?'

'No,' said the man, 'I'm not Jewish.'

'Are you sure?' asked Mrs Cohen.

'I'm absolutely sure,' replied the man.

'Could you be mistaken?' Mrs Cohen persisted.

'No way,' responded the man.

'I've got a feeling that you're Jewish,' said Mrs Cohen yet again.

'Listen, lady, get this, I am not Jewish.'

'Look, Mister, it's just between you and me, all right? You're Jewish, aren't you?'

Worn down, the man said, 'Okay, you got me, I'm Jewish.'

'That's funny,' said Mrs Cohen, 'you don't look Jewish.'

The wife of a Jewish immigrant who'd only recently arrived in Australia dies suddenly. One of the neighbours offers his condolences, mentioning to Isaac that it's an Australian custom to put an ad. in the Classified Columns. So Isaac phones the *Age* and, determined to save money, asks for a two-word message. 'Ruth died.'

When the operator explains that the minimum charge covers five words, he thinks for a moment and adds, 'Toyota for sale.'

The business executive jumps out of a four-storey building and splatters on the footpath. Within a few moments the ambulance arrives and the officers try everything – mouth-to-mouth, heart massage. An old Jewish lady comes up. 'Give him chicken soup. It won't help, it won't hoit.'

Mr Weinstein couldn't attend the final court case of a major commercial litigation, but instructed his lawyer to advise him immediately of the outcome. When he returned to his office, the following fax message was waiting for him. 'Justice prevailed.'

To which he immediately replied, 'Appeal.'

Mr Cohen and Mr Cohen are both hospitalised for severe attacks of sciatica. They share the same room and get the same daily massages, which are extremely painful. While Mr Cohen is crying out loud during the massage, the other Mr Cohen endures his with serenity and calm. After it's been going on for a few days, Cohen asks Cohen, 'How do you manage to take this treatment without yelling?'

'How do I do it? You think I'm such a fool to let them massage my sciatic leg?'

Sol Greenblat was hit by the recession. He was practically broke. He prayed on the Sabbath in the synagogue. 'God, I need your help. I've never asked you before and I promise not to bother you again. All I need is to win the lottery. Just once God, that's all I ask.'

On Monday he looked in the papers – nothing. So next Saturday he went to the synagogue again and his prayers were even more fervent. On Monday – nothing.

So on Wednesday he prayed, 'God, do you really want me to pray again? It's only just a small thing I ask. Please help me.'

And he heard a voice, 'Look mate, you'll have to co-operate a little. You have to buy a ticket.'

Abe Finkelstein had finished his hawking rounds for a week and had done very well. So he thought he would give himself a justly deserved reward and went to a well-known King's Cross brothel. The Madam said, 'Well, you can have this nice Chinese girl over there for $5, then I have a redhead for $10 and this terrific blonde for $15.' Abe decided to spend $10 and had a marvellous time.

More than twenty years later his wife had died and he felt lonely so once again he went to the brothel. He recognised the redhead who was now the Madam, and there was a friendly reunion. Whereupon a huge youngster of about 20 appeared and called out, 'Mum, does this guy bother you?'

'No, no,' said the Madam, 'in fact, John, I'd like you to meet your father.'

'What?' said John, 'this little Jewish bloke's my Dad?'

To which Abe responded, 'Watch your manners! If I hadn't been so generous, you'd have been a Chinaman.'

A big Texan steps off the plane at Ben Gurion airport and hails a taxidriver. He drawls, 'Ah want yew to take me to where yew people are weeping and wailing and rocking and beating your heads against the wall.'

And the taxidriver takes him to the Taxation Department.

Poor Isaac lay dying and his family were at his bedside.

'Are you there, Abe?'

'Yes, father, I'm here.'

'Are you there, Ben?'

'Yes, father, I'm here.'

'Are you there, Rachel?'

'Yes, father, I'm here.'

'Are you there, Anna?'

'Yes, father, I'm here.'

Isaac forces his way up onto his elbows. His eyes

open a little and he yells, 'Who the hell is looking after the business?'

A Jewish shopkeeper rented some space in one of the new shopping malls. Each new tenant was allowed one banner above their space. The retailer on the right asked for 'Best Quality'. The one on his left 'Lowest Prices'. After a moment's reflection, the Jewish shopkeeper demanded 'Enter Here'.

A group of Israelis were discussing recent wars. 'What a shame that we have no Tomb of the Unknown Warrior,' said one, 'representing the fallen who were never found.'

'Of course we have such a tomb,' said another. 'It's on the outskirts of the city. I'll take you to it.' And they came upon a well-kept cemetery, as green as an oasis.

'There,' he said, 'is the Tomb of the Unknown Warrior.'

The first man looked and immediately protested, 'What are you talking about? This is the tomb of Isaac Goldberg, the prominent banker.'

'That's right. As a banker he was remarkable, as a soldier – unknown.'

An old Jewish bloke is crossing the street in Berlin in 1936 when he accidentally bumps into a burly stormtrooper.

'*Schweinhund*,' snarls the Nazi.

'Goldberg,' the old chap replies offering his hand.

Mr Block approaches a Catholic priest regarding the funeral of his deceased sister.

'This must be an error, Mr Block,' says the priest, 'I am a Catholic priest and your sister, God bless her soul, was Jewish.'

'My sister was not only baptised but she entered a convent and died as a nun.'

'That makes, of course, things quite different. Particularly as she has been a bride of Christ, I will be happy to see her to her grave. My fee for the service will be $100.'

Mr Block gives the priest $50, saying, 'My brother-in-law will pay the other half.'

Young Moishe was never good at mathematics and at the end of Term 10 his grades were completely unsatisfactory. When his father took him to task, his explanation was that his teacher was anti-semitic.

'Fine,' said his father, 'if that is the case, I will have you baptised.'

But baptised or not baptised, Moishe again brought a completely unsatisfactory report at the end of the following term.

'Now I have had you baptised and things haven't improved,' reproached his father.

'Come on, father, you know we Christians are no good at maths.'

The President of Israel is visiting the Pope at the Vatican. On the Pope's desk he notices a green telephone. 'What is the purpose of that phone, Your Holiness?'

'Well,' answers the Pope, pointing skywards, 'that's a direct line to you-know-who.'

'Marvellous,' replies the President of Israel. 'May I make a call?'

'Certainly, my son,' replies the Pope, 'but it will cost you about $200.'

A few months later the Pope is paying a return visit to Israel and is in the President's apartments. He espies a green phone on the desk. 'My son, what is the purpose of that phone?'

'Well, Your Holiness,' replies the President, 'that is a direct line to you-know-who.'

'*Benissimo*,' replies the Pope, 'may I make a call? I will be happy to reimburse you.'

'Go right ahead,' replies the President, 'but don't worry about the cost. It's a local call.'

On a long flight, one of the passengers stood up and addressed the others. He said, 'My name is Brown B-R-O-W-N and I'm true blue. I'm an American through and through. I'm white as snow from the top of my head to the tip of my toes, and I hate blacks.' After a while he stood up and again made a speech, 'My name is Brown B-R-O-W-N Brown and I'm true blue, as white as snow from the top of my head to the tip of my toes and I hate Jews.'

After a while a little man stood up and also addressed the passengers saying, 'My name's Schmidt S-C-H-M-I-D-T Schmidt and I'm a Jew. I'm as white as snow from the top of my head to the top of my toes, except for my arse which is brown B-R-O-W-N brown.'

An Irish priest offered 10 cents to the boy who could tell him who was 'the greatest man in history'.

'Columbus,' said one.

'George Washington,' said another.

'St Patrick,' shouted a third.

'The 10 cents is yours. But as the only Jewish boy in class, why did you choose St Patrick?'

'Right down in my heart I knew it was Moses,' he replied, 'but business is business.'

An El Al jumbo jet takes off from London airport bound for Tel Aviv. After climbing a few thousand feet the captain gets on the blower. 'Good afternoon, ladies and gentlemen. Welcome aboard El Al. We'll be cruising at 35 000 feet for most of your journey. Heavy cloud below in some parts, but flying conditions should be very good. A little turbulence on descent maybe ... but that's all. Estimated time of arrival at Tel Aviv ... ah ... 1800 hours ... to you ... 1750.'

There are two Jewish business men who, although close friends, have been rivals all through their business lives. Each tries to outdo the other in every field of endeavour. When Max buys a home for one million dollars, Harry responds by buying one for a million, one hundred thousand.

It came to pass that Max went to Europe on his vacation and, on returning, couldn't wait to boast to his friend. 'I didn't want to disappoint the queen, so when she came to meet me at the airport, I agreed to let her put me up at the palace. She really couldn't do enough for me.'

Harry, at this point, is eaten with jealousy. Determined to outdo Max, he embarks on a European journey within days. When he returns after a few weeks he is met at the airport by his friend. 'Well,' asks Max, 'how was it? Was it as good as my trip?'

'I really don't know,' responds Harry. 'I didn't go

to London. I decided to go to Rome. And when I got there, the Pope came to the airport and insisted that I stay at the Vatican.'

This greatly impresses Max. 'The Pope?' he asks breathlessly, 'tell me, what is the Pope really like?'

'Well, I'll tell you,' says the storyteller, 'him I liked, but her I couldn't stand.'

For their fortieth wedding anniversary, Sadie gives Hymie a gift voucher to a high class brothel. Hymie is shocked. 'Sadie, what does this mean?' 'Well, Hymie,' says Sadie, 'our sex life has become so boring that I want you to take this, with my blessing, and go with one of these goils and learn something to put a little sparkle back in our schtupping.' Hymie is dismayed, but Sadie persists and eventually he goes.

The next morning he staggers through the door exhausted and, waving away Sadie's questions, stumbles to bed. By dinner, he's recovered enough to join Sadie and she asks, 'So? How was it?'

'Ahh, it was nothing,' he says.

'Nothing! All that money I spent and you say it was nothing. Surely you learnt something!'

'I didn't, Sadie,' says Hymie, 'I tried everything but everything I tried, we do already.'

'But surely,' says Sadie, 'surely there was one thing.'

'Well,' says Hymie, 'maybe there was one little thing.'

'Yes,' says Sadie, 'yes, what is it?'

'Well,' says Hymie, a little embarrassed, 'she moaned.' Sadie is speechless a moment. 'She moaned?' Hymie guiltily nods. 'And you like this moaning?' says Sadie, and Hymie shrugs and nods. 'Whoo boy,' says Sadie, 'for this I pay all that money. But, okay, if moaning is what you like then who am I to argue.'

That night Sadie and Hymie slide between the sheets and Sadie says, 'You want me to start moaning now?' And Hymie says, 'Not now, Sadie, not now.' Foreplay proceeds and Sadie says, 'Now, Hymie? You want I moan now?' 'Not yet, Sadie,' says Hymie, 'not yet.' And then Hymie climbs aboard Sadie and things, for him anyway, are building to a big crescendo as Sadie waits with wide-eyed anticipation. And then Hymie orgiastically calls out, 'Now, Sadie, moan now!' And Sadie shrugs and says, 'Okay, if that's what you want ... So, you're not going to believe it, but I went to the butcher's this morning and he had no veal and my corns were hurting and, *oi vey*! Mrs Silverstein wouldn't stop telling me about her son the doctor ... '

A Jewish socialite, Mrs Beckki Goldstein, had just learnt that she had six months to live. On hearing this she contacted her rabbi and asked him to find her a teacher so she could learn to speak Hebrew. The rabbi asked why she wanted to learn to speak Hebrew.

'Never mind,' she said, 'just find me a teacher.'

The rabbi organised a teacher for her and after six weeks she managed to master the Hebrew language, much to her tutor's amazement. Some time later, the rabbi paid her a visit and enquired how the lessons were proceeding.

'Excellent,' she said. 'I have mastered the Hebrew language in six weeks.'

'This is wonderful and amazing,' said the rabbi, 'after six weeks you have managed to learn Hebrew, a language that has taken scholars many years to perfect. Tell me, Mrs Goldstein, was there a reason for learning Hebrew at your age in life?'

'You bet,' Mrs Goldstein said. 'When I die and go to heaven I want to be able to speak to God in his native tongue.'

'Well, that's all very well, Mrs Goldstein, but what happens if you go to hell after you die?'

'It doesn't matter,' she said. 'I also speak Hungarian.'

As Hyram turned into his driveway, he was surprised to find a brand new Ford Laser parked there. He entered the house and called to his wife, 'Rachel! What's with the new car?'

Rachel ran to her husband, gave him a big kiss, and said excitedly, 'Oh, Hyram! It's all thanks to you. Since we got married, every time we made love I put \$50 away. Yesterday I'd saved enough to buy the Laser!'

Hyram looked dejectedly at his wife. 'Oh, Rachel,' he exclaimed, 'if only I'd known. I would have given you all my business and you could have bought a Rolls Royce!'

After twenty years delivering mail to the same area, Abe the postman was retiring. As he went from house to house on his final round, the neighbours gave him little gifts in appreciation of his service. When he arrived at Mrs Goldberg's house she said, 'Postie, for your last day I've made you a lovely lunch. Please come in.' Which he did.

After lunch, Mrs Goldberg then said, 'Now that you've eaten, would you like to come upstairs with me and make love?' Although somewhat surprised, he agreed to her request. As he was leaving, she picked up an envelope from the hall table and gave it to him. He opened it and found that it contained \$5.

'Mrs Goldberg,' he said, 'you made me a beautiful lunch; you took me up stairs and we made love. And now you want to give me \$5. You are too generous.'

'Oh,' she said, 'you really should thank my husband. This morning I said to him "Abe the postman is retiring. What do you think I should give him?" And my husband said, "Fuck him! Give him $5" but the lunch was my idea!'

Mr Cohen is on a skiing holiday in the alps and gets hopelessly lost. After a few days a search party is sent out to find him. They arrive in the first valley and call out, 'Mr Cohen! Mr Cohen! It's the Red Cross!' Silence.

They struggle on, through deeper and deeper snow, to a second valley. 'Mr Cohen! Mr Cohen! It's the Red Cross!' Nothing.

With immense difficulty they make it to a third valley where, once again, they call out, MR COHEN! MR COHEN! IT'S THE RED CROSS!!'

And they hear a little voice, from far in the distance, 'I gave at the office, already!'

Moses went back up the mountain. 'Excuse me, God, I just want to get this straight. The Arabs get all the oil, and we get to cut the ends off our what????'

Three retired ragtraders, who made a bit of money out of schmutter, meet every week in an Acland Street café for a chat. One tells his friends that he has terrible, terrible news. 'My son has become a Christian.'

'*Oi vey*,' says another, 'so has mine!'

Then the third confesses that his son, too, has traded in the yarmulke for a crucifix. Whereupon the rabbi wanders in and they tell him of their troubles. The rabbi looks shamefaced and says that his son, has also become a Christian. So they troop off to the Synagogue where the rabbi prays to God, reminding Him of the way He had helped the Israelites flee Egypt, taking them safely through the Red Sea and showing them the Promised Land. 'And now, just a few thousand years later, our sons have become Christians.'

'A funny thing,' says God, 'my son too . . .'

The priest in the confessional hears an old man's voice on the other side of the screen. 'I'm 79 years old, married to the same woman for 50 years, and always faithful – never looked at another woman. Yesterday, I made passionate love to a pair of 18-year-old twins.'

Priest: 'When was the last time you went to confession?'

Man: 'What confession? I'm Jewish.'

Priest: 'So why are you telling me?'

Man: 'I'm telling *everybody*!'

The recession hit hard and a Jewish couple getting on in years falls on very hard times. Rachel offers to help by going out on the streets. Abe protests feebly, but Rachel goes. The next morning he's counting the takings. There's $34.50. 'Which lousy schmuck gives you the 50 cents,' he asks.

'All of them.'

What do you get if you cross a Jewish American Princess with a computer?

A system that won't go down on you.

Why do Jewish American Princesses prefer to have sex doggy style?

Because they can't bear to see anyone else enjoying themselves.

Did you hear about the Jewish banker who bought his wife a solid gold diaphragm?

He wanted to come into his own money.

A New Zealander, trying to escape the shame of applying for the dole in an increasingly hostile Australia, approaches a local farmer for a job. He claims to be a great horseman, terrific with cattle and even better with sheep. 'I worked for sux farmers when I was in New Zulland,' he said. 'There's nothing around the farm that I can't do.'

The farmer decides to give him a go. 'I want you to go up to the top of the hill, herd all those cattle down into the yards and then round up the sheep and shear them.'

The New Zealander goes to it. Half an hour later the farmer sees that all the cattle are in the yards, but there's no sign of the sheep. So he goes up to the shearing shed and finds the New Zealander having intercourse with one of his ewes.

'You rotten swine,' yells the farmer, 'I told you to shear them.'

'Not on your life,' said the New Zealander, 'I'm not sharing them with anybody.'

What's long and hard and fucks New Zealanders?

High School.

How do you make a New Zealander successful in small business?

Give him a large business.

An American, an Australian and a New Zealander were walking down a country lane when they chanced upon a ewe caught in a wire fence with its bum facing out to the road. Commenting upon the sheep's gyrations and exertions to escape, the American said, 'Goddam, I wish that was Madonna. I'd give her a reason to wriggle!'

The Australian said, 'I wish that was Kylie Minogue – I'd be up that like a rat up a drain pipe!'

Said the Kiwi, 'I wish it was dark!'

Things were going badly in Te Maika, as in the rest of New Zealand. Brian decided to try his luck in Melbourne, and two months later, his brother Bruce got a letter from him, 'You must come over here. The streets are paved with gold.'

Bruce packed his few belongings, and travelled steerage from Auckland. As he stepped onto the quay at Port Melbourne, he saw a 50-dollar note on the ground. 'Good as gold!' he exclaimed as he bent to pick it up. Then he stopped, straightened up, wiped his brow, and said, 'Hang about. It's Sunday today. I'll start work tomorrow.'

There's a sign outside a Queensland garage, 'Fill up and get a free fuck.' A man fills up and says, 'Well?'

The attendant says, 'Law says there's got to be a little competition. Think of a number.'

'Eight.'

'Bad luck, it's nine.'

The man drives off, stops at the next pub, orders a drink and says to a bloke standing at the bar, 'That garage down the road – it's a bloody take. Signs says "Fill up and get a free fuck" and it's all bullshit.'

The bloke says, 'No, mate, you're wrong. It's fair dinkum. Ridgy-didge. No worries. My wife won twice last month.'

A chap walks into a bar, bubbling over with good humour and says to the barman, 'Look, I've got this incredible joke about banana benders. You set me up with my drink and I'll tell you my incredible joke.' So away goes the barman, prepares the drink and returns with it.

'Just one point, sir, before you start this joke, I think perhaps I ought to mention. I happen to be a Queenslander. And if you notice that gentleman at the end of the bar who is bigger than I am – I happen to know that he also is a Queenslander. And if you glance over to the far corner there and notice the gentleman in the blue shirt who is bigger than both of us put together – he also is a

Queenslander. I just thought you might like to know all that.'

'Oh, well, in that case,' says the chap glancing around, 'perhaps I'll just have the drink. Perhaps I'll not bother you with the joke.'

'Why not? It might be a very interesting joke.'

'Well, hell, I mean,' he says glancing around again, 'I don't want to have to explain it three times over.'

Stalin's corpse was having a very unsettling effect on Soviet citizenry, so Nikita rang President Kennedy and asked him if he'd help with his dilemma by taking Stalin's body. Kennedy said no, and suggested Krushchev ring Macmillan. But Prime Minister Macmillan also refused, as did President de Gaulle. Krushchev then called Ben-Gurion of Israel and explained his problem.

Ben-Gurion said, 'Send it to us, we'll take care of it. But remember, my country has the highest rate of resurrection in the world.'

A Russian official woke Mr Brezhnev one morning saying, 'Comrade Brezhnev, I'm sorry to wake you, but there are two very important items of news which you'll have to know about. One of them is good and one is bad. Which you do want to hear first?'

Brezhnev said, 'I'd better hear the bad news first.' The official said, 'Comrade Brezhnev, the Chinese have landed on the moon.'

Brezhnev said, 'God, that's awful, what's the good news?'

'All of them,' said the official.

Ivan was leaning on his front verandah chewing solemnly. His friend Yuri approached. 'You should be more careful, my friend. It is illegal to have imperialist, capitalist chewing gum in Mother Russia. You might get arrested for being in contact with the enemy.' Ivan looked at Yuri and said, 'It is not chewing gum. I am washing my underpants.'

A Russian decides to buy a motor car. He rings the car factory and asks for a delivery date if an order is placed now. The man at the car factory says five years, which would be a Monday in September. The car buyer asks, 'Would that be in the morning or the afternoon?'

The car salesman says, 'After five years, what does it matter morning or afternoon?'

The car buyer says, 'Because the plumber is calling in the morning.'

Two Russians, a man and a woman, met on the train taking them to work. Said the man, 'Vot are you working at?'

The woman replied, 'I work in a tractor factory. I paint tractors red. And last week my extra production earned me a medal and I was made one of the elite, a Hero Worker. However we are very proud of our achievements and if we keep our production tallies up we have been promised a tour of the salt mines.'

The man listened to all this, then exclaimed, 'Enough of this romance, down with your pants.'

President Gorbachev, at a news conference in London, was asked by a reporter, 'President Gorbachev, what effect on history do you think it would have had if, in 1963, President Krushchev had been assassinated instead of President Kennedy?'

Gorbachev thought for a moment and replied, 'I don't think Mr Onassis would have married Mrs Krushchev.'

Andy McTavish migrated to Australia and took up residence in a boarding house in Melbourne.

'Would y' like me to cut yer some lunch?' asked the landlady as he set out to work.

'Och aye, that would be verra guid.'

So the landlady made him a sandwich from a slice of cheese and put it in a neat paper bag. When he arrived home that evening he said nothing about the lunch. Eventually the landlady, consumed with curiosity, asked him if he had enjoyed the lunch.

'Och aye, it were verra guid, what there was of it.' Taking the hint, the landlady next day gave him two sandwiches. That evening the same question brought forth the same reply. And so this went on – three and then four sandwiches – and always the reply, 'Och aye, verra guid, what there was of it.' So the landlady decided on a desperate measure. She got a large loaf, cut it lengthwise, filled it with everything in the fridge – ham, cheese, salami, peanut butter, tomato, lettuce, hard-boiled eggs, olives – the lot, and wrapped it in several pages of the *Age*. That evening she asked, 'And how did y' like yer lunch today, Mr McTavish?'

'Och aye, it were verra guid, but I see you are back to one sandwich again!'

There were two Scotsmen in a pub in Glasgow comparing scars and old wounds on their respective bodies, legacies of the innumerable fights and brawls they'd been in, and for which much of working-class Glasgow is famous. Each was trying to outdo the other for former acts of bravado and daring.

'See this scar here,' said one in an accent that made Billy Connolly sound like an educated Pommie, 'I got that fra' a big bastard wi' a razor i' Gorbals one night!' He pointed to a white line that ran from below one ear to the middle of his chin.

'Och, tha's nothin',' said the other, 'take a look at this!' He turned his head to display a missing ear lobe. 'Bit off by a sailor in yon boozer doon at they docks!'

'See you and ya wee love bites,' said the former, 'I nearly lost ma nose fra' a chibbin' i' Brig-ton – see they stitches!'

And so it continued, the two so engrossed in their comparisons that they failed to notice they were being observed. Across the other side of the bar, but within earshot, was a monster of a man. Fully 2 metres tall, he had a face that looked like raw meat, hands like hams, and a chest as big as a barrel. He sat alone, his huge bulk dwarfing the table on which he leaned. He listened intently while the erstwhile warriors displayed more and more sections of their battered anatomy. Then he rose, finished his pint, and lumbered over to where they sat.

'See youse two!' he bellowed. Silence fell upon the bar.

'D'youse want ta see a *real* scar, instead o' they scratches on ya scrawny wee bodies?' The two nodded silently, almost paralysed with fear.

Slowly, the huge man unbuttoned his shirt, and then the belt of his trousers, eventually revealing an enormous purple scar that began from under his chin, ran the entire length of his torso, and terminated only centimetres above his pubes. The entire bar was transfixed, gazing unbelievingly at this ultimate trophy, this extraordinary badge of pugilistic pride. The giant completed a full 360 degrees display, ensuring that everyone got a good look.

Finally, one of our two warriors managed to break the silence. 'Jesus Christ!' he spluttered, 'where d'you get that?'

A broad smile split the face of the giant as he uttered but two words. 'Post mortem!'

Two 90-year-old Scotsmen meet in the street and Jock says to Sandy, 'What's this I hear about you being committed on a rape charge? You know that's ridiculous.'

'Och aye,' says Sandy, 'but I was too proud to plead Not Guilty!'

What is a Tasmanian man's idea of foreplay?

You awake, mum?

There was great excitement in Wynyard, Tasmania, as the local football team had won the preliminary final and, for the first time in twenty-nine years, would play in the Grand Final the following week. Discussion of the game had reached a fever pitch in the small coastal town and most of it centred on the injuries of the team's champion players, Ian and Trevor Dick, who were brothers. Ian had strained ligaments and Trevor a corked thigh. Would they be fit for the big day?

The burning question was answered on Friday morning before the game by the *Advocate*, which had the following banner headline on its sports page: WYNYARD TO PLAY WITHOUT DICKS. Not to be outdone, the other newspaper in the region, the *Examiner*, led with a similar headline on Saturday, the morning of the game. It read: WYNYARD TO PLAY WITH DICKS OUT. Needless to say the ground was jam-packed for the big game as people travelled from all over the state to see this historic clash.

How do you get a racist to laugh on a Sunday?

Tell him a racist joke on Friday.

What's the difference between a racist and a bucket of sludge?

The bucket.

Why is a racist like a drunk?

Because whatever he says ends in a slur.

Why is a racist like a dog?

They both mark out territory by spraying walls – and always with something offensive.

What's red and white and peels itself?

A white supremist trying to get a suntan.

What's the definition of 'confused'?

A white supremist watching the Olympic 100-metres men's sprint.

What do you get when you cross a white supremist with a donkey?

Someone who thinks the sun shines out of his own ass.

What do you call a bigot who does well in an IQ test?

A cheat.

Why is a bigot like the announcer at Rosehill?

Because they both start shouting the instant they see a new race.

What's the difference between a schoolyard racist and Adolf Hitler?

Opportunity.

What are the best four years of a racist's life?

Year 6.

Why is racist abuse like pooing your own pants?
Because you only do it when you're really scared.

Why do racists always hang round in gangs?
So they can form a dope ring.

Why *didn't* the racist cross the road?
Because she was afraid of seeing the other side.

Why couldn't the racist get work as a doctor?
Because every time he felt bad about himself, he'd try to put someone down.

How many racists does it take to change a light bulb?
None – because racists hate being enlightened.

Have you heard about the racist who choked on his yoghurt?
Someone told him it grew out of a foreign culture.

Why is a racist like a 'Neighbours' writer?
Because they're both involved in character assassination.

Why do racists compete with others on the basis of colour?
Because if they competed on brains, they'd lose.

Why did the racist punch-out the sophisticated immigrants?

Because if you can't join them, beat them.

Have you heard about the racist who was terrified of getting a culture shock?

That's why she only attacked people without power.

Why is a racist like a drug runner?

Because they're both terrified of foreign customs.

Did you hear about the racist who was invited to address the recycling conference?

He had a lot of experience in talking rubbish.

Two black doctors were walking along a hospital corridor in Johannesburg. One said to the other, 'You know that white fellow in Ward 5 who has cancer?'

'The one in the corner bed?'

'Yes. Have you broken the news to him he has a terminal illness?'

'Well, yes, as a matter of fact I have.'

'You bastard. I wanted to tell him.'

SOCIAL NICETIES

Scene: Collins Street, Melbourne, peak hour. A limo waits at a red light. A tramp knocks on the driver's window. Driver presses button, lowers window.

Tramp: 'Lend us a couple of dollars for a feed, mate.'

Driver removes cigar from mouth: ' "Neither a borrower nor a lender be" – William Shakespeare.'

Replaces cigar, presses button, raises window. Lights change to green, limo proceeds to next intersection, stops again at red light. Tramp runs after limo, again knocks on driver's window.

Driver presses button, lowers window.

Tramp: ' "Cunt" – D.H. Lawrence.'

A rich American family commissioned a well-known author to write a family history, but insisted he should soft-pedal on the case of one particular family skeleton. This was the late Uncle William whose life of crime ended with his death in the electric chair in the 1920s. 'Don't come straight out and say this,' the author was told, 'just skirt around it.'

So this is what he wrote, 'Uncle William occupied a chair of applied electronics in one of our leading government institutions. He was held to the post by the closest of ties and his death came as a real shock.'

Long before the Australian Government decided to let gays into the army, a couple of colonels were travelling in a first class compartment, each reading his newspaper. After a while, one put his paper down and called across to the other, 'Army?' The second put his paper down and replied, 'Yes, as a matter of fact.' They both returned to their papers.

After a while the first one put down his paper again and asked, 'Duntroon?'

'Yes, as a matter of fact,' replied the second. Back to their papers.

Some while later, the first put down his paper again and called across, 'Homo?'

'No.'

'Pity.'

During World War II the train from Liverpool to London was absolutely full and many soldiers had been standing in the corridors for hours. All this time a wealthy dowager in a first class compartment had been occupying two seats, one for herself and one for her tiny dog. A weary English officer asked her politely whether she would mind putting her dog on the floor. She replied, 'I have paid for Fifi's seat and she is going to stay there as long as she wants.'

Eventually the officer could stand it no longer. He picked up Fifi, threw her out the window and sat down. For a moment there was stunned silence. Then an American officer sitting opposite leant towards the English officer. 'You know,' he said, 'you English are a strange lot. You eat with your fork in the wrong hand; you drive on the wrong side of the road, and now you've thrown the wrong bitch out of the window!'

A wizard was strolling about the Botanic Gardens one day and noted two statues, a man statue and a woman statue, perched on each side of the path, staring at each other. 'Look at that,' he murmured to himself. 'There they have been since Federation, in sun and rain, heat and cold, droughts, floods and bushfires and never a move. I will reward them.' So he clicked his fingers and humanised the statues. 'As a reward for your patience,' he told them, 'you can have half an hour as humans.'

The man statue looked at the woman statue and said, 'Will we?'

'Yes, let's,' giggled the woman statue. So they retired behind some bushes, whence for some fifteen minutes came muffled sounds of gasps, giggles and grunts. Then they came out from behind the bushes, pink in the face, and dusting off turf and grass and ferns and lolly papers and beer can labels.

The wizard looked at his watch and said, 'You still have fifteen minutes before you're back to being statues.'

The woman statue said to the man statue, 'Again?'

'Too right,' said the man statue, 'only this time you hold the pigeon and I'll crap on it.'

The Dowager rings for her butler and asks him to:

'Please take off my dress.'

'Please take off my petticoat.'

'Please take off my bra.'

'Please take off my panties.'

All of her requests are answered by a respectful, 'Yes, Ma'am.'

Finally she says, 'And Jeeves, if I catch you wearing my clothes again, you'll be sacked.'

Lady Penelope of Sloane Street, London, is throwing a party. It is to be fancy dress and everyone is to come as an emotion. Lady Penelope has a big black butler called Jeeves whose advances to her are continually knocked back. Comes the night of the big party and a little group of close friends gather behind her at the door to welcome her guests. The doors are opened and first in the queue is dressed entirely in green. 'Let me see,' Lady Penelope says, 'you're green with envy!' The group at the door applauds elegantly.

The second guest steps up to the door dressed entirely in blue. 'Hmmm . . .' considers Lady Penelope, 'you've got the blues.' The group behind her titters and claps genteelly. Her jaw drops as the next to step up is Jeeves, stark naked. Around his waist is strapped a bowl of custard. He's got a cock on him like a sock full of sand and the end of it disappears into the bowl. She gasps, turns pale and puts her gloved hand to her mouth. There is a hush from behind.

Jeeves growls, 'I's fucken d'iscusted.'

Two Englishmen, two Scotsmen, two Welshmen and two Irishmen were stranded on a desert island. The Scotsmen started the Caledonian Club to celebrate all things Scottish – tossing the caber, bagpipes etc. The two Welshmen started an Eisteddford, the two Irishmen formed the IRA and agreed to blow up anything built by the English.

The two Englishmen went to the opposite ends of the island and would not talk to each other as they'd not been introduced.

Two old codgers took their wives along to the ladies' night at their very exclusive club. They chose the club's specialty from the menu – thick blue boiler pea soup made with lashings of ham from the bone. An hour later the inevitable happened. One of the gentlemen emitted a sound from his nether regions which would have been described in less-refined circles as a massive 'Doris Hart'.

'I say, old boy,' said his startled club mate, 'not in front of my wife.'

'Terribly sorry, old chap,' said the contrite offender. 'I wasn't aware it was her turn!'

The speaker was known for the brevity of his speech-making. It was claimed he once made the shortest speech on record. Introduced to a large and expectant audience as 'The World-wide Authority on Sexual Behaviour', he rose and said, 'Ladies and gentlemen, it gives me great pleasure.' And sat down.

An Australian, an Englishman and a Frenchman were arguing as to the meaning of *savoir faire*. The Australian said, 'I'll give you an example. A bloke comes home to find his best cobber screwing his wife in bed. He says, "G'day, Shirl! G'day, George! Never mind me, just carry on. I'll go and get a beer!" That's *savoir faire*!'

The Englishman said, 'Well, I'd almost go along with that, but I'd express it a little differently. A chap comes home, "Good evening, Shirley. Good evening, George. Never mind me, I'll just go and have a gin and tonic." That's *savoir faire*.'

The Frenchman says, 'No, no. A man comes home to find his best friend in bed making passionate love to his wife. He says, "*Ah, bonjour*. Never mind me. You just carry on while I go and get a drink." And if they *can* carry on, that's *savoir faire*!'

The Australian, the Frenchman and the Canadian were bragging about their sexual escapades with their respective wives.

'After I have zee sex wiz my wife,' said the Frenchman, 'I cover her wiz crepes suzette and eat it sensually off her silky bare skin. She becomes so excited she rises centimetres off ze bed.'

'When I screw my wife,' drawled the Canadian, 'I pour maple syrup on her and lick it off slowly. She's in so much goddam ecstasy she rises *feet* off the bed.'

'Me?' says the Aussie. 'When I've finished with my old lady I wipe my dick on the curtains and she hits the roof!'

John saw Bob in the pub. Bob had a black eye.

'What happened?' asked John.

'Well,' said Bob, 'I was in church last Sunday, and we stood up to sing a hymn. I noticed that the dress on the woman in front of me had caught up into the crack of her bum. I thought to myself, that will be uncomfortable when she sits down, and it wouldn't look good for her to be squirming on the seat in church. So I reached forward and pulled the folds of her dress out from where it was caught. She turned around and slugged me, whammo. Black eye.'

'Some people have no gratitude,' opined John.

The following week they meet again. Bob's other eye is blackened.

'Not that woman in church again?' asked John.

'Sure was,' replied Bob. 'Same deal. We stand up to sing a hymn, her dress is caught in the crack of her bum. Only this time it's the guy next to me who pulls it out.'

John asks, 'And did she think it was you and slug you for it?'

'Oh, no. You see, I knew that she didn't like her dress being pulled out of her bum, so I tried to poke it back in again. Whammo. Black eye.'

The Governor-General was visiting the State House for the Confused. In the main assembly hall the inmates were sitting about quietly but periodically one would stand up and shout out a number after which they would all fall about in paroxysms of mirth. When the G-G asked what was going on, the superintendent revealed that because they had all been there so long and had heard all their respective stories many times, they had numbered them. So all an individual had to do was shout out the number of his story and they all knew what it was about. Fascinated, the G-G said he would like to tell a story and see the reaction. The superintendent said, 'Okay, think of a number and when I introduce you, shout it out.'

Having got the attention of the audience, the superintendent introduced the G-G and announced he was going to tell a story. The G-G then shouted '69', which was greeted with a deathly silence. Embarrassed, the official party left the hall and when outside, the G-G asked why they hadn't laughed.

'They knew the story,' the superintendent consoled him, 'they just didn't like the way you told it!'

Two old blokes, obviously mates, were standing on the corner of Spring and Bourke Streets. It was a balmy day. The first bloke sniffed the air and remarked to his friend, 'You didn't fart just then, did you?'

To which his mate took considerable offence. 'Of course I did. You don't think I smell like that all the time do you?'

Two old ladies were sitting on a Sydney bus, circa 1960. 'What do you think of these new fangled tights, Glad?'

'Oh, I suppose they're all right, but the trouble is every time I fart I blow my shoes off.'

A very rich and respected Toorak lady held a tea party for her rich and influential friends, and ate more cucumber sandwiches than was good for her. During one of those deadly silences that happen in even the best of parties, a colossal breaking of wind came from the hostess's direction. Never one to be easily embarrassed, she quickly said to her butler, 'James, stop that immediately!' The butler turned slowly and replied in his most superior voice, 'Certainly madam, which way did it go?'

The Keatings go to London to see the Queen. Because of Paul's 'coming the grope' on her last tour, and because of all the fuss about the republic, relationships are pretty strained and Paul is trying to make the very best impression. Halfway down the Mall the lead horse farted so ferociously that people thought they'd heard a 21-gun salute. 'I do apologise, Mr Keating,' said HM as the smell filled the carriage. 'That's all right, Your Majesty,' replied the Australian Prime Minister, 'I thought it was the horse.'

A young man won $200,000 in the lottery. When he collected his cash he went home and sat down to count each note. On reaching $200,000, he peeled off just one note and gave it to his father. Dad looked at it and said, 'Thanks, son. I'm glad you're keeping thrifty ways like me. I've never taken drink, gambled or played about with loose women. In fact, when you were born, your mother and I were not married.'

Surprised, the son said, 'That's lovely! You know what that makes me?'

'That's right, son,' said his father, 'and what's more, you're a greedy one.'

An Arab gentleman in the doctor's surgery is having his severed left hand re-sewn to his wrist. Another doctor walks into the room and says to the patient, 'I see you won your appeal, Ahmed.'

A soldier in Queensland, training for the Vietnam war, jumped out of the grass and called out, 'Who goes there?'

An officer told him, 'You won't last five minutes in Vietnam. The idea is to stay lying down in the grass and call out "Ho Chi Minh is a bastard". Then, when the VC jumps up, you shoot him.' Some time later, in Vietnam, the officer came across the same bloke in hospital. He was in a very bad way. The officer asked him what happened.

'I did as you told me,' he said. 'Only the VC called out "and Arthur Calwell is a bastard". I jumped up to shake hands with him and we were knocked over by a tank.'

An Englishman, an Irishman and an Australian are at the beach together and see a mermaid sunning herself alluringly on the sand. They are all overcome by her charms. The Englishman marches up to her with great dignity and says, 'My dear, you are an exquisite creature and you must tell me if any man has ever kissed you.' The mermaid demurely answers, 'No, I've never been kissed.' So the Englishman bends down and plants a reverential kiss on her cheek then goes back to his colleagues, blushing with happiness.

The Irishman sidles over to the mermaid and says, 'Sure and you're the most beautiful little morrmaid I ever saw. Tell me, my beauty, has any man ever touched you gently on your perfectly formed, firm young breasts?' The mermaid lowered her gaze and admitted that she'd never been touched there. The Irishman bent down, gave her a feel and went back to the others beaming with satisfaction.

Then the Australian strode over to the mermaid. 'You ever been rooted?' he demanded.

'Actually, no,' said the mermaid.

'Well, you're rooted now, because the tide's gone out.'

A young couple rented a nice little suburban flat. They longed for a place in the bush but could not afford a mortgage. One day the husband came home very excited and called to his wife, 'Great news, I've been promoted and the rise is backdated. I also got a big bonus, so we can afford a mortgage and the deposit.'

After weeks of searching they found what they were looking for: Restored 19th century worker's cottage, on one hectare, easy reach of city by rail or road. So they arranged to inspect the property.

The cottage was beautiful, with stone walls and a newly painted tin roof. A crazy-paving path led across an immaculate lawn to the front verandah. An elderly man opened the door and invited them in. The hallway was hung with genuine horse brasses and Victorian prints. Each room was freshly painted and tastefully furnished. 'I really must compliment you on the condition of the property,' said the young man to the owner but, even as he spoke, his wife tugged his sleeve and reached up to whisper in his ear.

'My wife,' he said to the owner, 'observes that there appear to be no toilet facilities.'

'That's right,' said the owner, 'we haven't got the mains and the dirt's no good for septic. We've got a dunny down the back. Come and see.'

He led them into the back garden, past herbs in pots and neat rows of vegetables, down a brick path at the end of which stood the dunny, resplendent in a new coat of white paint and red roof, flanked by frangipanis in full bloom. The dunny was superbly made of cedar chamfer-board. Its receptacle gleamed inside and out and the seat was more cedar, smoothed and polished through years of use.

'Again,' said the young man, 'I must compliment you on the condition of this, er, facility.' Again his wife tugged and whispered.

'What's the matter this time?' asked the owner.

'My wife observes that there is no lock on the door,' the young man replied diffidently.

The owner considered this question carefully; the demonstrable lack of security appeared to imply considerations that had never previously exercised his mind. 'She's right, you know, there is no lock on the door. But I'll tell you something, mate, I don't know what people are like where you come from, but I've lived here man and boy for seventy years and I've never had a bucket of shit stolen yet.'

Bruce had been to a party held by the friend of a friend of a friend. He had had a wonderful time, and much of the evening had vanished in an amiable alcoholic haze. The next morning he discovered that he had left his wallet at the house, and although he could remember the street the house was in, he couldn't remember the house number or the name of the owner. However, he did remember one unusual feature – the house had a gold-plated toilet seat.

So he started at one end of the street, knocking at doors and asking whether this was the house with the gold-plated toilet seat. He was met with reactions ranging from hostile incredulity to helpful indifference. After he had repeated his litany for the seventy-sixth time, he was met by a stony gaze lasting a full ten seconds.

Then the man in the doorway turned and called over his shoulder, 'Hey, Harry, here's the bloke that pissed in ya tuba!'

OUT OF THE MOUTHS OF BABES

Little Johnny hadn't spoken a word in all his six years of life. Finally, one morning at breakfast he cried out, 'Mum, the toast's burnt!' His amazed and delighted mother hugged him joyfully and asked, 'Johnny, why haven't you spoken before?'

'Well,' he replied, 'everything's been all right up till now.'

Two little boys are sitting on the beach examining each other's navels. 'What are they?'

'Well, when you're born there's a piece of rope hanging out there. And they cut it off and twist the end around and tape it inside.'

'What for?'

'So you won't go psssshhhhh and go down.'

A little girl was sitting at the table drawing. Her mother said, 'What are you drawing, darling?'

The little girl said, 'I'm drawing a picture of God.'

Mother said, 'But how can you do that, dear? Nobody knows what God looks like.'

'They will when I've finished.'

'Where did I come from, Mum?' asked a six-year-old.

Mum had been dreading the question but decided against euphemism. She gave the little boy a very frank, candid description beginning with the sex act and concluding with the dramas of the delivery room. She then awaited his reaction.

'I just wondered,' said the child. 'The boy who sits in front of me came from New Zealand.'

Little Johnny was sitting in the dirt tormenting ants and spiders and things, pouring liquid on them and watching them sizzle. The parish priest, Father Murphy, walked past and enquired, 'What's in the bottle, Johnny?'

'Sulphuric acid, Father,' said the boy with savage glee.

The priest, wishing to deter the lad from these savage entertainments, said, 'You shouldn't use that. You should use this wonderful Holy Water I have here in this bottle.'

'What bloody good's that?' the lad asked querulously.

'Well,' said the priest, 'yesterday I poured some of this on a woman's stomach, and she passed a baby!'

'That's nuthin,' said Johnny. 'I poured some of this on the cat's arse and it passed a fuckin' motorbike!'

A four-year-old was in church on Sunday when the wine and wafers were passed out. His mother leaned over and told him that he was not old enough to understand and was not allowed to take part in the Communion.

Later, the collection plate came by and stopped in front of him. His mother leaned over and tried to coax the coin out of his clenched fist. He shouted, 'If I can't eat, I won't pay!'

Two little kids meet on the corner. She is a very pretty little girl, he is your average boy walking his dog. They are both quite shy of each other, but eventually start talking.

'Hello.'

'Hello.'

'What's your name?' asked the boy.

'My name's Petal,' replied the girl, betraying a very cute young girl lisp. 'What's your name?'

'My name's Troy.'

'What's your doggie called?'

'He's called Porky.'

They both stand there awkwardly for a minute, turning on their heels, hands behind their backs, looking at the ground. Then, 'Petal's a really pretty name. How come you're called Petal?'

'Well,' the little girl said, her lisp getting cuter and cuter as she talked. 'A long, long, long, time ago, before I was ever born, my Mummy and Daddy went on a picnic in the woods. It was a beautiful day – the birds were singing, the sun was shining, the butterflies were fluttering around. So Mummy and Daddy lay down in the long cool grass to talk. After a while the fairies came along and picked a petal off one of the trees and floated it down to where Mummy and Daddy were resting in the grass. "Gee that's pretty," they said, "if we ever have a pretty little girl, we'll call her Petal." And that's how come I'm called Petal.'

The little boy was all teary-eyed as he said, 'That's *beautiful*.'

'Mmmm,' Petal agreed. 'Hey, how come your dog's called Porky?'

Very matter-of-factly Troy answered, 'Because he fucks pigs.'

Bobby and Billy have progressive parents who don't believe in discipline and, as a result, the language of the children leaves a great deal to be desired. One holiday they go to stay with their grandmother, a conservative old lady who scarcely knows the meaning of some of the words she hears. After a week she's on the edge of a nervous breakdown, and seeks advice from a friend.

'If it's that bad,' he says, 'there's only one answer. Next time one of them says something you don't like, wallop him! You'll feel better, and they'll get the message.'

She's hesitant, but nothing else has worked, so she decides to try the new approach. Next morning they're all in the kitchen as usual.

'Bobby,' she asks, 'what would you like for breakfast?'

'Oh,' says Bobby, 'give me some of them fuckin' cornflakes.'

Bang! Next moment he's sitting on the floor looking at Grandma with astonishment.

'And Billy,' she says sweetly, 'what would you like for breakfast?'

Billy looks down at Bobby and up at Grandma. 'Well, I'm not exactly sure,' he says, 'but you can bet your sweet arse it won't be them fuckin' cornflakes . . .'

A small girl went out to where her father was working in the garden and said, 'Daddy, what does sex mean?' Dad scratched the side of his jaw and wondered if he'd heard right.

'What does what mean?' he asked.

'Sex,' she repeated.

'Why . . . er . . . why do you want to know what sex means?'

'Because Mummy told me to tell you lunch will be ready in a couple of them.'

Little Gregory wakes up in the middle of the night feeling alone and scared. He goes into his mother's room for comfort. He sees his mum standing naked in front of the mirror. She's rubbing her chest and groaning sensuously, 'I want a man, I want a man.' Shaking his head in bewilderment, Gregory takes off back to bed. Next night the same thing happens. Little Gregory wakes up feeling scared again and goes to mum's room for company. There she is again, standing naked in front of the mirror, rubbing her chest and groaning, 'I want a man, I want a man!' Little Gregory gives up and goes back to bed. The third night it happens again. Little Gregory wakes up, goes into his mum's room but this time there's a man in bed with his mum.

Gregory's eyes widen. He hoofs it back to his room, whips off his pyjamas, rubs his naked chest and groans, 'I want a bike, I want a bike!'

The lady running a preschool kindergarten was staging a nativity play. The scene was the Inn, and George, aged 5, was the reluctant innkeeper. He was angry because he hadn't been given the part of Joseph. There was a knock at the door.

'Who's there?' growled George.

'It's me, Joseph and Mary, and she's going to have a baby. Can we stay here tonight?'

'No,' snapped George. 'Piss off.'

A young boy came home from school and asked his mother, 'What is vice?' She stammered that his father knew more about that sort of thing.

When Dad got home she said, 'Now's the time to tell our son about the facts of life.' So he took his son into the garden and decided to go the whole hog. He told the lad about sexual intercourse and masturbation and oral sex and prostitution and ejaculation and multiple orgasms and the G-spot. The boy stood there with his mouth open. 'Gee, thanks, Dad.'

'That's all right, son, but why did you ask about vice?'

'Cos they made me Vice Captain at school!'

Mum was having the dickens of a time getting her son ready for school. 'I'm not going,' he screamed. 'The teachers all make fun of me and the kids all hate me. I'm just not going anymore.'

'I'll give you two reasons that you will go, son,' said the mother. 'First you are 49 and second you're the headmaster.'

Little Johnny came home from school to find the family's pet rooster dead in the front yard. Rigor mortis had set in and the rooster was flat on its back, with its legs in the air. When his Dad came home, Johnny said, 'Dad, our rooster's dead. And its legs are sticking up in the air. Why's that?'

His father, thinking quickly, said, 'Johnny, that's so God in his infinite wisdom can reach down from the clouds and lift the rooster straight up to heaven.'

'Gee, Dad, that's great,' said Johnny.

A few days later, when Dad came home from work, Johnny rushed out yelling, 'Dad, Dad, we almost lost Mum today!'

'What do you mean, Johnny?'

'Well, Dad, I happened to come home from school early and walked into your bedroom and there was Mum, flat on her back, legs in the air yelling "Jesus, I'm coming, I'm coming." And if it hadn't been for Uncle George holding her down, we'd have lost her for sure.'

The little boy was to start school and his mother, anxious to give him confidence, said she would take him to meet the teacher. 'Then you'll stay at school until you're 15 and might, in later life, become Prime Minister.'

The little boy started to quiver, his eyes moistened and a tear rolled down his cheek. His mother asked him, 'What's wrong?'

And he stammered, 'Mum, you won't forget to come and get me when I'm 15, will you?'

A boy applied for a job as a men's convenience attendant after his mother had seen an ad in the paper. He was interviewed by an old bloke sitting by a kerosene fire who said, 'Right oh, you can start. Fill out this form.' The boy said, 'I can't write.'

'Well,' said the old bloke, 'you don't qualify for the job.' So the boy went away. On the way home he bought some apples for 20¢ and thought he'd try to sell them for 40¢. Years passed, and he finished up with twenty fruit shops and finally became a millionaire. One day at the bank the manager asked him to sign some papers. 'Sorry,' he said, 'I can't write.' The manager said, 'You can't write? Good heavens, what would you have become if you'd been able to write?'

'A bloody toilet assistant,' replied the man.

The kindergarten teacher with a new class thought the kids should tell each other something about their families.

Said little Johnny, 'Well, Miss, my Dad has two penises!'

'Don't be silly, Johnny, that's just not possible.'

'It's true, Miss,' he persisted. 'He's got a little one he does wees out of, and he's got a really big one that he cleans Mummy's teeth with!'

A young school teacher asked her infant class to nominate some beautiful things. The answers came thick and fast.

'Kittens.'

'Moonlight.'

'A rose in the morning.'

'Young chickens.' etc.

The only other response was little Kevin who proposed, 'A 17-year-old girl who's pregnant.'

'Yes,' said the young school mam, 'a pregnant woman is beautiful at any age, but why did you suggest that?'

'Well,' said Kevin, 'my big sister is 17 and the other night when she told Dad she was pregnant he said, "that's just bloody beautiful, that is!"'

A teacher asked a Grade 4 class to spell whatever they had for breakfast. In response, one spelt B-A-C-O-N. Another spelt E-G-G-S. But Jimmy spelt B-U-G-G-E-R A-L-L. 'Miss' was mortified and ordered him to come in front of the class.

'Now, Jimmy, as your punishment you can be the first in the geography test. Where is the South Australian border?'

'At home in bed with Mum,' replied Jimmy. 'And that's why I had bugger-all for breakfast.'

A young boy asked his father if he could explain the difference between potential and reality. So his father said, 'Go and ask your mother if she would sleep with the milkman for $1 million.' The boy protested, saying he couldn't ask his mother that sort of question. But his father insisted. When the boy returned he said his mother had said yes.

His father then said, 'Now go and ask your sister if she'd sleep with the milkman for $1 million.' Again the boy protested that he couldn't ask that of his sister. And again his father insisted. Once again he told his father the answer was yes.

Then his father said, 'Now go and ask your brother if he'd sleep with the milkman for $1 million.' The boy said, 'But Dad, they're both males.' Father insisted.

So the boy went off and asked his brother the same question. He returned to say that his brother had said he, too, would sleep with the milkman for $1 million.

Father then explained to the young boy, 'Well that's potential and reality. We have the potential to make $3 million. But the reality is we live with two sluts and a poofter.'

'Tomorrow morning, *mes enfants*,' says the teacher at a Paris primary school, 'we will be having our weekly English lesson. And tomorrow the word we'll be studying is "probably".' (This she pronounces as pwobably.)

'Tonight, I want you to think of a sentence that shows you understand the meaning of this interesting English word, pwobably.'

The children copy the word she's written on the blackboard and head for home. Next day she asks Jacques to use 'pwobably' in a sentence.

'Last night my father came into my bedroom just before I was going to sleep. He was *pwobably* going to tell me a story.'

'*Très bien*, Jacques! And now *petite* Bridget?'

'Last night, my mother came into the bathroom when I was having my bath. She was *pwobably* going to dry me with the towel.'

'*Très bien*, Bridget! And now, let us hear from Henri.'

'Yesterday my sister was having a music lesson *avec le* music teacher, Monsieur Chirac. Suddenly the music stopped and I went into *la chambre*.

Monsieur Chirac had his trousers around his ankles and my sister had pulled her skirts up very high. They were *pwobably* going to shit in the piano.'

Several boys from Maribyrnong State School spend their lunchtime playing by the Maribyrnong Creek. When they arrive back late the headmaster hauls them up to his office for an explanation. The first boy explains, 'Sir, we were just throwing peanuts into the creek.'

The headmaster lectures him severely, first for being late and, more especially, for wasting good food in a world where so many are starving. He orders him to write a hundred lines: 'Waste not, want not.' The second boy offers the same excuse and receives the same censure and penalty.

Now it's the third boy's turn to be questioned. Looking a bit bedraggled, he looks up at the headmaster and says, 'Sir, I'm Peanuts.'

It's the new teacher's first morning in class and she's keen to make a good impression on the kids. So she asks a pretty little blonde girl her name. She replies, 'Apple Blossom, teacher.' Noting the teacher's surprise, she explains, 'When I was a baby an apple blossom fell on my head and so Daddy named me his Apple Blossom.'

The teacher then asks a little brunette girl her name. Not to be outdone, she says it's 'Cherry Blossom', explaining it in much the same way. As a baby, she'd been sitting beneath the cherry tree.

The teacher then turns to a poor, miserable-looking little bloke with a twisted nose, lop ears, snaggle teeth. 'And what's your name?' And the poor little bugger says, 'Wardrobe.'

After a series of sex eduction lectures, tapes and videos, the primary school teacher asked the kids to prepare a short burst on the subject and present it to the class next morning. She nominated children to speak. The first was adorable little Jenny who told the class that her cat had had kittens. 'Very good, Jenny,' said the teacher, 'and very appropriate.' And thus it went as the teacher pointed to children around the classroom. A pet budgie had just laid an egg. A cow had given birth to a calf. And all through the simple little stories, the class terror, Freddy, had been waving his hand to be picked. 'Ask me,' he'd chanted over and over. Finally the teacher acquiesced.

'It's an hour before sunset. My dad was in Vietnam when the VC attacked his position. Hundreds and hundreds of them. Dad shot about fifty with his rifle, killed another twenty with hand grenades, stabbed ten to death with his pocket knife and finally strangled the rest.'

'Freddy,' interjected the teacher, 'that's a very

interesting story. But it was supposed to be about the birds and the bees. How does your story relate?'

'It goes to show, Miss,' said Freddy, 'that you shouldn't fuck around with my dad.'

Don Chipp was driving through the Victorian countryside a couple of years ago. With the honesty of a Democrat he conceived [sic] his speedometer needle was perilously close to 120 kph. On the left hand side of the road he noticed two typical 11-year-old boys. At 11 years of age, boys seem to achieve their most unspeakable and insufferable and yet most lovable selves. They also seem to master the cheekiest of toothy grins. These two chaps were no exception. They were wearing red peaked caps and holding up a large homemade sign roughly printed in texta colour SLOW DOWN POLICE CHECK AHEAD. Instinctively Don's foot came off the accelerator and he negotiated the next bend within the speed limit. As he passed the police trap, complete with radar and other paraphernalia, Don gave a royal wave and the smuggest of smiles.

He was having some thoughts of these altruistic lads when he passed the next bend. Here on the left hand side of the road were two other 11-year-olds with a roughly printed sign NOW WASN'T THAT WORTH A BUCK.

ANIMAL CRACKERS

A bear and a rabbit were walking together down a jungle track. The bear suddenly stopped and said, 'Excuse me, old man, call of nature y'know,' and left the track. He came back a few minutes later and they both continued their walk. 'Tell me,' the bear said, 'are you rabbits bothered by shit sticking to your fur?'

'Not at all,' the rabbit replied. 'It doesn't affect us – dry pellets, you know.'

'Good,' said the bear, 'that's all right then,' and picked up the rabbit and wiped his bum with him.

A merchant banker has his apartment redecorated, following a jungle theme. As a finishing touch he buys a brilliantly coloured parrot and sets up its elaborate cage in the loungeroom. The bird is quite chatty, and screeches comments about all manner of things. One evening, when his owner brings a woman home, the parrot screams, 'Hey, you look like a good fuck!'

The banker apologises and cautions the parrot, 'Any more of that and you go into the freezer to cool off.'

The following week the banker brings home another date. 'Hey!' screeches the parrot. 'Great tits!'

The banker grabs the parrot and stuffs him into the freezer, saying, 'A few minutes in there should give you something to think about.'

When he opens the freezer door five minutes later the parrot looks suitably subdued, and with beak chattering, squawks, 'What the hell did that chook in there say?'

What do you do if a bird shits on your windscreen?

You don't take her out again.

A magician is hired to entertain passengers on a long ship voyage. The first night out, he starts his show in the lounge in front of an enthusiastic (if captive) audience. He has just produced a pack of cards out of nowhere, and is about to take his bow, when the ship's parrot, in a cage but also in the lounge, squawks, 'I saw what you did! You pulled those from up your sleeve!' Laughter and derision from the audience.

The next night, the magician was opening with another trick, hiding a coin and making it re-appear. As he prepared to take his bow, the parrot squawked again, 'I saw that! You hid that in your shoe!' More laughter and derision from the audience. The magician had had enough. He went to the captain and said something had to be done. 'Very well,' was the reply, 'we'll cover the bird up with a blanket.'

Well satisfied, the magician appeared again on the third night. Just as he was about to launch into one of his disappearing tricks, the ship hit a reef and sank. The magician managed to survive by clinging to a piece of wood, and after a couple of days of floating on his improvised raft, what should float by but the cage, enveloped in the blanket. The magician pulled the cage onto the raft, and whipped off the blanket. The parrot sat in the cage, blinked several times in the light and turned his head slowly from one side to the other, looking round in a puzzled manner. 'All right,' said the parrot, 'I give up – where'd you hide the ship?'

While on a visit to a shopping centre, an elderly bush spinster bought a pair of talking parrots from a pet shop. On her return home she rang back and asked how she could distinguish the male bird from the female.

'Simple,' replied the dealer, 'wait until they're mating and fasten something around the male's neck so he'll be easy to spot.'

The lady bided her time, and in due course tied a strip of white ribbon around the male bird's neck.

A few days later the parson came to visit. The cock bird took one look at him and croaked, 'Ha ha! So the old girl caught you at it too, eh?'

A bloke goes into a pet shop, looking for something suitable for his wife. He spots a very attractive rosella. 'I'll take the parrot.'

'A present?' asks the pet shop owner.

'Yes, for the missus.'

'Well, this is a very intelligent parrot, it's a very talented parrot. You'll be able to teach it to say all sorts of things, but there is a problem.'

'What's that?'

'It's got no feet.'

'Well, how does it sit on the perch?' asks the bloke.

'If you look closely, sir, you'll see that it's grasping the perch with its pecker.'

'I didn't know parrots had peckers.'

'Well, this parrot has a pecker. Look, see how it uses it to balance itself,' says the pet shop owner.

The bloke takes the parrot home and his wife is thrilled to bits. And not only does it learn to talk, it learns to keep an eye on things. So one night when the bloke gets home the parrot tells him that his wife has had a visitor.

'What happened?'

'Well, this chap came in and started kissing your wife.'

'Then what happened?'

'Then he started to undress her.'

'And then what happened?' asked the bloke.

'I don't know,' says the parrot, 'that's when I fell off my perch.'

Squatter Fraser was exhibiting his prize bull at the annual Western District Agricultural Show as he did every year. Two hours before the judging, he noticed the bull's eyes were crossed and knew that this would rule out any chance of a prize. He hurriedly called in the vet, who took one look at the beast and fished a plastic tube out of his black bag. The vet shoved one end of the tube into the bull's bum and blew vigorously through the other end. Instantly, the animal's eyes uncrossed and Squatter Fraser walked off with the blue ribbon.

At the following year's show, the same thing happened. Hoping to save a few bob, Fraser hunted around and found a piece of plastic tubing, knelt down and repeated the vet's routine. But the bull's eyes stayed firmly crossed. In desperation he called in the vet who quickly appraised himself of the situation, pulled the tube out of the bull's rectum, reversed it, pushed it in again and blew.

Hey-presto, the bull looked at the vet straight in the eye, but Squatter Fraser was puzzled. 'Tell me,' he asked the vet, 'why did you turn the tube around?'

The vet regarded him with astonishment. 'You surely didn't think I'd be crazy enough to blow into the same end of the tube as an arsehole like you!'

Four young bulls were boasting of their plans for the future.

'I'm going to Rome to become a Papal bull,' said one.

'I'm going to become a stock market bull,' said another.

'I want to be a bull in a china shop,' said the third.

'Well, I'm not going anywhere,' said the fourth. 'I shall stay here for heifer and heifer and heifer.'

Bruce and Simon were checking out the junk shops in the hope of finding something of value for their antique stall at the Paddo Market. In the doorway of a particularly grotty shop, Bruce noticed a cat lapping milk out of a really great Royal Doulton saucer. He nudged Simon and gave him a knowing wink. Then, acting very casual, Bruce said to the old codger running the shop, 'That's a very nice cat. Like to sell him?'

'Well,' said the old codger, 'I might be willing to let you have him for, say, ten bucks.'

Simon picked up the cat and said, 'We might as well take the saucer as well, seeing that he's used to drinking from it.'

'No way,' said the codger.

'Well, could we buy it from you?'

'No way.'

'But why?'

'Because thanks to that saucer I've already flogged eighty-seven cats.'

How do you make a cat go 'woof'?

Soak it in petrol and throw a match on it.

A young man lived in a garden flat in Paddington with a dog and three cats. He named the dog and two of the cats George. The third cat had no name.

'Why such an odd arrangement?' asked his next-door-neighbour.

'Well,' replied the young man, 'when I return home from work in the evening, I go to the back door and call "George, George, George", and they all come in.'

'But what about the third cat?' queried the neighbour.

'Oh,' said the young man, 'he never goes out.'

In response to sounds of unusual activity in next door's backyard, a neighbour looked over the fence. A great deal of shovelling was taking place. A very large hole was being excavated.

'What are you doing?'

'I'm burying my dead cat.'

'Oh, what a pity. But Tiddles was only a little cat. Why the big hole?'

'Because,' solemnly explained the neighbour, 'he's inside your bloody great Alsatian!'

What is the difference between a coyote and a flea?

The coyote howls about the prairie.

The boys were on a trip to Kakadu and decided to go fishing. On the way to the moorings, they saw a great pair of shoes in a tourist shop window. 'Look at the price,' said Davo, 'five hundred bucks.'

'They're crocodile shoes,' said Wocka, 'I know where we can get plenty of those.'

They headed upriver and Wocka dropped the boys off by a deep pool where they could catch some fish. He headed upstream in the boat. When he hadn't returned in a couple of hours, they went looking for him. And they kept finding crocodiles floating belly up in the water, but no sign of Wocka. Finally, round the next bend, they spotted him, wrestling a huge crocodile in a rock pool.

'What the bloody hell are you up to?' they yelled.

'Well,' said Wocka, 'if this bastard isn't wearing shoes, I'll give up.'

A meeting was arranged by the Western Australian Department of Agriculture aimed at trying to come up with a solution to the dingo problem in WA. The meeting was also attended by representatives from CSIRO, pastoralists and environmentalists with the intention of coming up with a mutually acceptable solution. The pastoralists wanted to kill the dingos while the greenies wanted a 'biological' solution, such as castration of the dingos, as a strategy of population control. At this point one of the pastoralists lost his temper and blurted out, 'Listen, lady, the dingos are eating the sheep, not fucking them!'

How do you make a dog 'meow'?
Pass it quickly over a circular saw.

A man went to the movies to see a re-run of *Gone With the Wind* and was very surprised to see a large dog sitting next to a woman in the row in front of him. What was even more surprising was that the dog seemed to be following the story, sitting with ears pricked, wagging its tail at the happy parts, and sitting downcast with bowed head during the distressing or emotionally intense parts of the story.

At the conclusion of the movie the man could contain his curiosity no longer and, as the audience was filing out of the cinema, walked over to the lady.

'Excuse me, madam. I couldn't help noticing your dog in the movie. He seemed to understand the story and really enjoyed it. It was amazing!'

'Yes,' replied the woman enthusiastically, if a trifled puzzled. 'I was amazed, too. He hated the book!'

I saw a dog sitting with three of my friends playing poker.

'Isn't it amazing,' I said, 'a dog playing poker.'

One of my mates looked up and said, 'Aw, I dunno, every time he gets a good hand he wags his tail.'

A duck walks into a chemist. 'Give us a jar of Vaseline,' it quacks.

'That'll be five dollars,' says the chemist, without batting an eye.

'Put it on my bill, please.'

'Certainly sir. Anything else?'

'Yeah, give me a packet of condoms, too.'

'Yes sir. Shall I put them on your bill?'

'No thanks. I'm not that kind of duck.'

What's grey and comes in pints?

An elephant.

An elephant and a mouse were walking through the jungle when all of a sudden the elephant fell into a hole. It was very deep and steep-sided and the elephant couldn't pull himself out. So the mouse said he'd hail the first car that came along. After a while a shining new Porsche came roaring through the jungle. The mouse hailed it, they got a rope, dropped it down the hole and the Porsche towed the elephant out. The elephant thanked the Porsche driver who went on his way.

Shortly thereafter the mouse fell into a hole and he couldn't climb out. So the elephant dropped his dick down the hole and the mouse climbed up it, and they continued on down the road.

The moral of the story is: if you've got a big enough dick, you don't need a Porsche.

A bloke blundered into a pub in tow with an emu and a cat. He ordered a beer, a vodka and a rum and the three sat at a table. Shortly after, the emu went to the bar and re-ordered, then returned to the table. This happened several times. The barman scratched his head, wondering why the cat didn't buy a shout. So, the next time the bloke fronts up the barman asks, 'Hey, why isn't the cat buying?'

The man sort of smirks, saying, 'It's a long yarn. Y'see, I found this vase, rubbed it and a genie pops out. The genie says "Okay, you got me out. So what do you want?" Well, like any normal bloke, I asked for a bird with long legs and a tight pussy.'

A man driving in the outback sees a farmer staggering from tree to tree carrying a huge emu. The emu is eating acorns from the trees. He stops the car and says, 'Why don't you put the emu down and shake the tree? Then the acorns will fall down and that would save a lot of time.'

The man says, 'What's time to an emu?'

What is the difference between a mountain goat and a goldfish?

The goldfish mucks about the fountain.

A fish goes into the bar. The barman says, 'What do you want?'

The fish croaks, 'Water!'

Two beautiful girls were walking down St George's Terrace when they heard a cry for help. They had some trouble working out where it was coming from, but eventually found a green frog sitting on a window ledge. The frog was in a pretty emotional state and explained that it had been a Perth entrepreneur. He had fallen under the spell of the NSCS and been turned into a green frog. Only one thing could save him. To be kissed by a beautiful girl. They seemed rather doubtful about his approach but he assured them that he was, truly, a Perth entrepreneur, and he promised them anything and indeed everything if one of them would only kiss him and restore him to his previous condition. The girls looked at him for a while. Suddenly one of them opened her handbag, picked up the frog, dropped him inside and snapped it shut. 'Good heavens,' said her friend, 'what are you doing?'

'Well,' said the girl with the handbag, 'I'm no fool. I know that a talking frog is worth a lot more than a Perth entrepreneur.'

The wide-mouthed frog sets out on his travels around Australia. First he meets a kangaroo.

'Hullo,' says the wide-mouthed frog (mouth stretched wide by hooking a forefinger in each corner). 'Who are you?'

'I'm a kangaroo.'

'What do you do?'

'I sleep under a bush all day and hop around the countryside at night, having a wonderful time.'

'That's very nice,' says the wide-mouthed frog and goes on his way. Next he meets a wombat.

'Hullo, who are you?'

'I'm a wombat.'

'What do you do?'

'I sleep in my burrow all day and come out at night to forage around for a good feed.'

'Pleased to meet you,' says the wide-mouthed

frog as he continues his journey. Then he meets a snake.

'Hullo, who are you?'

'I'm a snake.'

'And what do you do?'

'I eat wide-mouthed frogs.'

Wide-mouthed frog, hastily becoming a narrow-mouthed frog (by pushing lips together vertically with forefingers), 'Bet you don't see many of them around.'

Why do you wrap guinea pigs in masking tape?

So they don't burst when you fuck them.

The Director of Taronga Park Zoo called in his deputy.

'Look,' he said, 'we've got a major problem. The gorilla's on heat and we've only got a couple of weeks to mate her. Contact all the leading zoos and see if they can lend us an active male. Tell them we'll cover all the expenses.'

After a couple of days spent telephoning and faxing zoos all over the world, the deputy director reported. 'No luck,' he said. 'All the males are too young to breed or past it.'

'Bugger it,' exclaimed the Director, 'I thought we

were going to be the first zoo successfully to breed a gorilla in captivity.'

'I've got an idea,' said the deputy director. 'You know old Charlie the Pom, the cleaner?'

'What, that dirty, hairy old bastard who cleans out the cages?' 'That's him. He's a simian, if ever I saw one. How about we offer him a couple of thousand dollars?'

'Well,' said the Director, 'it's worth a try.'

So they called in Charlie and explained the problem.

'I dunno,' said Charlie, 'I reckon it would cost a lot more than that to bring a gorilla over here.'

'Oh, all right,' said the Director, 'how about five thousand?'

'Okay,' said Charlie, 'but there are three conditions.'

The Director sighed. 'Righto, what conditions?'

'Number 1, she's got to be chained down, otherwise she might get stroppy and attack me. Number 2, she's got to have a bag over her head, 'cos she's an ugly cow.' Charlie paused.

'All right,' said the Director, getting exasperated, 'what's the third condition?'

'Any children of the union must be brought up Protestant.'

An Australian diplomat living in West Africa was disturbed by a hell of a racket on his roof. He went outside and looked up to see a gorilla ripping off tiles and hurling them down into the garden. He rang the local police station. 'Sorry, sir,' said the sergeant, 'I'm afraid we can't help you. I suggest you look in the yellow pages and under "G" you'll see Gorilla Catchers. Just ring one of those.' The chap did as suggested and the gorilla catcher said, 'Sir, I'll be there in fifteen minutes.'

Sure enough, fifteen minutes later around the corner came a small van. When it pulled up a fellow stepped out built like Tarzan, wearing only a small piece of leopard skin around his hips. In one hand he carried a revolver. Then out of the van jumped a small corgi.

'Good lord,' said the diplomat. 'I would have expected a German shepherd or a bull terrier, but not a corgi.'

The gorilla catcher said, 'Just hold this gun will you?' Then he opened the back of the van and the fellow saw that it was made into a cage with heavy bars. The gorilla catcher opened the barred door and turned to the diplomat. 'Now look here, I'll tell you how it goes. I will climb up onto the roof and wrestle with the gorilla. When I see the opportunity I'll throw him off the roof. As soon as he hits the ground the corgi will race in and bite him in the groin. The gorilla will give a scream and leap up and jump into the cage. Then he'll slam the door shut between himself and the dog. All we have to do is walk up and slip the lock.'

The diplomat was most impressed. 'That's incredible,' he said. 'It's so cleverly worked out. Does it always go like that?'

'Always,' said the gorilla catcher.

'Well, what have I got this gun for?' asked the diplomat.

'Well,' said the gorilla catcher, 'it's always worked out like this in the past. However, just in case, if instead of me throwing down the gorilla, he should throw me down, YOU IMMEDIATELY SHOOT THE CORGI.'

A bloke goes to the CES to get a job. The only one that's available is at Taronga Zoo. On arrival he's told the gorilla has just died but, luckily, they've managed to preserve its skin. His job is to wear it, to pretend to be a gorilla until another can be shipped from Africa.

The days went by and he settled into the new job, coming to thoroughly enjoy his carefree existence, munching bananas and swinging from branch to branch, watched by enthralled spectators. However, he became too enthusiastic and, swinging too far, landed in the lions' cage. As he pulled himself to his feet one of the lions growled fiercely and he ran to the bars screaming for help. Whereupon he heard one of the lions snarling, 'If that dopey bastard doesn't shut up, we'll all lose our jobs.'

An American with a very sick horse went to his Australian neighbour's place and ask him what he gave his horse when it got sick. The neighbour said turpentine. So off went the American. He came back several days later and said, 'My horse died.'

'That's funny,' said the Aussie neighbour, 'so did mine.'

An old horse was employed by the Maitland Cricket Club. Every day a match was scheduled, the horse had to pull a dirty great roller so as to prepare the wicket. Naturally the horse got very bored and so began demanding that he be selected for the Maitland team. Needless to say the captain and the selectors refused. So the horse said, 'No game, no roll. ' Finally the selectors had no choice but to relent.

The local team won the toss and went in to bat. After losing three quick wickets the captain sent in the horse. He struck form at once, began hitting fours and sixes to all points of the compass, taking the Maitland team to a very good score. The visitors didn't fare well, owing to the fact that the horse ran around and caught out most of their best batsmen and even managed to run out a couple of them. In fact, their score was so low that they were obliged to follow on.

Well, Maitland's captain was so delighted with the horse that he asked it to open the bowling in the second innings. The horse only laughed and said, 'Wake up to yourself, horses can't bowl.'

What is the difference between a cavalry horse and a draught horse?

The cavalry horse darts into the fray.

A weary penguin, bleary-eyed after a hard day's fishing in the Ross Sea, hauls his exhausted little body up onto the penguin rookery where he sits looking around him in a somewhat bewildered fashion. After a while he says to the nearest penguin, 'G'day mate, I'm a bit snookered and not sure exactly where I am. Have you seen my wife?'

After a pause the other penguin replies, 'Dunno – what does she look like?'

A stranger walks into the Phillip Island pub and orders a scotch. 'You look a bit upset,' says the barman. 'What's wrong?'

The stranger says, 'I reckon I just ran over a couple of penguins.'

'No way,' says the barman. 'Not at this time of the year.'

'Then you better make that a double scotch,' says the stranger, 'it must have been a couple of nuns.'

An English tourist finds a bedraggled penguin on the beach at Bondi and asks a nearby cop what to do with it. 'I'd take it to the Taronga Park Zoo, mate.' Off goes the tourist.

Next day, to the policeman's astonishment, there's the Pom and the penguin waddling along Bondi Beach together. 'Hey, you,' says the cop, 'I thought I told you to take the penguin to the zoo.'

'I did,' said the tourist, 'and he enjoyed it so much that I'm taking him to the pictures today.'

A young man gets a job assisting the keepers at Taronga Park Zoo.

He is put in charge of the porpoises and given special instructions about their diet; the porpoises are very partial to seagull chicks, which must be collected surreptitiously from the harbour foreshores and fed to the porpoises very early in the morning, before the zoo is open, to avoid trouble with the RSPCA and animal rights activists.

One morning, as the young man is returning to the zoo with his bag of chicks he sees that one of the lions has got out of the lion pit and is sprawled across the entrance to the zoo, snoozing in the sun.

The young man prods the lion, trying to wake him, but when the animal doesn't budge, he decides to feed the porpoises first, and steps over the lion. Just then a siren sounds, a police car screeches to a halt and an officer leaps out to arrest the young man. On what charge? Transporting underage gulls over a prostrate lion for immoral porpoises.

Two lions escaped from Taronga Park Zoo. They went in different directions. One was caught a few hours later and returned to its cage, but it was six months before the other one was captured.

'How come you were able to remain free for so long?' asked the first lion.

'It was no problem. I simply made my way over the Harbour Bridge after dark, then I holed up in an empty room I found on the top floor of some government offices. The place was packed with advisors and advisors to the advisors. Every time I got hungry I just nipped out and ate one and slipped back to my room again. I could have stayed there for years.'

'How come they finally realised that something was going on?' asked the first lion.

'Oh, I made a terrible mistake. One day I ate the tea lady!'

Bullen's lion tamer was performing his new act, one that had never been seen before by the public. The crowd were wildly appreciative, clapping noisily at almost every move he made. Well satisfied and egged on by the crowd response, he approached his finale for the evening. He made the largest of his lions sit in front of him. When he hit it on the head with the handle of his whip, the powerful animal opened its huge jaws. The lion tamer immediately opened his fly and extruded his genitalia, which he promptly put into the lion's mouth. He then hit the lion on the head again with his whip handle and the animal very gently locked its jaws on its master's genitals. The lion tamer flourished his whip and the crowd burst into rapturous applause. He then hit the lion on the head again, the lion opened its jaws and he packed away his genitalia.

Again with a flourish, he quietened the crowd and asked, 'Is there anyone in the crowd who is game enough to try this?' There was a short silence as most of the men in the audience looked embarrassed, but eventually a little old lady put up her hand and nervously said, 'Can I try?'

The lion tamer was rather taken aback and stumbled over his reply, 'Well, um, that's very brave, but you, um, haven't got the required, um . . .' The little old lady defended herself, 'Don't tell me that I can't do it, young man! I am sure I can! But don't you dare hit *me* on the head!'

The circus advertised for a new lion tamer and had two applicants – a young woman, and an old man. The circus manager decided to test their skills with the lion so he first asked the young woman to show him what she could do. She entered the cage, removed all her clothes and the lion walked up and nuzzled her bare legs. The astonished circus owner then said to the old man, 'Can you do that?'

'You're damned right I can,' said the old man, 'just get that lion out of there first.'

What's the difference between the Prince of Wales, a bald man and a monkey's mother?

The Prince of Wales is heir apparent, a bald man has no hair apparent and a monkey's mother is a hairy parent.

A woman wanted to purchase a woollen jumper. As she walked through the mall she saw an attractive jumper in the window of a boutique. She asked the price of the garment and decided it was far too expensive. So she walked on and saw exactly the same garment in another shop for half the price. Having purchased it, she returned to the boutique to complain. The sales woman's response was haughty. 'But Madam, our garment is made from virgin wool.'

'I don't give a damn what the sheep do at night,' said the woman, 'I just want a reasonably priced jumper.'

What does a dingo call a baby in a pram?
Meals on wheels.

Did you hear about the Irish dingo?
It ate the azaleas.

Did you hear about the Italian dingo?
It ate the pastor.

A SPORTING CHANCE

A husband and wife are doing the dishes. She's washing, he's wiping. She hands him a saucer which slips from his fingers and smashes on the floor. Her reaction seems out of all proportion to the incident. 'Tell me, you bastard, where you've been going every Tuesday and Wednesday night? And where do you go on Saturdays when you head out of the door without a word and aren't home for hours?'

The husband looks somewhat embarrassed but brushes off his mysterious absences by saying, 'They're not important. It doesn't matter.'

'I demand an explanation,' she says.

After a few moments' embarrassment, the husband says, 'It's really nothing. I just go to brothels and have sex with prostitutes for money. That's all. Then I come home.'

'You're a liar!' screams the wife. 'You're secretly playing with the Sydney Swans. You go off to practise during the week and you play with the Swans on Saturdays.'

'No! No!' the husband protests his innocence.

'I'm not doing that, I promise you. I'm just going off to fuck hookers.'

'You promise? Cross your heart that's all your doing? That you're not really going off and training and playing with the Swans?'

'Darling, I promise you. Faithfully. All I'm doing is spending hundreds and hundreds of dollars on professional sex.'

She throws herself into his arms, sobbing with relief against his chest. 'Darling, darling, forgive me for being suspicious. I'm sorry that I didn't trust you.' He makes soothing noises and they resume doing the dishes. She hands him another saucer which, once again, he fumbles. It sails up in the air, he grabs at it without success and, once again there's a breakage.

'YOU BASTARD,' she screams. 'YOU ARE PLAYING WITH THE SYDNEY SWANS!'

(The Swans were the first VFL team to move interstate. After initial successes, their downward slide has been spectacular. This joke hints at the magnitude of their humiliation.)

What has thirty-six legs and can't climb a ladder?

The Swans.

During the Queen's first visit to Australia, she was taken to a game of Aussie Rules. At half-time, when introduced to the players, she asked a country boy how he developed his skills.

'Started kickin' mallee roots around. Could hoove the bastards 50 metres across the back paddock.'

The President of the VFL said to the player, 'Now, that's a bit strong.'

To which the player replied, 'Ah, well, 40 bloody metres then.'

Two old mates were barramundi fishing up in the Gulf in the summer. Unfortunately one dropped dead so his mate loaded him in the four-wheel drive and drove to Brisbane, which took him two and a half days. He called at a police station to notify the death and the Sergeant said, 'He must be very smelly by now.'

The mate said, 'He's not too bad – I gutted him.'

Four mates were playing golf. One of them was bending over a putt, concentrating like mad, when a funeral procession passed by on a nearby road. He straightened up, removed his hat, held it over his breast and remained at silent attention until the cortège had passed. His three mates were amazed. They'd never known him to be a man of particular sensitivity and praised him for his respect for the dead. 'It's the least I could do,' he said modestly, 'we would have been married twenty-eight years tomorrow.'

As the golfer trudged towards the 19th hole at the Royal Melbourne, he muttered, 'That was my worst game ever.' To which the caddy replied, 'You mean you've played before?'

A distinguished Australian barrister had always dreamed of playing the St Andrew's course in Scotland. Finally, he received an invitation from a British barrister who was a member and headed immediately for Mascot. Sadly, on arriving in Scotland, he found his friend had died. He was admitted to the clubhouse and told to see a gentleman in the corner, who was reading *The Times*.

'I beg your pardon, your lordship, but my name is Fleetwood-Jones. I'm from a leading law firm in Sydney, Australia, and have always yearned to play a round here, but unfortunately my friend, who was a member here, has just died, and so . . .'

His Lordship lowered *The Times* and asked 'Church?'

'Anglican, sir.'

'Education?' his Lordship continued.

'Cranbrook, sir, and then Oxford.'

'Athletics?'

'Rugby, sir, played for the Wallabies in 62. And rowed number 4 in the crew that beat Cambridge.'

'Military?'

As a matter of fact, got the VC.'

His Lordship considered briefly, then nodded to the Club Secretary and said, 'Nine holes.'

A husband and wife were playing golf together when, unfortunately, the husband smashed a ball straight into her face. Panic-stricken he ran to the club house for a doctor.

'Doctor, come quickly ... my wife's been hit by a golf ball.'

'Where was she hit?' asked the Doc.

'Between the first and second holes,' gasped the man.

'Oh dear,' replied the doctor, 'that won't leave much room for bandages.'

A big bloke strides up to the bar of a golf clubhouse and orders a beer. As the barman starts pouring the beer the bloke notices a friend, drinking alone at the other end of the bar. He takes his beer up to that end of the bar, taps his friend on the shoulder and asks how he has been. The friend replies in a very hoarse croak, 'Up until today I've been fine.'

The big fellow, surprised at his friend's difficulty in speaking, asks, 'What happened to your voice? It sounds terrible.'

The friend replied, barely audible, 'I'll tell you. I teed off on the sixteenth and sliced the ball badly over the boundary fence and into the trees. So I swore, picked up the tee, grabbed the buggy and went to look for my ball. Just as I was about to walk into the trees, and not knowing how long it would take me to find the ball, I turned around and waved the following group through. I looked for the bloody ball but couldn't see it anywhere. In fact, I was so intent on looking for the ball that a passing cow made me jump with fright. Unbelievable as it may seem, as the cow turned away, I noticed what looked like a ball stuck under its tail. I walked slowly up to the cow, lifted its tail and, sure enough, there was a golf ball. But it wasn't mine! Mine was a white one and this was orange.

'While I still had hold of the cow's tail, I noticed a woman from the following group come into the trees, obviously looking for her ball. I called over to her and she came my way. As she got closer, I lifted up the cow's tail and said, "Does that look like yours" and she wrapped a nine iron around my neck.'

An Irish golfer wasn't very good at the game, which he found pretty frustrating. Then, one day, a leprechaun appeared and said, 'I'll help you become a greater golfer, but every time you do, you'll have to give up part of your sex life.' The golfer agreed.

'Firstly, it's time you sank a ball in par,' said the leprechaun, 'and the cost is one week of celibacy.' So off the golfer drove and with four shots he had his ball in the hole.

They met again in a month's time and the wee feller said he'd decided it was time for the golfer to achieve a birdie. 'But the penalty would be eight weeks of celibacy.' He teed up with considerable enthusiasm and, three shots later, the ball was in the hole.

It was some months later until they met again. The leprechaun said, 'Today, a hole in one. But you'll have to give up screwing for a year.'

'A hole in one is every golfer's dream,' said the golfer. He drove off and straight into the hole went the ball.

'I'll have to leave you now,' said the leprechaun, 'but for the record, what's your name?'

'Father O'Flaherty,' was the reply.

There were two men golfers being held up by two women who wouldn't wave them through. Finally one of the blokes said he'd go up and ask to be let through. But he came back looking very worried. 'What's the matter?' asked his friend.

'Well, it's very awkward. You see, one is my wife and the other is my mistress.'

'I've never met your wife – I'll go up,' said the other.

Shortly thereafter he came back and said, 'It's a small world.'

An elderly member breezed into his golf club late one afternoon when there were still a number of golfers in the lounge. He slapped a $50 note down on the bar and said, 'Drinks all round, barman, if you please.'

The golfers accepted readily, so the old gent pushed the change across the bar and said, 'Let's have another round, barman.' Whilst the party was consuming the second round, the barman came back and said, 'Tell me, sir. You don't often come into the club these days, yet here you are, shouting for the bar. What's the celebration?'

'Well,' replied the old member, 'as you know, I'm a retired army major of 69, and tomorrow I'm being married to a delightful young lass of 19 – daughter of an old army colleague of mine. So I have reason to celebrate. Let's have another round.' So they did, and eventually the major staggered off home.

Some time later, the major reappeared at the club, produced a $100 note and repeated the performance. After the second round, the same barman said to him, 'Major, I remember last time you came in and shouted because you were being married the next day. So what's the celebration for this time?'

'Well, my boy, this morning my wife gave birth to a fine bouncing baby boy. So again I'm celebrating. Another round, please.'

Whilst this round was being served, an experienced golfer, with a good memory for scores, came over and said, 'Major, I overheard your conversation, and I was here last time you were celebrating your impending marriage. Wasn't that only seven months ago?'

'Yes,' said the major, 'and that's what I'm so bloody delighted about – two under par, on a strange course, with concealed holes, using two old balls and an old club with a whippy shaft.'

A young woman decided to take up golf, but had never had a golf club in her hand. So she joined a club and was advised to have some lessons. The pro took her to the practice nets to show her how to stand in relation to the ball and how to swing the club. Unfortunately she had no idea of an acceptable swing, so the pro stood behind her, reaching around to place his hands over hers on the shaft of the club. He then showed her how to commence the backswing, then released his grip and went to step back so she could try again on her own. But he found he was unable to move because the zipper on his fly had caught in the zipper of the young woman's skirt. The more he struggled to separate the zippers the more tightly they became meshed. So with great embarrassment he decided the only thing to do was to return to the pro shop where he would be able to disengage the zippers with the aid of a pair of plyers.

Off they frogmarched back towards the pro shop in view of a number of onlookers who viewed their progress with mixed feelings – wonder, surprise, embarrassment, mirth. As they rounded the corner of the clubhouse, a big Alsatian dog rushed out and threw a bucket of water over them!

An Australian, keen to have a holiday abroad and wishing to improve his golf handicap, takes a holiday in Japan where the excellence of the golf courses is well known, if expensive. He is soon on the first tee of the superbly groomed fairways of the Osaka Resort. This resort specialises in tuition for the average golfer and has introduced a system where the golfer is assigned a little silver robot which accompanies the player around all eighteen holes of the course. The robot is programmed to do everything from dragging the golf buggy around the course to advising on club selection; how to play the shot, correcting errors in the player's swing, scoring and, of course, looking after the player's comfort needs.

After a few basic instructions from the pro, and a substantial hiring fee, the Australian tees off at the first, after taking on board the robot's concern at the bunkers some 192 yards from the yellow tee markers on the left side of the fairway. He smacks his second onto the green (it's a par four and he's on the green for two – rarely happened before) after the robot draws his attention to a basic and easily corrected fault in his grip.

After some further constructive advice as to his stance, a few tasteful but nevertheless funny jokes from the robot and a can of his favourite Aussie beer, our player was feeling pretty good. His score card was steadily improving and halfway through the round he was actually sinking some of the birdie putts which had been bogie putts in previous rounds. He was also beginning to enjoy the ooohs and aaahs and the applause which seemed to him to come from an invisible gallery which was following his every shot, but which in reality was supplied by courtesy of the little silver robot. It was his own British Open, and he had triumphed. By the time he had finished he was three under the card! This from an 18 handicapper.

As he returned to the pro shop he was actually toying with the idea that perhaps a life in golf was not just a dream. A bit more practice on the tips from the robot and who knows? He tipped the pro and (although he still felt a bit silly doing it) bade a fond farewell and thanks to the little silver robot. The robot passed a typically courteous remark and looked forward to 'tearing the course apart' next time with the Aussie.

Well, it was so overwhelming and he played so well, the Aussie booked immediately for holidays next year and even advanced the deposit right there and then. He only asked that he be assigned to the same little silver robot next trip. Not a problem, said the pro, happy to be of service.

It was a difficult year at work, which made the time go slowly, however he was out on his home course at every opportunity and, although playing better than in previous years, he never quite captured his Japanese form of a year ago. It was time to once again take his leave, so off to the Osaka Resort he went. After check-in he was on the doorstep of the pro shop, somewhat alarmed that there were no little silver robots to be seen. So he asked the pro about his robot and was appalled at what he heard.

The pro recounted the whole tragic story thus. Although the little silver robots had proved to be a great success in everything they were supposed to do, on sunny days the glare from their silver panels was off-putting to other golfers and sometimes caused players to hit poor shots. So something had to be done. The Committee met and decided to come up with the ingenious idea of painting the robots black, matt black in fact. 'That must have solved the problem,' said the incredulous Aussie. Matt black paint, no reflection from the sun. What was the problem?

'Problem was,' replied the pro, 'one night the bloody black little robots broke into the clubhouse, got drunk, stole the poker machine takings and did not come back to work next day!'

What do you call a lady who can suck a golf ball up a garden hose?

Darling.

The Englishman, the Scotsman and the Australian were trying to get into the Barcelona Olympic Games without paying. The Englishman got a long stick and sharpened the end to a point. He went to the gate and said, 'David Mitchell, England, javelin.' And was allowed to enter.

The Scot got a tennis ball, rubbed off the fluff and went up to the gate. 'Sandy McGregor, Scotland,' he said, 'shot putt!' He too was allowed to enter.

The Australian found a scrap of barbwire left behind by the building contractors and said, 'Bluey Morgan, Australia, fencing.'

Chap with an impediment in his speech rushed up to a bookmaker after the fifth race and said, 'I bbbbacked a fffive-ttt . . .' 'Look,' said the bookie, 'there was no 5 to 1 winner, so buzz off.'

Not to be deterred the punter said, 'Bbbut I bbbacked a fffive . . .' The bookie got somewhat heated, but the punter persisted. When the bookie could take no more, he pulled a $20 note out of his bag, gave it to the punter and said, 'Now piss off and stop annoying me!'

The punter accepted the note rather reluctantly, and as he left the ring, a mate asked him how he was making out. 'I just met a bloody gggood bbbookie,' he said. 'I tried to tttell him I bbbacked a fffive ton tttruck into his cccar and he gave me twwwenty bucks.'

A Queensland grazier employed a boundary rider with whom he could not resist gambling. Every week when he paid the boundary rider he found himself drawn into some ridiculous bet which involved him in paying his employee two or three times his wages. And the fame of the 'unbeatable' gambler spread throughout the land.

Finally, one day the grazier took the boundary rider aside and said, 'Look, I like you, but I can't go on losing all the money. So I've had a chat with my old mate, Brown, over on the next property. He's agreed to give you a job – same wages and conditions – and he's rather looking forward to the challenge of employing the Great Queensland Gambler. Is that okay?'

'Sure, Mr Smith, that's fine,' said the boundary rider. He shook hands, collected his final wages and rode over to the Browns' property. Mr Brown met his new employee at the boundary fence and they rode together to the homestead. As they were dismounting the Great Queensland Gambler said,

'By cripes, you've got piles badly, haven't you Mr Brown?'

'No,' said Mr Brown. 'Never a suggestion of a pile in my life.'

'I'll bet you you have,' said the gambler. 'I can see by the way you ride. I bet you twenty bucks you've got piles.'

And before he could think of the consequences, Brown said, 'Done!' And shook the hand of the Great Queensland Gambler. Then Brown recovered his presence of mind.

'How are we going to prove that I haven't got piles?' he asked.

'Well, Mr Brown, a bet's a bet. I guess you'll have to let me examine you.'

'Come on,' said Brown. 'I've only just met you. You can't expect me to let you . . .'

'Well, a bet's a bet. We can call if off if you like . . .'

But Brown's desire to beat the unbeatable gambler overcame his inhibitions and, there being nobody else about at the time, he submitted to the indignity of the examination. The boundary rider paid up like a lamb and with good grace.

'No, not a suggestion of a pile, Mr Brown. Here's the twenty bucks,' he said.

Brown was ecstatic. He raced into the homestead and rang Smith. 'You know the great gambler you sent over to work for me,' Brown exalted. 'He wasn't here twenty minutes and I won twenty bucks from him.'

'Cripes!' said Smith, 'How did you do that?'

'Well, he was silly enough to tell me I had piles,'

said Brown, 'and I've never been bothered with them.' 'Now wait a minute,' said Smith, 'how did you prove that?'

'Well, promise me you'll never tell another living soul. I had to let him examine me. But it was worth it to see his face when he lost.'

Smith snarled, 'He didn't lose. He won. And you've just won it for him. You see the last thing he did before he left here was to bet me a hundred bucks that he'd have his finger up your arse within an hour of setting foot on your property.'

The little man walked onto the building site in response to the sign 'Bricklayers Wanted', presented his union ticket and was signed on by the large and unsmiling foreman. About an hour later he called his new brickie over.

'Okay, bloke, your work's all right, but you talk too much for mine. Where do you come from anyway – I haven't seen you around?'

'I don't do much bricklaying these days,' was the reply.

'Oh yeah, what do you do then?'

'Gambling mostly – I'm a professional gambler.'

'Come again – you do what?' The veins on the foreman's temples were swelling.

'Professional gambling – I bet on anything. For instance, I'll bet you ten bucks that by lunchtime you'll have a serious hernia.'

'You're mad – I'm the fittest man on a building

site anywhere in Victoria – Australia for that matter,' said the foreman.

'Do you want the bet or don't you?' replied his new brickie.

'Just to teach you a lesson, I'll take it – a tenner it is – by 12 o'clock, and in the meantime get back to work and keep your trap shut.'

All went well from then on and, as the gangs knocked off for lunch, the foreman couldn't wait to call the little bloke over.

'Okay smart stuff, I want your tenner and I hope you've learnt your lesson.'

'No hernia eh?' said the little bloke, 'I could have sworn. But a tenner's a lot of money – I reckon you ought to allow me to check.'

The foreman looked murderous but the little bloke persisted and so, reluctantly, the big fellow lowered his tweeds for the inspection. 'Seems okay,' said the little bloke as with the tip of his trowel he tested the weight of each testicle. 'I guess I lose this one – here's your tenner.'

'Yeah – and you're fired anyway – so get lost,' said the big man.

'Suits me,' the little bloke said, stepping a pace or two out of the foreman's range, 'I'll just collect my winnings off the fellas and I'll be going.'

'What bloody winnings?'

The little bloke was suddenly cheerful, 'Don't you get it? There's eight blokes over there each owing me a tenner for betting that I wouldn't have your balls on the end of my trowel by lunchtime. Eighty, er seventy bucks is not a bad morning's work!'

Fred and his mate were having a drink in a pub at the Gold Coast when a very wealthy American walked in. They invited him over and got yarning. During the course of the conversation Fred's mate told the American that Fred knew everyone that was important in the whole world.

The American said, 'I just can't swallow that.'

'It's fair dinkum, mate,' said Fred's mate, 'and what's more I can prove it.'

'Well, then, how about you prove to me that Fred knows the President of the United States of America,' said the wealthy American. 'And if you can I'll give you $200,000.'

'Okay then. We'll have to fly to Washington to do that,' said Fred's mate.

'Hold on there,' said Fred, 'it's not right to take this man's dough like that. Everyone knows that I know Bill Clinton.'

'No, I insist,' said the wealthy American. 'I've got a jet waiting for me at Brisbane airport. We'll catch a cab out to the airport and fly to Washington so that you can prove Fred knows Bill Clinton and the $200,000 will be yours.'

They caught the cab, jumped into the plane and headed off to Washington. The next day they all fronted up at the White House, introduced themselves to the guards and were ushered into the President's waiting room. Bill Clinton came to the door of the waiting room and said with a big welcoming smile, 'How are you, Fred? Golly gosh, it's been a long time! Come in, come in.' Fred and Bill were closeted for close on an hour in the Oval Office. When he finally came back to the waiting room, the wealthy American said, 'Well, Fred, you sure proved that you know Bill. I'll write out your cheque. No, on second thoughts, what I'll do is this, I would like you to prove to me that you know Maggie Thatcher. If you can do that, I'll double the $200,000 to $400,000.

Fred looked doubtful at this and said, 'Yeah, I know Maggie Thatcher. She's a good friend of mine. But I don't like to take your money.'

'I insist,' said the wealthy American, 'my jet is all fuelled up. We'll catch a cab to the airport and fly to Heathrow immediately.'

'It's your money,' said Fred, 'let's go.'

They flew to Heathrow and caught a taxi to Parliament House. On the way they were stopped by a cavalcade of official vehicles. They got out of the taxi and started walking past the Rolls Royces, the Jaguars, the Daimlers. They'd only passed a couple when a darkened window of a Daimler was wound down and it was Maggie. She called out, 'Fred! Hello there! Fancy seeing you in London. Come over here and ride with me and we'll catch up on the news.' Fred jumped into the Daimler and off they drove. Fred's mate and the wealthy American went to their hotel and a couple of hours later Fred turned up. The wealthy American said, 'Well Fred, you certainly know Maggie Thatcher. I'll either pay your $400,000 now or I'll double it if you can prove you know the Pope.'

Fred said, 'Sure I know the Pope and if you're silly enough to bet me $800,000 I'll prove it to you. We'll have to fly to the Vatican City though.'

The wealthy American said, 'Done!'

They headed for Heathrow and took off for Rome. When they got there Fred wanted to know what proof the wealthy American needed. The American said, 'I want you to come out on the balcony of the Vatican with the Pope when he makes his daily appearance before the crowds.'

Fred agreed and disappeared into the Vatican. At 2 o'clock the wealthy American and Fred's mate were waiting with the crowds in the square beneath the balcony to see Fred and the Pope. When Fred emerged from the Vatican a few minutes later, he found his mate standing over the body of the collapsed American.

'What happened?' asked Fred.

'Well, everything was fine until this dago standing behind us said, "I know who Fred is, but who's that fella with him?"'

A midget walks into the pub, reaches up and taps on the bar and asks the publican, 'Can a bloke get a bet on here?'

The barman leans over the bar, peers down at the midget and asks, 'You're not a copper, are you?'

There was a bloke who, although he punted on every race every Saturday, had not backed a solitary winner for many years. Every race he'd front up to a bookmaker, slap a tenner on his selection, and then watch it race as if it had rabbit traps attached to all four legs. Lesser gamblers would have given up, but this fellow persisted.

One day, a kind-hearted bookie decided that he would let the punter win for a change. He called the punter over and said, 'You've been backing horses with me for ten years and never had a collect. I'll tell you what I'm going to do – I'm going to put the names of all the fancied runners in next week's big race on slips of paper and place them in my hat. You can draw one of them out and I'll give you – free of charge – the odds about it to $1000. In other words, if you select a 7 to 1 pop and it wins, I'll pay you $7000.'

The punter was thrilled with this arrangement and readily agreed. The slips of paper with the horses' names on them were placed in the bookmaker's hat and the punter drew one.

'What horse did you draw?' asked the bookie, as the punter sadly surveyed the paper.'

'Akubra!'

The producer of *Phar Lap*, John Sexton, restaged the 1930 Melbourne Cup. On looking at the rushes, he realised that not all the horses in the re-enactment finished in the proper sequence. So he called all the jockeys together. 'Gentlemen, we have a problem. The horses must finish in exactly the same order as they did in the original race.'

There was a long silence broken finally by the leading jockey. 'What's the problem?'

Fred got a job driving a racehorse transport truck. He had to take horses to Flemington and Moonee Valley. He was running a bit late one day and had his foot flat to the floor when he was caught in a radar trap and pulled over. 'You were doin' 150, driver, ' said the police officer. 'What's the story?'

'Sorry, sir, but I was late for the first race at Flemington. And the trainer said I'd lose me job if the horses weren't there in time.' Whereupon the cop walked to the back of the truck and looked in.

'What the bloody hell are you talking about?' he yelled. 'There are no horses in here. It's empty!'

'Bugger it,' said Fred, 'they've given me the scratchings again.'

POLITICS AND POWER

Politicians are like a bunch of bananas. They start off green, quickly turn yellow, and there's not a straight one in the whole bunch.

Two rival politicians met face-to-face on a narrow pavement. Neither was willing to step aside for the other, especially since it had been raining heavily and the street was awash. So they glared at each other for a while until, finally, one said, 'I never step aside for fools!'

'Oh, really,' said the other, 'I always do!' and stepped off into the wet street.

A school class was shown over Parliament House and, when they returned to school, the students were asked to write an essay about what they'd seen. One lad wrote just one line, 'All politicians is bastards.' Rather than scold him, the teacher decided to apply psychology and sent the boy back, where he met the Speaker, was introduced to the Premier, sat in the Speaker's chair, met the Leader of the Opposition and was given an official lunch. After this red carpet treatment he went back to school to write another essay. It also consisted of one line, 'All politicians is cunning bastards.'

The leader of the opposition droned on and on, despite warnings from the speaker, who eventually was banging his gavel repeatedly. Finally the speaker lost his temper and hurled his gavel at the politician. He missed and hit someone in the front bench. As he slumped to the ground, the injured man said, 'Hit me again. I can still hear the bastard.'

There are two squashed corpses on the Hume Highway. One is a dead possum, the other a dead politician. What's the difference?

There are skid marks before the possum.

It happened in the early 1970s. There was this almighty flood. In one of the rescue helicopters – apart from the pilot – there was an odd group of three people. A young hippie, a simple country clergyman and a half-sozzled bloke in a crumpled suit. Suddenly the machine developed a serious fault. Ashen-faced, the pilot turned around and said, 'I'm terribly sorry, but you'll have to bail out because we're going to crash. The problem is that we've only got two parachutes.'

Before he finished speaking, the business-suited bloke spoke up, 'I'm a Rhodes scholar,' he said, 'and I'm in charge of all the workers in Australia. I have the brains, the drive and the connections to become the PM of this great country. I am clearly indispensable.' So saying, he grabbed the pack nearest to hand and jumped out.

'Son,' said the padre, 'I am an old man, I suffer from arthritis and am near the end. You have your life ahead of you – you take the other parachute.'

'What's with you, man?' asked the hippie, 'there's still two chutes. That self-important idiot jumped out with my back-pack.'

Once upon a time, a little nonconforming swallow decided not to fly south for the winter. He was unsure of the rationale behind the annual pilgrimage of his contemporaries and, being suspicious of unproved advice, decided to test the claim that it was necessary to avoid the life-threatening winter. So he wouldn't budge.

Gradually the winter started to close in. The swallow grew colder and colder. Finally he decided to head south after the others. But he'd left it too late. As he flew, the winter became more and more bitter. Ice formed on his wings. Eventually, he fell to earth in a frost-covered field. As he gasped his last breath, a cow wandered through the field and crapped on him. The warmth of the manure thawed his wings, warmed his body and revived him. He was so overjoyed by this turn of events that he raised his little head and whistled a happy little bird song. Just at that moment, a cat walking through the field heard the happy little chirping sound. It found the mound of dung, uncovered the little swallow and ate him.

There are three morals to this story:

1. Everyone who craps on you is not necessarily your enemy.
2. Everyone who extricates you from crap is not necessarily your friend.
3. If you are warm and comfortable in a pile of crap, keep your mouth shut.

A medical doctor, an engineer and a politician were discussing their professions. Which was the oldest? The medical officer reminded the others that the Book of Genesis clearly states that the first woman was created from the rib of a man. This was a medical function, so one must agree that his profession was the oldest. Whereupon the engineer argued that earlier in the Book of Genesis there was reference to the fact that God created order and calm out of chaos and mayhem. 'That would take an engineer.'

'Oh no,' cried the politician. '*We* go back further. Who do you think created the chaos?'

There was a young couple typically in love who had an all-consuming problem. That is, she was a staunch Liberal and he was a dedicated Labor supporter. They decided to marry under the solid rule that politics would not be discussed, but immediately after the reception they had a fierce political argument. Later that night in the nuptial bed the girl relented and tapped the fellow on the shoulder and said, 'There is a split in the Liberal Party ranks and it is likely if a Labor member stood then he would get in unopposed.' To which there was a prompt reply, 'It is too late, he stood independently and has blown his deposit.'

A politican was driving a constituent and her young son through Kings Cross when the son pointed out some women loitering on the footpath and asked her, 'What are those ladies waiting for?'

To which she replied, 'Son, they are waiting for their husbands to come and pick them up after work.' Whereupon the politician, obviously Labor, cut in and said, 'Lady, you can't shield your son from the real world. Admit to him that they're prostitutes.' The boy then asked, 'Mother, do prostitutes have babies?' To which the mother replied, 'Of course, son, where do you think politicians come from!'

A New Zealand Minister had been forced to resign, and while he was packing up he looked out the window of his office, high above the streets of Wellington, and said to his staff, 'See that new school over there? Well, last year I persuaded Cabinet to vote the money for that school. Yes, I built that school. But do you think the voters will remember me for that?

'And see that new hospital down the street? Well, the year before I built the school I had to call in every political debt owed me to get Cabinet to back that hospital. But I did it. And I built that hospital. But will the voters ever remember me for that? Course they bloody won't!

'And see that six-lane freeway out to the airport? Well, the first year I was a Minister, the year after we just managed to win the election, I had to squeeze Cabinet like you wouldn't believe to get the money for that, and I built that freeway, and you can bet the voters won't ever give me a second thought for that either.

'But screw one sheep and they never forget!'

The political candidate knocked hopefully on the door of a prospective supporter in the electorate and introduced himself. Much to his surprise, the lady of the house remarked, 'I'm certainly not going to vote for you!'

'But,' said the candidate, 'you've never seen my opponent.'

'No,' said the lady, 'but I've had a damn good look at you.'

My favourite jokes are one-liners which can be pinned more or less at random on one's political opponents:

'He's always been insufferable. In fact, he was so insufferable as a child that at the age of nine both parents ran away from home.'

'When he was born he was so unprepossessing that his parents hired a team of lawyers to try to find a loophole in his birth certificate.'

A businessman, disappointed in his career, decided to volunteer for the first brain transplant. A brilliant surgeon offered him a choice of three samples from his brain bank: one from a leading brain surgeon at $1000, one from a leading research scientist at $1000 and one from a retired politician at $5000. He enquired why the last one was so much dearer. 'It's never been used,' said the brain surgeon.

Why do so many people take an instant dislike to Senator Bishop?

Because it saves time.

Senator John Button was staying at a hotel in Los Angeles where there was a convention of comic book superheroes – Batman, Spiderman, Wonderwoman, etc. At breakfast Button was interrupted by the arrival of Superman, who said he was feeling the worse for wear after a heavy night. Button enquired what had taken place. Superman said that he'd come back to his room after a party and was preparing for bed when his X-ray vision revealed that Wonderwoman was lying naked in the next room. Superman said he could do nothing else but crash through the wall, landing on the bed. So Button said to Superman, 'Well, that must have surprised Wonderwoman!' To which Superman replied, 'Not nearly as much as it surprised the Invisible Man!'

Hillary Clinton was out jogging one morning. As she passed a small boy she saw that he had a boxful of puppies. She stopped and asked the young man what kind of puppies he had. He looked up proudly and said, 'They're all Democrats.' Hillary was pleased as she jogged away. She returned home and told her husband the story.

About a week later Bill was jogging by a young man with a box of small puppies. He stopped and asked the young boy what kind of puppies they were. The boy looked up confidently and said, 'They're all Republicans.' Somewhat puzzled, Bill asked him if he was the same boy that had told Hillary about his Democrat pups. The boy said that, yes, he was the same boy. Bill then asked him if he had a new box of puppies.

'No,' said the boy, 'they are the same puppies.'

Bill asked, 'How can they be Democrats last week and Republicans this week?'

The small boy said cheerfully, 'Last week, when they had their eyes closed, they were Democrats. Now that their eyes are open they are Republicans.'

Whilst campaigning in 1992, Bill Clinton discovered that his wife, Hillary, had almost married a small town mechanic. On pointing out to Hillary how close she came to not being First Lady, she replied that had she married the mechanic, *he* would have been President.

Nick Greiner was having great difficulty getting any good press coverage. So he called his press secretary and demanded that all the press be assembled under the Harbour Bridge for a major announcement at noon the next day. The due time arrived and all the State's media were assembled. The Premier said, 'I'm sick and tired of all this bad coverage, so I'm going to do something that nobody here can complain about.' He then proceeded to walk on the water across Sydney Harbour. The Premier awoke next morning to find that the *Sydney Morning Herald* proclaimed: GREINER CAN'T SWIM while the *Telegraph* was emblazoned with the banner GOVERNMENT RORTS; GREINER DOESN'T PAY THE TOLL.

A prostitute decides to undertake a new marketing technique by applying tattoos to her inner thighs. On one thigh is tattooed the face of Nick Greiner, on the other that of Wal Murray. Any client identifying one or the other receives a 50 per cent discount. If they can identify both, they get a freebie. A succession of customers identify either Nick or Wal. Then the lady happens to pick up an off-duty policeman who can't recognise either. 'Nup, I give up,' he says, 'but the one in the middle looks like Ted Pickering.'

Bob Hawke visited George Bush during the Gulf War and couldn't help but be impressed by the quality of the White House staff. So he said to Bush, 'George, where do you get all these great staffers?'

Bush replied, 'It is very simple. Every morning I ask a staff member a trick question. Watch this . . .' Bush then called for Dan Quayle. The VP walked in and Bush said, 'Dan, your mother has a child. It's not your brother, it's not your sister, who is it?'

Quayle replied, 'That's very simple, George. It's me.'

'Well done, Dan,' said the President, and Hawke was duly impressed. 'I've got to try that out.'

On his return to Canberra, he took his car straight into the office and put the same question to Paul Keating. 'Paul, your mother has a child. It's not your brother and it's not your sister. Who is it?'

Keating said, 'Gee, Bob, that's a tough one. I don't know the answer but I'll find out.' So he ran down to Johnny Button, well known as the brightest man in the Government, and said, 'John, your mother has a child. It's not your brother, it's not your sister. So who is it?' Button looked at him, half took off his glasses like he always does, and said, 'Paul, you moron, it's me!'

Keating was delighted. 'Right! I've got it!' He ran back to Hawke and said, 'Bob, my mother has a child. It's not my brother and it's not my sister. But I know who it is.'

Hawke said, 'Well, who?'

Keating responded, 'John Button!'

Hawke looked at him and said, 'Don't be bloody silly, Paul. It's Dan Quayle!'

If an intelligent politician, an intelligent woman and the Easter Bunny got into a lift together and discovered a $10 note lying on the floor, who would pick it up?

The intelligent woman. The other two don't exist.

There was a meeting between Bob Hawke, Presidents Bush and Gorbachev. While they were discussing world problems, the Angel of the Lord appeared to announce that God was not pleased and intended destroying the world in three weeks. Each travelled back to their respective countries to make the announcement. George told the Americans that he had good news and bad news.

The good news was that he had proof of God's existence. The bad news was that He was going to pull the plug. President Gorbachev told the Russians that he had bad news and worse news. The bad news was that God existed, despite Communist beliefs to the contrary, and the worse news was that the world was to be destroyed. Bob Hawke, meanwhile, appeared on national television to tell us that he had good news and terrific news. Although he hadn't believed it previously, there really was a God. And the terrific news was that no child would be living in poverty in a month's time.

Bob Hawke was flying home to Canberra after a particularly successful day kicking the shit out of the left wing. And since he was in such a good mood he decided he would do something to make an Australian happy. So he asked the steward if he could toss a $10 note out of the plane, so that whoever found it would share in some of his joy. The steward suggested that he throw ten $1 coins out of the plane since that would make ten Australians happy. Bob said, 'What a great idea. Maybe some poor kids will find them and I'll have less of them to worry about being in poverty by 1990.' A left-winger sitting behind him overheard all this and piped up with, 'Why don't you throw yourself out of the plane? Then you'd make all Australia happy.'

I've had a lot of trouble knowing when Bob Hawke is telling the parliament lies,' said the journo. 'When he raises his eyes he's telling the truth. When he rolls his eyes he's telling the truth. When he scratches his chin he's telling the truth. Now I know when he's lying. It's when he opens his mouth.'

Gary Hart meets Margaret Thatcher. Mrs Thatcher tells him, 'I want your hands off Nicaragua, your hands off Afghanistan and your hands off my knee.'

Why does Dr Hewson's Ferrari go backwards?
Because it's negatively geared.

A specially chartered Lufthansa flight arrives at Buenos Aires airport. It taxis away from the main terminal and, under cover of darkness, a number of shadowy figures emerge. They immediately pile into a Mercedes and are driven off into the night. They arrive at an impressive mansion outside of town purchased some years earlier by the local BMW agent. The men knock nervously at the door. After a time, steps approach. The door opens and reveals an old man with a familiar lock of hair dangling over the forehead. Except after all these years the lock is thin and grey.

'Yes?'

'*Mein Führer*,' says the spokesman, 'we have come to beg you to return to Berlin, to lead your people in the Fourth Reich!'

'No,' snarls the old man, 'been there, done that.'

'But, *Mein Führer*, the entire population is ready for you. The neo-Nazi movement has never been stronger.'

'The German people were not worthy of me,' snarls the old man.

'True, *Mein Führer*. But now a United Germany is ready to follow you anywhere, to fulfil your greatest dream.'

The old man ruminates. He talks about having a peaceful, private life with Eva and the great-grandchildren, about how well BMW sales are going. But, finally, he is prevailed upon.

Then he makes one proviso. 'Okay, but this time, no more Mr Nice Guy.'

David Hill is going to work one day and he gets in the David Hill lift and goes up to the David Hill suite. The lift makes an unscheduled stop on the third floor and in walks a very attractive blonde who David had never seen before. The woman obviously doesn't work for the ABC because she is not carrying anything in triplicate.

She and David look at each other and she says, 'David Hill?'

And he says, 'Yes.'

And she says, 'I'd like to give you a blow job.'

And this is the mark of the man. David Hill looks at her and says, 'Yes . . . fine, but what's in it for me?'

David Hill and his wife were in bed today.

'God . . .' she said, to which he responded, 'You may call me David when we're in bed.'

Saddam Hussein disappeared down the bunker where he addressed his magic mirror, 'Magic mirror on the wall who is the biggest bastard of them all?' The magic mirror said, 'Saddam Hussein, you are the biggest bastard of all.' Saddam was so delighted with the response that he raced out and ordered a thousand of his faithful followers to be put to the sword.

The next week he disappeared down the bunker again. 'Magic mirror on the wall, who is the biggest bastard of all?'

'Saddam Hussein, you are still the biggest bastard of all.'

Saddam again was so delighted he declared war on the Kurds. The next week he went into the bunker, but didn't return. His worried aides finally decided to seek him out. When they arrived there was Saddam crying uncontrollably in the corner.

'Sire, sire,' they cried, 'what's wrong?'

'Who's Paul Keating?' sobbed Saddam.

Keating dies and turns up at the pearly gates. He asks for admission, explaining that he was 'the world's greatest Treasurer' and undoubtedly Australia's greatest Prime Minister. Peter sends him down below because he isn't on the list. Up comes an old man with a long white beard who insists that *he* is the real Keating. And Peter lets him in. A man who's been watching goes up to Peter and asks why he let in this imposter whilst denying the genuine article. 'No, he's not Keating. He's God. But he thinks he's Keating.'

Three plastic surgeons meet at a conference. The first, an American, talks about the latest triumph in Californian reconstruction. 'A guy was shot to pieces in a shoot-out. All we had left was his right ear. We took that ear, reconstituted the entire body and now he's back at work. As a matter of fact, he replaced six men.'

The English plastic surgeon promptly tops the story. 'We had a nuclear accident at a power station, and all that was left was a single hair. We took that hair, reconstructed the entire human being and now he's back at work at the power station. Where he's replaced *twenty* men.'

The Australian plastic surgeon is unimpressed. 'I was walking down Collins Street a few weeks ago and smelt a fart. I trapped it in a bottle, got back to the hospital, managed to constitute it into an arsehole and then into an entire human body. That bloke's now the Prime Minister of Australia, and he's put a million people out of work.'

Paul Keating entered a pub with a pig on a leash. He ordered two beers, one for him and one for the pig. After a couple of rounds, the barman's curiosity got the better of him. 'Where did you get him?' he asked. 'I won him in a raffle,' replied the pig.

The former Treasurer of Australia, Paul Keating, rushed into the office of the Prime Minister, Bob Hawke.

'Bob! Bob! I've just seen your new business card and you've got C^3I after your name. I thought that was a high-tech buzz word standing for Command,

Control, Communications and Intelligence. You don't have any of those qualities.'

Bob Hawke pompously replies, 'Paul, you've got it all wrong again. Those letters stand for Charisma, Credibility and Integrity.'

'But, Bob, what does the other C stand for?' blurts out the former greatest treasurer on the planet.

'I couldn't think of another suitable word beginning with C,' says our esteemed leader. 'You suggest one.'

Paul Keating, the Indian High Commissioner and the Israeli Ambassador are forced to seek emergency accommodation when their car breaks down in the middle of the bush. A farmer is happy to help, but has only two spare beds ... 'So someone will have to sleep in the barn.'

The Israeli Ambassador volunteers. 'We Jewish people are used to sleeping in barns – it is part of our history.' But he returns to the house when he discovers that he'll be cohabiting with a pig, which just isn't kosher. Then the Indian High Commissioner steps forward, only to be knocking at the door a few minutes later, protesting the presence of a cow. 'The cow is sacred to us Indians,' he exclaims. 'I couldn't possibly sleep with one.' 'Okay, scumbags,' says Paul, 'I'll go and sleep in the barn.'

After five minutes there's another knocking on

the door. The farmer opens it only to be confronted with the pig and the cow.

Paul Keating visits the Canberra cemetery to negotiate a plot. He's taken to a grassy knoll, beside a eucalypt, with a splendid view. 'How much is this one?' he asks.

'Five thousand dollars,' says the cemetery official.

'Have you got anything cheaper?'

'Well, yes, there's one down the hill for $2000. But the view isn't very good.'

'Two thousand is still too much. What else have you got?'

'The only other plot we have is behind the tool shed.'

'How much is that?'

'Two hundred dollars. But sir, an ex-Prime Minister of Australia can't be buried in a $200 plot.'

'No worries,' says Keating, 'I'm only going to be there three days.'

Paul Keating took his Cabinet colleagues into the parliamentary dining room for dinner. The waiter approached the Prime Minister and asked for his order.

The PM said, 'The steak.'

'Well done or rare?' asked the waiter.

'Rare,' said Keating.

'And what about the vegetables?' asked the waiter.

'They'll have what I have,' replied Keating.

Senator Graham Richardson has just explained his actions about the Marshall Islands affair to a forgiving Prime Minister.

Richo says, 'Paul, mate, you've got a hole in your pants.'

Keating replies, 'Richo, I told you to take that damn cigar out of your mouth before you kissed me goodbye.'

Paul Keating was tripping along a country road when the car ran over a pig. He told the chauffeur to go to the nearby farmhouse and explain what had happened, apologise and offer to pay for the animal. The driver was gone a long time and when he returned had lipstick all over his face, was smoking a cigar and clutching an empty champagne bottle. 'I had a marvellous time, boss,' he said. 'The farmer gave me a cigar, his sons kept giving me champagne and his daughters made passionate love to me.'

'Good grief,' exclaimed Paul, 'what on earth did you say to them?'

'Just what you told me, boss,' said the chauffeur. 'I knocked on the door and said, "G'day, I'm Paul Keating's chauffeur and I've just killed the pig."'

Henry Kissinger was midway through one of his diplomatic marathons. He was sitting at the airport at Tel Aviv, waiting for a jet to take him to a small but important sultanate. Oddly enough the airport terminal was all but deserted except for a rather serious-looking young Israeli who reminded Henry of Woody Allen. 'And what do you do, son?' enquired Henry, to pass the time. 'Oh, I've just passed my university course and I'm looking for a job,' said the boy. 'And what do you do?' Though stunned by the boy's ignorance, Henry made a joke of it. 'Oh, I'm a sort of marriage broker.'

'Gee, do you think you could get me a good marriage?'

'Certainly. Just watch me.' Whereupon Henry had the airport officials contact the head of the Rothschild family in Paris. After a few pleasantries, Henry told Baron Rothschild that he had a young friend who'd be the perfect husband for his attractive daughter.

'Ah, Henry, everyone says that. Can you imagine how many suitors that girl has?'

'Ah, yes, but how many of her suitors represent David Rockefeller here in the Middle East?'

Whereupon Baron Rothschild agreed that the young man should press his suit.

Next Henry rang David Rockefeller in New York and said, 'David, I've got a young bloke here who wants to be your representative in the Middle East.'

David Rockefeller laughed. 'But Henry, there are hundreds of young men who want to be my representative in the Middle East.'

'Perhaps,' said Henry, 'but how many of them are engaged to Baron Rothschild's daughter?'

Talleyrand once asked Napoleon, 'Why is it that your brothers hate you so much?' After a pause, Napoleon said, 'They believe that I have robbed them of the inheritance of our late father, the King.'

Mr Dan Quayle landed at Sydney airport carrying a personal letter to Paul Keating from the President of the United States. Standing on the tarmac, he handed it to Keating as the photographers captured the moment. What did the letter say?

'Please ignore this man, he is an idiot.'

President Reagan wakes one winter's morn and goes to the window of his bedroom to look at the freshly fallen snow on the White House lawn and is aghast to see, written in what is obviously urine, the legend 'Reagan sucks'. Furious, he calls in his CIA chief and bellows that this incident has ruined his whole day and they'd better find the culprit immediately. The CIA chief scuttles off and later that day fronts Reagan in the Oval Office and says, 'Sir, we have good news and we have bad news. The good news is we can unequivocally tell you who the culprit is. We've run the piss sample through spectrometers, the CIA computers and a urine-inspect-o-nalysis doo-dad and without a shadow of a doubt I can tell you, it was Frank Sinatra!'

President Reagan reels in shock and gasps, 'Frank Sinatra! That's the good news. What on earth could be the bad news?'

'Well, sir,' says the CIA chief, 'the handwriting's Nancy's.'

During the Fraser years, when John Stone still led the Treasury, a small dispute between clerical officers and the government resulted in a one-man picket at the bottom of the Treasury steps. The lone picketer was having limited success convincing his fellow unionists to join the strike, but even Stone's arrival at work did not deter him. 'SCAB!' he called after Stone, who turned around to give the striker a lengthy lecture about the distortion of allocation of labour, the imbalanced power of unions and the benefits of government labour policy. Satisfied he had made his point, Stone continued up the stairs only to hear the cry 'SCAB!' again at his back. Patiently he returned to the picketer and again (with more emotion) gave the man a diatribe on the many benefits of Tory labour policy. This time the striker would surely understand. Stone returned to his climb up the stairs. 'SCAB!' the call came for the third time. Exasperated, Stone returned to the picket, saying with conviction, 'You have heard my views. I just don't know what to say to people like you,' and he turned on his heel to stomp up the stairs. The picketer paused before calling after Stone 'INARTICULATE SCAB!'

A Short Poppy asked a Tall Poppy over to his place to swim in his pool. When the TP got there the pool was one of those squat, low vases. The SP had a lovely time, but the TP barely wet his toes.

The TP asked the SP over to his place to swim in his pool. When the SP got there the pool was one of those long thin vases you use for single red roses. The TP had a lovely time, but the SP was floundering, struggling, sinking.

Finally, as the SP was going down for the third time, he shouted, 'Help me! I can't touch the bottom!' 'Oh you can touch the bottom all right,' said the Tall Poppy, 'it's the top you can't touch!'

A Short Poppy and a Tall Poppy went to the Cenotaph. The TP said, 'Look at those mosaics on the ceiling; those fine, athletic soldiers looking like Greek gods! And look at those stained glass windows; pure artistry in light, it makes you feel close to God!'

The Short Poppy was looking down at their reflections in the polished marble floor.

'I don't know about that,' he said, 'but my balls are twice as big as yours!'

Four things wrong with being a Tall Poppy:

You take twice as long to grow to your full height.

While you're growing the short poppies are down in the dirt having all the fun.

When you do reach your full height everybody sneers at you and says you don't deserve it.

Then, on every 11th November, an old man cuts you off at the knees, sticks you in a hole in his jacket, and when you ask him why, he falls silent.

THE LAW IS AN ASS

The Pope dies. As he mounts the stairs to the Pearly Gates he wonders why he doesn't hear any trumpets. Nor is St Peter waiting for him. However, the gates are ajar so His Holiness pushes his way in. Needless to say, he's in his best outfit, complete with his most impressive papal crook. Well, you only die once, and he wanted to make a grand entrance. So he's very, very disappointed by the reception. Perhaps they'll jump out from behind a cloud and chorus 'Welcome to Heaven'. Perhaps they're going to have a surprise party for him.

But for twenty minutes absolutely nothing happens. Suddenly a bloke runs by with a big tray of sandwiches. And the Pope yells out, 'Hey you, over there!' The fellow stops and says, 'Oh, Your Holiness, we were expecting you. I'm sorry we weren't there to meet you, but we're holding a brunch for you tomorrow around 11 o'clock. You'll enjoy it. Welcome to heaven.'

The Pope says, 'Hang on, I'm the bloody Pope!'

'We've got lots of popes. We've got hundreds of popes here. You'll meet a lot of them at the brunch. Anyway, welcome to heaven, but right now we've got to go and meet Mr Meyers.' And off he goes. And the Pope is left wondering who the hell Mr Meyers is.

So he follows the bloke around the corner where a band's tuning up and there's St Peter with a list in his hand organising things 'The anchovies ... not many people like anchovies. Put them down at the end of the banquet table. The artichokes are very puny. That won't do for heaven, and certainly not for Mr Meyers. Get bigger artichokes – do a miracle, or something.'

Just then St Peter looks up and says, 'Oh, Your Holiness. Hi, I'm St Peter. Awfully sorry I wasn't there to meet you, but Mr Meyers is coming.'

The Pope says, 'Who is this Mr Meyers? And why is he more important than the Pope?'

'Well, he's our first lawyer.'

And the Pope says, 'A lawyer? What's a lawyer doing in heaven?'

'Oh, here he comes now, Your Holiness. Excuse me I'll be right back.'

St Peter runs off to the gate and the Pope catches a glimpse of a fellow in a pinstripe suit with a briefcase in his hand. He's led into heaven looking a bit puzzled. But St Peter couldn't be nicer. He takes the briefcase from him, shakes his hand, puts an arm around his shoulder and says, 'I'm St Peter. Welcome to heaven.'

Mr Meyers looks really puzzled and says, 'How did I get into heaven?'

'Believe me, Mr Meyers, it's not based on your work or your character or anything you've done during your life. But it's because you're the oldest man ever to come to heaven.'

'What do you mean? I was 46 when I died of a heart attack just this afternoon. What do you mean old?'

'Well, according to our records you're over 500 years old.'

'Nonsense,' protests Mr Meyers, 'I told you I'm 46.'

St Peter said, 'Well, we have your office records right here.'

Mr Meyers says, 'Oh no, you've just added up the hours I charge my clients.'

A lawyer was sitting in his office one afternoon, all by himself, doing some paperwork, when suddenly there's a big puff of smoke in the corner and the smell of brimstone. When the smoke cleared the lawyer saw – the Devil.

He said, 'What can I do for you?'

The Devil said, 'I want to offer you a great deal.'

'I'm a lawyer, I'll tell you whether this deal is great or not. What are the terms?'

The Devil said, 'Well, first of all, I guarantee that you'll live to be at least 150 years of age and that you'll have the body and lust of a teenager and an endless succession of nymphomaniacal secretaries, each one of which will be more beautiful, voluptuous and enthusiastic than the last one. Women will do anything you want – all you'll have to do is think about it. Moreover, you'll have a job with the biggest law firm in Melbourne. You just name it, you'll be the head of that law firm on the most fabulous six-figure salary. You'll have eight weeks holidays every few months if you want.'

The lawyer said, 'Hold on, this sounds too good. What do I have to give in return?'

The Devil said, 'Oh, it's very simple. Your faithful wife of twenty-four years and your two beautiful children will have to die right now. In extreme agony. And go to hell to burn for the rest of eternity.'

The lawyer paused for a minute and said, 'Oh, all right, but what's the catch?'

What happens to a lawyer who jumps out of a plane at 35 000 feet with no parachute?

Who cares?

A couple of blokes set off in a balloon. They're determined they are going to stay up longer than anyone else in ballooning history. But two days later there's a huge storm that wrecks all their radio equipment. And while they're being buffeted around, their food falls overboard. Worse still, they don't know where they are. They might be anywhere. On the other side of the world. So they decide to lose altitude until they come in sight of land. Down they go, very slowly, descending through the clouds. And they sigh with relief because they're over land. Peering down from the basket they see cars and think, 'Well, they're driving on the left side of the road. That means we're probably in the UK or Australia. And they're playing tennis. So it must be a civilised country.'

They come within hailing distance of the tennis court and call out to one of the players, 'Hello, down there!'

The two fellows stop playing tennis and look up. 'Yeah, what do you want?'

'Where are we?'

'You got any money?'

'Yes, what do you want with money?'

'Throw it down,' says the man on the ground.

So they throw a wallet down and one of the blokes on the ground picks it up, takes the money out, splits it with the fellow on the other side of the net and puts the wallet in his pocket. Finally he says, 'Now, what was your question?'

'Where are we?'

'You're in a balloon.'

At that moment they rise above the clouds and the two partners look at one another helplessly. 'That was useless,' said one.

'No, at least we know where we are.'

'What do you mean we know where we are?'

'Well, we're over a civilised country. They drive on the left hand side of the road. And those two fellows are lawyers.'

'How can you tell they're lawyers?'

'Well, first of all, they wouldn't do a thing for us until we paid them. And what they said was absolutely true and totally useless.'

University research psychologists decided not to use white rats in experiments any more. They opted to use lawyers instead.

First, they're much more plentiful – you can get lawyers anywhere. Second, sometimes experimenters get a little too attached to their white rats and if something nasty happens to them you feel bad. And with lawyers you just don't have that problem. Third, they've found out there are some things that white rats just won't do.

But the latest development is they've stopped using lawyers. They're back to using white rats again. The reason's simple. They weren't into it very long before they found out that lawyers aren't that close to human beings.

An engineer, a doctor and a lawyer were on a ship. It began taking water and sinking, and the cowardly crew abandoned the ship and the passengers. The three found themselves trying to stay afloat in a two-man dinghy. It was obvious that it was not going to work, and that sacrifice by one of the three was necessary to enhance the survival prospects of the other two. Without fuss, the lawyer went over the side and struck out confidently for what looked like a smudge of land on the horizon.

Suddenly, several menacing triangular fins broke the surface and the two in the dinghy thought the lawyer was about to pay the ultimate price. To their amazement, however, two of the sharks started leading the way to the island in the distance, while the remainder formed a protective circle around the lone swimmer.

Watching dumbfounded from the dinghy, the doctor stammered, 'That's the most amazing thing I've ever seen!'

'Not amazing,' replied the engineer, 'simply a matter of professional courtesy.'

A lawyer working for the family court forgot that he was due at a divorce settlement. By the time he arrived he saw his Aboriginal client, a woman, leaving the court holding a sheet of rusty galvanised iron.

'I'm terribly sorry I wasn't here in time,' he said.

'It's okay,' said the woman, 'I managed fine without you. Look, I got half the house.'

Two 88-year-old pensioners visit the lawyer. 'We want a divorce,' they chorus in quavering voices.

The lawyer is both amused and curious. 'Why on earth have you waited so long?'

'We were waiting for the kids to die.'

Two Justices of the Peace, having become slightly 'point-o-pissed' together one Friday evening, were promptly arrested by the unsuspecting new plod who had arrived in town to enforce the law. All parties were embarrassed when the facts emerged. However, the question of bail was not in issue, since each of these gentlemen, with a stroke of the legal pen, granted the other co-offender freedom on the condition that he would appear in the magistrates court on the following Monday morning. On Monday morning the question arose, who should sit on the bench first.

'*I* will,' said the first gentleman of the law, hoping that he could set a precedent for his brother justice. 'This is a serious matter, this drunkenness in a public place,' he said. 'However, as this is your first offence, I shall treat the matter with a degree of leniency and place you on a good behaviour bond.'

He then stepped down from the bench and took his turn standing in the dock. His brother justice, with whom he had previously been imbibing, stepped up and sat on the bench. 'There is a prevalence of this type of offence coming before the courts, and something must be done about it. Why, this is the second example of such behaviour that the court has had to listen to this morning. Fined $100!'

A Queensland farmer is seeking damages for injuries sustained when his horse was hit by a car. In court, the defence counsel asks, 'After the accident, didn't someone come over to you and ask how you felt?'

Farmer: 'Yes, I believe that is so.'

Defence counsel: 'And didn't you tell him that you never felt better in your life?

Farmer: 'Yes, I guess I did.' The defence counsel then sits down and the plaintiff's counsel stands up.

Plaintiff's counsel: 'Will you tell His Honour the circumstances in which you made the response?'

Farmer: 'Yes. Not long after the accident, my horse, which had sustained broken legs, was thrashing around. A policeman came up to the horse, put his revolver to its ear and shot it dead. Then he went over to my dog, which had a broken back and was howling miserably. He put his revolver to the dog's ear and shot it. Then he came over to me and asked, "How do you feel?"

I said, "I never felt better in my life."'

Three Sydney men, who were called for jury service but failed to attend, were summoned to appear before a judge and account for themselves. The first of them to front the judge was lectured on the seriousness of the offence and asked for an explanation. 'Your Honour,' he said. 'I realise how serious this matter is. The night before I was due to report for jury service I set my alarm clock to wake me in plenty of time. But the clock broke down – it didn't go off and I slept in. Even so I hurried and got ready to leave without breakfast, but I couldn't start my car. The battery was flat. I immediately phoned for a taxi. When it came I told the driver the situation and asked him to hurry. We were doing fine until we reached Pyrmont Bridge, but then we ran into a milk cart and killed the horse.'

The judge muttered something about that being 'a likely story' and told the man to sit down and wait while the second man was interviewed.

This man's story started off exactly the same way: the alarm clock that didn't ring, the car that wouldn't start, the taxi ... The judge interrupted, 'And when you got to the Pyrmont Bridge,' he suggested, 'you ran into a milk cart and the horse was killed?'

'That's right,' said the man. 'How did you know?'

'Never mind,' said the judge, 'sit over there and wait.'

The third man appeared before the judge, who eyed him sceptically and said, 'Did you set an alarm clock that failed to go off?'

'Yes, sir.'

'And then your car wouldn't start because the battery was flat?'

'Yes, sir.'

'So you called a cab and told the driver to hurry.'

'Yes, sir.'

The judge smiled sourly. 'I can hardly wait to hear what happened at Pyrmont Bridge,' he sneered.

'Ah,' said the man, 'that's where the hold-up happened – there were two dead horses on the bridge.'

What do you call a bigot in a wig?

Your Honour.

What do you call a few hundred bigots in wigs?

The Australian judicial system.

Why are Australian judges like Mother Teresa?

Because everything they say makes you want to launch an appeal.

Why is an Australian judge like a dyslexic?

Because they both stuff up their sentences.

Why is an Australian judge like a drunk?

Because his judgment suffers from too many years at the bar.

Why is an Australian judge like Old Sydney Town?

Because both offer a variety of 18th-century views.

Why is a woman in the court system like a ship on the ocean?

Because, at the end of it all, it will be her in the dock.

What do you call a judge driving through a working-class suburb?

Lost.

Is it true that Australian judges are all from the same class?

Yes. Mr Tompkin's Latin class at Melbourne Grammar, 1914.

Why are Australian judges so prejudiced against women?

Because they never met any at Melbourne Grammar.

What is right and old and goes round and round in circles?

An Australian judge endeavouring to blame the victim.

What is black and angry and going nowhere?

An Aboriginal Australian expecting a fair trial.

Why do white men get such lenient sentences?

Because the judges have to save prison space for the blacks.

Have you heard about the Australian judge who got confused?

He was prejudiced in favour of a woman.

Why is an Australian judge like a remedial speech teacher?

They both worry that men won't be able to cope with a long sentence.

Why do people address judges as 'the bench'?

Because they're both about as sensitive as a block of wood.

How many Australian judges does it take to change a light bulb?

None – the judiciary hasn't changed anything in years.

Why is an Australian judge like Halley's Comet?

Because they've both spun out of touch with the real world.

Why did the judge stop his wife plugging in the iron?

Because he couldn't cope with a woman being close to power.

What do you call fifty sexist, racist judges stuck at the bottom of the ocean?

A bloody good start.

Why are Australian judges often called wharfies?

They sit on cases.

There are two farmers over in C Division – Farmer Fred and Farmer Pete. Farmer Fred is doing six months for rooting a cow. Farmer Pete is in for aiding and abetting. He held up the cow's tail.

The little accountant had got three years for some heavy embezzlement, and went into prison with horror stories of prisoner assault. He was sure he was going to be reamed out. His worst fears were realised when his cell mate turned out to be a monster bikie – 2 metres tall, tatts, scars, and missing teeth and various other bits. But his fears were allayed slightly when the bikie revealed himself to be a bit simple, and invited the accountant to play with his toys – his jigsaw, his trains, and his comics. Eventually, the bikie said, 'Right, now we'll play Mummies and Daddies. Do you want to be the Mummy or the Daddy?'

A little uneasily, the accountant opted to be Daddy.

'That's fine,' said the bikie, 'now come over here and suck Mummy's cock!'

Two lawyers meet up in the Executive Lounge before a flight. One is looking slightly flustered and his friend enquires about the problem.

Says the first lawyer, 'I've just done something very embarrassing. You know how sometimes your words can get all jumbled and you say something you didn't mean to? I was at the check-in counter – there's a very beautiful young woman on duty – and I said, 'Good morning. Two pickets to Titsburg, please.'

His friend smiled. 'Yeah, similar thing happened to me at breakfast this morning. I poured myself a coffee then said to my wife, "You fucking bitch, you're ruining my life. I want out", when what I *meant* to say was, "Pass me the sugar bowl please, darling."'

A new partner in a law firm was known for bragging and attempting to outdo anyone else's stories at social functions.

At a dinner to entertain a potentially lucrative client, all progressed smoothly while the guest of honour held the floor. He described the new saltwater pool being installed at his beachside retreat – black slate, landscaped surrounds, spa. As he paused for a drink, the lawyer launched in, 'Oh, they're great, of course, but you should be looking at a pool larger than 20 metres. I had one installed last year, 30 metres long' – his boss mouthed the word FIRED at him across the table – 'and ah, 5 centimetres deep.'

A motorist is cruising along the Hume Highway at normal speed when he notices a police car right behind him. So he accelerates to 100 kilometres, and then to 115 kilometres, and so on. No matter what the increment in speed, the police car remains close behind. Finally it overtakes and passes the motorist and signals him to stop. A very angry constable demands an explanation of this erratic and illegal behaviour.

'It's like this, Sarge. Last week one of your officers ran away with my wife and I was afraid he was bringing her back.'

A few years back there was a mug local cop who hadn't made an arrest in a long, long time. His sergeant was crooked on him. The young cop said, 'There's no one around my beat doing anythin' wrong.'

So the Sergeant says, 'Next Saturday night, when the pub's closing, you'll see a bloke go down the back lane. Follow him, flash your torch on him and arrest him for urinating.'

Come Saturday night, the young constable saw a bloke and his girlfriend going down the lane. He followed them, flashed his torch on them and said, 'What are you up to?'

'I'm having sex with this young lady,' the bloke replied.

And the young cop said, 'You're damn lucky you weren't pissing. I'd have to run you in.'

A surgeon from outback Queensland is apprehended by police for driving his Rolls Royce in an erratic manner.

'Now, sir, would you blow into this breathaliser?'

'No, I cannot.'

'Why?'

'Because I have emphysema.'

'Well, sir, you must submit to a blood test.'

'Sorry, that's not possible.'

'Why?'

'Because I'm a haemophiliac.'

'Well, you must get out of your car and walk along a straight line.'

'No.'

'Why?'

'Because I'm pissed!'

CRIMINAL: A person found at home in bed at 3 a.m.

DESPERATE CRIMINAL: An Aboriginal person found at home in bed at 3 a.m.

WHITE VICTIM: A person whose family should be given $50,000 compensation.

BLACK VICTIM: A person whose family should be given no compensation.

POLICE INTELLIGENCE: Something used in order to raid the wrong house.

THE LAW: A system devised by do-gooders to hamper police operations.

INNOCENT PERSON: A person whose background requires further investigation.

INNOCENT VICTIM: An innocent person who's been shot by the Tactical Response Group and whose background thus requires *substantial* further investigation.

A bloke was in court in the backblocks of Queensland charged with cattle duffing – taking somebody else's unbranded cattle and whacking his own brand on them. The jury consisted of local farmers who'd all done a bit of duffing in their time, and the accused was a drinking mate from the Linga-Longa Pub. So when the judge sent them off to consider the verdict, their deliberations took about five minutes flat.

The clerk of the court says, 'Have you reached a verdict?

'Yeah,' said the foreman of the jury.

'Do you find the defendant guilty or not guilty?'

'We reckon he's not guilty, but he's got to give the cattle back.'

The judge was infuriated and started banging away with his gavel. 'You cannot reach a verdict with such conditions attached! The man is either guilty or not guilty. Now go away and reconsider your verdict.'

The jury shuffled grumpily out of the court, only to return seconds later.

'Well!' said the judge. 'How do you find?'

'We find him not guilty, and he can keep the bloody cattle!'

A bloke was driving home after a long lunch. He knew he'd had a few, so he was being particularly careful, doing everything by the book. Inevitably, he was pulled over. Before the cop reached the window, the driver was explaining how he'd really only had a couple and he was ... The cop cut him short. 'If you'd just get out of the vehicle please, sir.'

The man tried to explain how watchful he was being. The cop insisted. The man got out of the car. The cop led him around to the back and pointed.

'Are you aware, sir,' he said, 'that your left-hand brakelight is not working?' The man slumped to his knees and burst into tears.

'It *is* only a brake light, sir,' the cop said.

'Oh, fuck the brake light,' said the man, 'where's my bloody caravan?'

A vintage car buff had broken down and a fellow in a Porsche offered to tow him, 'but', he said, 'I'm in a hurry. If you see a police car, give a hoot.'

A little while later a traffic policeman returned to his base. 'I thought I'd seen everything,' he said, 'but today I give up. I was chasing this vintage car at 120 kilometres, but when I started my siren, the crazy guy starts hooting to overtake a Porsche.'

THE WORK ETHIC

Tarzan comes home pooped and says to Jane, 'It's a jungle out there.'

If a magician's wand is used for cunning stunts what is a policeman's baton used for?

There was a long drought in Central Africa. The witch doctor had tried all his rainmaking dances, imprecations, but to no avail. One of the elders observed that rain was never a problem in England, so why not send the witch doctor to London to learn the secret. Off he went to England, learned the secret, and returned to the tribe. He informed the leaders that these crazy white men had a big paddock of grass enclosed by a white picket fence. In the middle were two lots of sticks driven into the ground. Two men, each with a club, stood next to these sticks and waited for a lot of other men to spread themselves all over the paddock. Then two more men, wearing black trousers, four sweaters and six hats, came out to keep a close watch on the men with the clubs. Then one man got a red rock and threw it at one of the fellers with a club. AND DOWN CAME THE RAIN!

Why is it a good thing that there are female astronauts?

When the crew gets lost in space, at least the woman will ask for directions.

What does NASA stand for?

Need Another Seven Astronauts.

What's the difference between NASA and Margaret Fulton?

Margaret Fulton teaches cooks and NASA cooks teachers.

What's the difference between a rottweiler and a social worker?

The rottweiler eventually gives the child back.

(Joan Kirner, then Premier of Victoria, told this story when a large number of children had been seized from parents who belonged to a religious cult. The joke proved as controversial as the police action.)

What's an astronaut's favourite drink?

Seven-up.

When Australia got its space program going up the Cape, the scientists decided to send up three astronauts with a monkey. Before blast off, each was given an envelope, not to be opened until they'd got into orbit. Everything went pretty well, so they opened their envelopes.

The monkey's letter listed his tasks:

1. Recheck fuel supplies.
2. Review the instrument panel.
3. Adjust the solar power.
4. Recycle all urine for drinking purposes.
5. Check the automatic guiding systems.
6. Conduct the ten scientific experiments outlined on the next page.

The three astronauts opened their letters containing identical instructions. 'Don't forget to feed the monkey.'

It seemed like an appalling affront to the dignity of the upper class bank in an upper class area of Melbourne when a scruffy-looking male, about 25, walked in. Noses sniffed in disdain. He approached the upper class, snooty-looking female teller and said, 'I wanna open a fuckin' cheque account.' Her surprise was barely contained by her practised dignity. She told him she would most certainly not serve a man so rude and would he please leave the establishment. Instead, he repeated his request. 'I wanna open a fuckin' cheque account, ya bitch.' She left her cage with icy decorum and fetched the grey-suited, silvery-looking manager who approached with a supercilious expression. In an accent appropriate to the suburb, he chastened the young guy and impressed upon him the bank's strong belief in manners, decorum, cleanliness and presentation.

In spite of this the scruff repeated, 'I just wanna open a fuckin' cheque account, arsehole.'

The manager raised an eyebrow and asked, very icily, 'And how much would your initial deposit be, perchance?'

The reply came, 'Three-and-a-half million dollars. I just won Tattslotto.'

To which the manager said, 'And what cock-sucking little slut refused to serve you?'

A bloke walked into a bank and joined a very long queue. Finally he made it to a teller and asked for an appointment with the bank's manager. The teller apologised. 'Sadly, the bank manager passed away last week.' Whereupon the man thanked her and rejoined the still lengthy queue, only to be given the same message by the second teller. He then joined the long queue yet again, finally putting the same question to the third teller, who protested, 'But I just overheard my colleague explaining that the bank manager recently passed away!'

The gentleman thanked him but explained he just liked hearing the good news.

What do you call a bank manager with a big dick?

A tight-fisted wanker.

A woman goes into a bank and hands the teller a $100 note.

He looks at it closely. 'This is a forgery,' he says.

'Oh no,' cried the woman, 'I've been raped again.'

A wealthy and unusually idealistic merchant banker was pottering around the backyard of his mansion one day when an itinerant handyman came round and asked him for a bit of casual work. Feeling sorry for the fellow, the banker produced 5 litres of enamel paint and a brush and told the handyman he would like him to go and paint the front porch.

An hour later the handyman was around the back again to collect his earnings. The banker commended him on the speed of his work and handed him ten dollars. As he was leaving the handyman remarked, 'By the way, it's not a Porsche, it's a Mercedes.'

A couple of burly Melbourne brickies, Mick and Tiny, had the reputation of being the fastest in the trade. They could've dammed the Yarra overnight at the drop of a hod. One Friday night they were bragging as usual about their prowess with the trowel. Come closing time, they were about to stagger out into Lygon Street when a swarthy gent sidled up to them. 'You wanna make lotsa money?' he asked.

'Yeah, yer not wrong there, mate,' said Mick.

'Good. I have heard of your reputation. Fantastic. I represent the richest Sheik in the Middle East, and he wants a 10-metre brick wall built round his 200-room harem. The British want tea-breaks, the Americans leave gum all over the place, the Italians would serenade the concubines, the Germans speak German, and the French complain about the food. So we're trying Australians.'

'Good on yer,' said Tiny.

'But you must leave tonight.'

'We weren't doin' anythin' partic'lar.'

'And you must finish the wall within twenty-four hours of starting, otherwise you will be used to plug an oil well.'

'No worries, mate. Lead us to it.'

Mick and Tiny found themselves bundled aboard a private Concorde, and settled back into a beer-induced stupor. Next thing they knew, the cabin door was opened, and in streamed the Sahara sunlight. The first desert they'd ever set eyes on. They stared at it in total disbelief, dune upon dune as far as the horizon.

'Christ!' breathed Mick, 'will you look at all that sand!'

'Yeah,' said Tiny. 'Let's get the hell outta here before they bring the cement!'

The civic councillors of a small country town are reviewing the architectural plans for a new amenities block in the local park. One of the councillors is bemused by the terms being bandied around and finally quietly asks a fellow councillor what the architect means by the word urinal. When this is explained, the first councillor nods wisely, then announces, 'Well, why stop at a urinal? We should probably build an arsenal, too!'

An American, a Frenchman and an Australian were sitting in a bar overlooking Sydney Harbour. 'Do you know why America is the wealthiest country in the world?' asked the American. 'It's because we build big and we build fast. We put up the Empire State Building in six weeks.'

'Six weeks, *mon dieu*, so long!' snapped the Frenchman, 'ze Eiffel Tower we put up in one month *exactement*. And you,' he continued, turning to the Australian, 'what has Australia done to match that?'

'Ah, nuthin' mate. Not that I know of.'

The American pointed to the Harbour Bridge. 'What about that?' he asked.

The Australian looked over his shoulder. 'Dunno, mate. Wasn't there yesterday.'

An economist is a person who marries Elle Macpherson for her money.

An engineer and a scientist met in a pub to discuss a mathematical problem. On a table 4 metres away was a carton of beer. The problem was to reach the table, with a first step of any size, a second step half the first, a third step half the second and so on.

Quickly the scientist said that this was a geometric progression, was asymptotic to zero, and no matter how many steps you took, you'd never actually reach the table, and said it couldn't be done.

The engineer leapt 2 metres, strode 1 metre, minced half a metre, leaned over, picked up the beer and triumphantly declared, 'Fuckin' near enough's good enough.'

A workshop foreman was sent a young man for 'work experience' and, being busy for the moment, handed the young fellow a broom with the polite request to tidy up the floor a bit until someone could show him some proper work.

'But I'm a graduate engineer!' protested the young man.

'I'm so sorry, I didn't think,' apologised the foreman, taking the broom. 'Look, this is how you do it.'

The Italian-Australian retired from his factory job. He went to the nearest chicken hatchery and said, 'I ama retiring to open a chicken farma. Please sella me 10 000 day-olda chicks.' He took delivery and went on his way. Three days later he approached the hatchery sales clerk again. 'I wanna 10 000 day-olda chicks.' He took delivery and went on his way. Three days later he was back at the counter. 'I wanna 10 000 day-olda chicks.' The salesperson enquired, 'You certainly have bought a lot of chicks. Have you got a very large farm?'

The old man replied, 'No, all the others died. I think I might be planting them too deep.'

Propelled by two rows of sweating galley slaves straining at the long oars, a Roman warship glided across the sparkling Mediterranean. Suddenly one of the older chained rowers gave a strangled cry, clutched his chest and collapsed over the oar, stone dead. The guards released him from his chains, carried him on deck and threw the body into the sea.

Meanwhile the slave master strode rapidly up and down the aisle separating the two banks of rowers, giving each slave a lash with his whip. Then he said, 'Right, you know what to do.' Whereupon each slave released his grip on the oar, lay back on his seat and urinated into the air. Everyone was drenched. A recently-sentenced slave whispered into the ear of a neighbour. 'What was all that about?' Speaking from the side of his mouth, the neighbour replied, 'An old Roman tradition, son. Every time there's a death on board, we have a quick whip around and a piss-up.'

On his first day as a member of the galley crew, a slave remarked to the oarsman beside him that it was a beautiful day to be sculling around the Mediterranean. 'Won't be tomorrow,' said his mate, 'we're booked to take Antony and Cleopatra waterskiing.'

Four insurance companies decided to amalgamate. At the first joint board meeting it was agreed that the new company should have its own coat of arms. So the College of Heralds was called in and the requirements stated, which were that it should embody some element identifying each company while also indicating their union. In due course the College of Heralds representative returned and unrolled a vellum scroll to be viewed by the board members. On it was a large shield suitably decorated and divided into four quarters in each of which was depicted a double bed occupied by a couple.

'What on earth is this?' asked the Chairman. 'It's not at all what we asked for. How does it show the identity of the original companies?'

'Quite simple,' was the reply. 'The first quarter shows a man in bed with his wife. That's Legal and General.

'The second quarter shows a man in bed with his fiancée. That's Mutual Trust.

'The third quarter shows a man in bed with his secretary. That's Employers Liability.

'The fourth quarter shows a man in bed with a prostitute. That's Commercial Union.'

A young man can't believe his luck when he is allocated a seat beside a very attractive girl on a flight to Sydney, and decides to strike up a conversation. So he starts by asking her where she's going.

'I'm going to a nymphomaniacs' convention in Sydney,' replies the girl.

He suddenly becomes very interested, and asks her, 'What sort of men do you like?'

'I like policemen,' she replies, 'because they're big and strong and honest.'

'I see,' says the young man, 'well, what's your second choice?'

'Cowboys,' she says, 'because they look so manly with their leather and spurs and horses.'

'What about your third choice?' he asks.

'Well, I like Jewish men because they're artistic, sensitive and caring.'

'What's your name?' she asks the young man.

'I'm Sergeant Hopalong Bernstein.'

A businessman was faced with the dilemma of firing two of his three secretaries. All were good at their jobs, and he didn't know how he was going to choose between them. Finally he decided to put an extra $100 in each of their pay envelopes and judge their reactions. The first secretary surreptitiously pocketed the extra money and didn't say a word. The second came to him and said, 'Look, I've been overpaid $100, so I went out and invested it in bonds at twelve-and-a-half per cent.' And the third secretary came to him and said, 'Look, I was overpaid $100. It's not mine. I haven't earned it. I want to give it back.'

Which one kept her job? The good-looking one with the big tits.

A man was visiting Sydney for the first time in 30-odd years. He wanted to drive down Martin Place in style, but when he got there Martin Place had vanished under acres of amenities. The old Hotel Australia had gone, so had the privy and the clock, too. Sadly he drove to Railway Square, but the tram shelters were no longer there. Marcus Clarke had disappeared and the Empire was now Her Majesty's. He was about to leave forever when, in the corner, he saw the shop of Gus, the cobbler. He went in and, sure enough, there was Gus, mouth full of nails. Nothing had changed.

'Gus,' he said with some emotion, 'remember me?'

Gus shook his head.

'I went bush over thirty years ago and I've never been back. Matter of fact, I left some shoes here.'

'Aw,' said Gus, 'well, I never throw anything out. What was your name again?' And he rummaged in the shadows. 'Brown plain toes?'

'Yes, yes,' cried the bloke.

'About size 9?'

'Yes.'

'And with lace-up fronts?'

'Yes, that's them!'

Gus called out, 'Be ready next Tuesday.'

The locals were drinking prior to closing time when an obviously English gent with a monocle entered through the swinging doors. An awed hush fell upon the assembled throng as the visitor announced in clipped British tones, 'I'd like a whisky and soda, please.'

One local approached the visitor and asked him, 'Whaddaya doin' up 'ere, mate?'

'Well,' he replied, 'I'm a taxidermist and I'm having a wonderful time. Yesterday I stuffed a kangaroo and today I stuffed a koala and they do tell me, if I can stay a few more days, I'll be able to stuff a wombat.'

The inquisitor returned to his group and said, 'The bastard reckons he's a taxi driver. But, if you ask me, the bugger's a bloody drover just like the rest of us.'

They had so many strikes on the Melbourne wharf that they asked the workers not to clock on or off. Instead they suggested they might like to sign the visitors' book.

Two wharfies are unloading a container. One checks a consignment document, scratches his head, and says, 'What's a cubic foot?' His mate frowns then replies, 'Dunno. Reckon we can claim compo for it though.'

Woman: 'Officer, I've been half-raped.'

Policeman: 'What do you mean half-raped?'

Woman: 'It was a wharfie and it started to rain.'

Four union members were discussing how smart their dogs were. The first, a member of the Vehicle Builders' Union, had a dog called T-Square. He said he could do maths calculations. He told him to go to the blackboard and draw a square, a circle and a triangle. This the dog did with consummate ease.

The Amalgamated Metal Workers' Union member had a dog named Slide Rule who he thought was even cleverer. He told him to fetch twelve biscuits and divide them into four piles, which Slide Rule did without problems.

The Liquor Trades' Union member admitted that both were quite good, but he thought his dog could outperform them. His dog was named Measure, and he told him to go and get a stubby of beer and to pour half a litre into a 1-litre bottle. The dog did this without a flaw.

They turned to the Waterside Workers' Union member and said, 'What can your dog do?' The waterside worker called his dog, who was named Tea Break, and said to him, 'Show these bastards what you can do, mate.'

Tea Break went over and ate the biscuits, drank the beer, pissed on the blackboard, screwed the other three dogs, claimed that he'd injured his back, filed a worker's compensation claim form and shot through on sick leave.

After a former leader of the Liberal Party retired from Parliament, he became internationally known for producing some of the world's best daffodils. He was often asked if he could send daffodil bulbs around the world but, in most cases, they'd perish before they'd arrive. As the years rolled on, he became more and more crippled with arthritis and needed to use his crutches to get around. This disability did not deter him from his enthusiasm for producing daffodils and one day he struck upon a perfect way to export the bulbs – he used a condom with a little water in it. The daffodil arrived at its destination hale and hearty. Having proof that the experiment worked, he then collected all his orders, which amounted to 144.

On a Friday evening he walked with some difficulty into the local chemist shop, and asked the chemist for 144 condoms, not explaining the purpose to which he intended putting them. The chemist was somewhat taken aback but handed over the cache. The old man spent the weekend filling each condom with a daffodil and, as well, received a phone call from a customer ordering a further 144 bulbs. He returned to the chemist on Monday morning and asked him for another 144 condoms, adding, 'And this time give me 144. You short-changed me by 5 on Friday night!'

Two men formerly employed at a sheltered workshop that has been closed front up to Social Security to claim unemployment benefits. The counter clerk addresses the first man: 'What was the nature of your previous work?'

'I sewed the crotches into ladies' underpants,' he replies.

'Right, you're entitled to $100 a week as a compensation for lost wages,' says the clerk.

He turns to the second man: 'Previous work?'

'Diesel fitter,' he replies.

'You're entitled to $200 a week compensation,' says the clerk.

The first man objects, 'Why is he getting more? I had the really skilled job, with the sewing. When I finished a pair of pants, all *he* did was pull them over his head and say, "Dese'll fit 'er."'

FOOD FOR THOUGHT

There is a very famous international restaurant in London, just off Berkeley Square. They claim they can serve any national dish and, if they fail, the customer is given £100 reward. So an Australian bloke called Bruce thinks he'll try them on. He asks for kangaroo balls on toast. The waiter receives the order without blinking an eye, but after a very long time has elapsed, the dish fails to appear. Bruce then does his lolly and demands his £100. The waiter slips it to him hidden in a starched serviette, so that no other restaurant guest can observe the transaction, 'Please take the money,' says the waiter, 'but don't tell anybody. It would be very, very bad for business. You see, it's never happened before, never in our history.'

'Well,' said Bruce, in a conciliatory voice, 'I suppose that kangaroo balls are a bit hard to . . .'

'You don't understand, sir,' interrupted the waiter, 'we ran out of bread.'

A traveller staying at a rough bush pub was annoyed when the girl who brought his customary morning tea failed to materialise. After waiting some time, he dressed and made his way to the kitchen. 'Say, where's the chambermaid?' he asked the swarthy, barefoot cook.

'Blowed if I know, mister,' replied the woman, busily wiping out cups with her greasy apron. 'But the rest of the crockery comes from Japan.'

A city bloke was visiting the outback and he booked into an old hotel with an outside toilet. After he'd put his suitcase on the bed, the first thing he did was go to the toilet. Trouble was, he couldn't get near it for blowflies. So he went and saw the manager to make a complaint.

'I just went to the toilet and couldn't get near it for blowies.'

The manager looked up at the bar room clock and said, 'It's only 11.30, mate. Could you hang on for another half hour? Until 12 o'clock? The blowies will all be in the dining room then.'

Cucumbers are better than men because:

* the average cucumber is 15 centimetres long
* cucumbers stay hard for a week

* a cucumber never suffers from performance anxiety
* you can follow a cucumber in the supermarket – and you know how hard it is when you take it home
* cucumbers can get away any weekend
* a cucumber will always respect you
* you only eat cucumbers when you feel like it
* cucumbers don't need a round of applause
* cucumbers don't ask 'Am I the best?' How was it? Did you come?' and 'How many times?'
* a cucumber won't mind hiding in the fridge when your mother comes over
* a cucumber can stay up all night – and you never have to sleep in a wet patch.

The worst things about being an egg are:

* you only get laid once
* you come in a box with eleven other blokes
* only your mother ever sits on your face.

Tarzan, having swung through the trees all day, was feeling a bit crook, so he went home early. 'What's for tea?' he asked Jane. She pointed at a pot. He lifted the lid and saw that it was full of tiny finches. He pulled a face. 'What else have you got going?'

Jane pointed to a bigger pot. Tarzan lifted the lid and discovered chimpanzees floating around in the thick sauce.

'Oh, bugger,' he said, 'boring old finch and chimps again.'

Two roadworkers sit down for their lunch break. One opens his brown paper bag and exclaims in disgust, 'Aw, look mate! Flamin' raspberry jam sandwiches again!'

His mate says, 'Why don't yer go crook at yer missus and git her to give yer somethin' else?'

To which the first bloke replies, 'That's me trouble, mate. She's away and so I have to cut me own lunch!'

A little old lady with slightly failing eyesight was in the butcher's shop. 'Can I help you?' said the butcher.

'Yes, please. I would like a kilogram of your pissoles.'

'My dear lady,' said the butcher, indicating the appropriate sign. 'That is an "R", not a "P"!'

'Oh, all right then – give me a kilogram of arsoles.'

For the best part of six months, Mrs Martin had religiously visited her local butcher shop on Saturdays and bought four slices of bacon, half a kilo of sausages, three lamb chops and fourteen tins of Dinky-Di dog food. Curiosity eventually got the better of the butcher who asked how many dogs she had at home to eat all the tinned stuff she bought every week. A little embarrassed, Mrs Martin whispered to the butcher that the dog food was actually for her husband who ate two whole tins of it day in, day out.

The butcher was horrified. 'You shouldn't let him eat that,' he cautioned. 'It's not meant for humans, just dogs. At the rate he's putting it away I wouldn't be surprised if it killed him before much longer.'

'Don't you think I've told him that?' replied Mrs Martin. 'But it's all he wants and I'm tired of the arguments, so he can eat all he likes. Anyhow, it's none of your concern. Just fill my order, please.'

And so it continued, until one Saturday some six weeks later, Mrs Martin told the butcher she didn't want the fourteen tins of Dinky-Di any more, just the usual meat order. 'Great,' said a much relieved butcher, 'you've finally talked some sense into your old man and he's given up eating dog food.'

'If only that was true,' said a sad Mrs Martin. 'Actually, my husband is dead.'

'Ha hah,' mocked the butcher, 'I told you. Didn't I tell you the dog stuff would finish him off one day? I knew it'd happen. Why didn't you listen to me?'

'It wasn't the Dinky-Di at all,' sobbed the widow Martin.

'Okay, then,' roared the butcher, 'if it wasn't the blasted dog food, what killed your husband?'

Mrs Martin touched a tissue to her eyes, sighed deeply and said, 'Poor old thing. Last Wednesday he was quietly sitting in the middle of the road licking his dick and a car ran over him.'

A man went into a pub and ordered a dry martini. The olive went into a small glass jar he had brought with him. He drank quickly and ordered another. And another. Always putting the olive into the jar. After about an hour the jar was full and the man staggered out with it.

'What a weirdo!' exclaimed a customer.

'Not really,' said the barman. 'What would *you* do if your wife sent you out to get a jar of olives for tonight's party, and the shops were all shut?'

A woman who had eaten at a country pub visited the Ladies. On the way out as she was leaving the place she said to the waitress, 'You can tell the owner of this dump that I found your graffiti in very bad taste.'

'Okay,' said the waitress, 'but next time you should try our spaghetti.'

A road train heading west to the Channel country struck and killed a wild boar. The carcass was in pretty good nick so the driver decided to offer it to the publican at Cungamilla.

'Yeah, I'll give you 20 bucks for it,' said the publican, 'we're almost out of meat.'

A commercial traveller was stopping at the pub. At dinner the publican offered him the choice of roast pork, grilled pork chops or ham on the bone. 'Fresh killed, local wild boar,' said the publican proudly.

The traveller chose the roast and complimented the publican on the pork. 'Glad you liked it,' said the publican. 'You can have chops, or bacon, or ham, or brawn for breakfast. We don't waste anything out here.'

'Sounds good,' said the traveller, 'could I have a drink of water?'

'Yes, mate, but we've only got bore water.'

'Crikey,' exclaimed the traveller, 'you're right – you don't waste anything, do you?'

A cattle buyer and his mate were travelling back through northern New South Wales late one afternoon. They came across a pub and dropped in for a few well-earned ales. After a few drinks the offsider said to the barman, 'Can a man get a bite to eat around here?'

The barman said, 'Sure, what would you like? Steak and eggs or steak and onions?'

They settled on steak and onions and had one or two more drinks in the interlude. When the tucker finally arrived the buyer, who was hungry, grabbed the dish and started in to eat, only to spit out the first mouthful in disgust and exclaim to the barman, as he threw the plate on the floor, 'That would have to be the worst bloody meal I have ever tasted!'

By this time the pub dog is scurrying around and starting to lap up the food, so the barman retorted in know-all fashion, 'I don't know about the food being crook – the dog's enjoying his, isn't he?'

'Sure, he is eating it,' says the buyer, 'but look at the way he keeps licking his arse to get the taste out of his mouth.'

What's green and red and goes round and round at 100 kilometres an hour?

A frog in a blender.

What's hot, yellow and dangerous?

Shark-infested custard.

A traveller arrives at a country pub hot and very dusty. He orders a meal and a glass of water. After a while the meal arrives but not the water. 'What do you do to get a glass of water in this dump?' says the traveller. The cook replies, 'Well, you could try setting fire to yourself.'

A feller walks into the bar with his mate – an alligator on a chain. He says to the publican, 'Would you serve John Elliott?' 'Blood oath I would,' replies the publican, well aware that John Elliott owned one of Australia's greatest breweries.

'Well, I'll have a schooner for me, and John Elliott for the croc.'

The honeymooners looked at the list of meal times in their hotel.

Breakfast 6 a.m. – 11.30 a.m.
Lunch 12.30 p.m. – 3.30 p.m.
Dinner 6.30 p.m. – 9.30 p.m.

'Kevin,' wailed the bride, 'we'll be kept in eating so long we won't have time to go anywhere.'

A traveller arrives at an outback hotel and orders a meal.

'Only got corned beef, mate,' said the cook.

'That'll do,' said the traveller. He took a seat and when the meal arrived found it consisted of a slab of ancient corned beef and very little else.

'Could I have some tomato sauce to put on it?' the traveller asked. And the cook yelled out to the publican, 'Hey, boss, bastard out here thinks it's Christmas!'

During World War II in North Africa, an officer and twenty diggers were detailed to make a 21-day patrol in the desert. The question of who would be the cook arose. Bluey, who was known to have been a shearers' cook was suggested as eminently suitable. 'Not on your bloody life,' Bluey said, 'pick it out of a hat.' But the others all professed inability to boil water.

After a lot of argument, Bluey agreed to do it, with the provision that 'the first bastard who complains will have to take over the job'. He dished them up all sorts of concoctions and they got all sorts of pain and diarrhoea, but no one complained. Desperate, one morning, Bluey served them up what he said were rissoles.

As one bloke bit into his portion, he cried out, 'Jeez, it's camel shit!' But quickly recovering, he held up a finger and said, 'But mark you, very well cooked.'

The famous artist, Sir Russell Drysdale, is painting away in the Northern Territory thousands of kilometres from nowhere, when he becomes aware of somebody's eyes burning a hole in his back. Sir Russell turns around and there, on the other side of the gully, is an old swaggy. He's watching with fascination as the picture emerges on the canvas. They strike up a very one-sided conversation. Eventually, Sir Russell prevails upon the painfully shy traveller to join him around the campfire later that night.

'I hope you like curry,' he says, 'I've got a really good one simmering away. All I've got to do is get some rice on.'

Later on they're sitting eating by the light of the fire and Sir Russell notices that the old bloke is pushing all the sultanas to one side of his plate. 'Don't you like sultanas?'

'Aww,' says the swaggy, peering closely at his plate in the firelight, 'I thought they were blowies.'

THE DEMON DRINK

A member of the Temperance League was haranguing his audience about the evils of alcohol. Holding two glasses with transparent liquid in front of him, he declared the first glass to be filled with water, aqua pura! But the second contained pure alcohol. He then removed a tin containing worms from his pocket. He put the first worm into the water and it swam around happily. He then put a second worm into the alcohol and it instantly shrivelled up and died.

'There,' he thundered, 'what's the moral of that?'

There was complete silence until an old fellow at the back of the hall called out, 'it looks as if you drink alcohol, you won't have worms!'

The customer, rather the worse for wear, was staggering out of the pub just as a pair of pretty girls, identical twins, was about to enter. Observing his condition, they parted to let him through.

'Now how,' murmured the drunk, 'did she do that?'

A drunk, reeling his way homeward along a country road, came upon a large truck bogged at the side of it. A similar type of vehicle had driven up behind and was endeavouring to push it clear. The engines roared, wheels spun and their chassis quivered. The drunk stood watching in amazement and then became articulate, 'Stone the crows! Them things sure kick up a fuss, and a helluva din, when they're mating!'

A well-dressed man, having overindulged, was wandering alone in the city. He couldn't remember where his car was and couldn't remember where he lived. Floundering along, he was approached by a tall, bearded, distinguished-looking man who said, 'My son, let me help you.'

'Impossible,' said the man. 'I don't remember where I am or who I am.'

'My son, let me take you home.'

'How can you?'

'My son, I know all these things.'

And he did. And it came to pass that he found his home, knew where the key was, unlocked the door and put the man to bed. The man was thankful and though the room was spinning, he recognised it as his room. 'I've got to thank you,' said the man to the kind stranger. 'You've been wonderful. Tell me what is your name?'

'My name is St Paul,' said the stranger.

'That's a nice name – the same name as the bloke in *The Bible*.'

'The same,' said the stranger, 'for I am St Paul.'

The man sat up. 'You're St Paul? That's fantastic. I've always wanted to meet you because I have a question I wish to ask. May I ask you a personal question?'

'Certainly, my son.'

'Tell me, did those bloody Corinthians ever answer your letters?'

Mrs Briggs' hubby, Fred, worked night shift at the CUB. One night, around 1 a.m., a policeman knocked on her door with bad news. 'I'm sorry, Mrs Briggs, but Fred has had an accident.'

'Oh, sweet Jesus, what's happened?'

'I'm afraid he fell into a large barrel of beer and died.'

'The poor darling. Did he suffer a lot, do you think?'

'We don't think so, Mrs Briggs. You see, he got out six times for a pee.'

'I don't like one of the blokes who comes in here after work,' said the barmaid to the boss of the hotel.

'Why?' asked the boss.

'Oh, he orders a beer, drinks it, screws up his face, slams the glass down on the bar and yells out "Piss" very rudely and then walks out. He does it almost every night!'

'Well, you point him out when he next comes in,' said the boss.

The next afternoon, the bloke arrives and the barmaid points him out to the boss who walks up to him and says, 'Ay, you! Piss off!'

'Okay,' says the bloke, 'give us a small scotch then.'

Why did God invent beer?

So ugly girls could get screwed.

It's Dad's 90th birthday, and he and his son are celebrating at the pub. The father says that he will pay for all the drinks that night and says to the barman, 'We'll have double scotches please.' The barman serves them and asks for $10. Whereupon the father hands over a couple of bottle tops.

This outrages the barman who says, 'What the hell's this?' Whereupon the son takes the barman aside and says, 'Look, it's his 90th birthday. Just humour him. Allow him to keep paying with bottle tops and I'll fix you up at the end of the night.' The barman reluctantly agrees and, all night, the father pays for expensive drinks by throwing bottle tops onto the bar. At the end of the night they're walking out the door when the barman yells to the son, 'Come back here!'

'What's up?'

'Look, I've got all these bloody bottle tops and you said you'd fix me up at the end of the night.'

The son says, 'Sorry, I've had a few too many and I forgot. How much do I owe you?'

The barman says, 'Well, 465 bucks.'

'No problem,' says the son. 'Have you got change for a manhole cover?'

A devoted off-roader was showing his buddy the kit and preparations for a venture into the farthest reaches of the Sturt Desert. 'You've forgotten the most important thing,' said the friend.

'How's that?' said the adventurer.

'You've forgotten the gin and the vermouth,' came the reply.

'Gin and vermouth are important? How come?'

'Well, if the worst comes to the worst and your engine's blown up and your water and food are all gone and your radio equipment has failed and you're stuck in the middle of the boiling desert hundreds of kilometres from the nearest help, you get a glass and pour two fingers of gin into it, add one full finger of vermouth and before you get the glass to your lips, faces will pop over every hill and from behind every rock and say, 'That's not the way to make a martini.'

Two women walked into the Ladies' Lounge and ordered a couple of beers. 'Are ya gonna have another, luv?'

'Nah. It's only the way me coat's buttoned.'

A loudmouth Yank, looking for properties to buy around Barcaldine, is in the bar of the Shakespeare Hotel.

'Yeah, ma'am,' he says to the barmaid, 'ah'm looking to buy me a ranch – stations, you call them, they tell me. Ah come from Texas and ah'm looking for a big spread because where ah come from in Texas, everything is big. Why, do you know, mah ranch in Texas is so big, it takes a whole week to ride around it on a horse.'

'Yeah, ' said the wizened little ringer. 'We used to have a 'orse like that. We shot the bastard.'

A man goes into a bar with his wife and, immediately on sitting down, says to the bartender, 'Give me a drink, before it starts.' The bartender pours him a beer. The man drinks it.

'Give me another beer,' he says, 'before it starts.'

The bartender is puzzled. 'There's no entertainment here tonight, sir. The strippers come on Fridays.'

Again the man demands, 'Another drink before it starts.' Whereupon his wife interjects with, 'I think you've had enough to drink, dear.'

And the man says to the bartender, 'See! It's started!'

Two mates meet in a pub, one from Melbourne, one from Sydney. They have an intense debate over the relative virtue of their cities' beers. To settle the question of quality, they decide to send a sample of their favourites to a chemical analyst. After several days the document arrives back from the expert. It reads as follows: 'After exhaustive analysis of the respective properties of both fluids, I and my colleagues have reached the common conclusion that both Clydesdale stallions are too old for work.'

A guide on a coach tour said, 'On my left is the Opera House. On my right is the Town Hall. On my left is Hyde Park. We are now passing Darling Harbour. We are now passing the Rocks. We are now passing the oldest licensed hotel in New South Wales.' And a voice at the back shouted, 'Why?'

LOVE, MARRIAGE AND THE SEX WAR

Bruce enters a chemist shop. 'I want a deodorant.'

'Ball or aerosol,' asks the chemist.

'No,' says Bruce, 'armpits.'

The Bastard from the Bush was in the paddock when he saw the Grim Combine Harvester bearing down on him.

'Just let me have one last root with my wife, and then I'm ready to die!' he begged.

'Okay,' said the GCH, 'you've got ten minutes.'

So the BFTB races home, saying, 'Honey, I'm dying, this is our last root,' leaps on her and comes within minutes.

Then a voice from outside the bedroom window says, 'Your time is up!'

'Goodbye, honey!' says the BFTB, and heads for the door.

'Oh, that's all right for you,' says the wife. 'What about my orgasm?'

A tough-looking bloke turned up at the red light district in Kalgoorlie and said to the Madam, 'Give us the roughest sheila you've got.'

Pretty soon he's ensconced with a great big brassy-looking blonde, and as she slips her dressing-gown off, he strikes a wax match right across her breasts and lights a cigar. He's pleased that she doesn't seem surprised or at all concerned. So he turns away from her with a grin and proceeds to rip off his gear. When he's finished, he turns around, still puffing away and finds her with her back to him, bent double, clutching both her ankles.

'What are you doing?' he says.

She casually replies, 'I just thought you might like to open a bottle of beer before we got started.'

A shearer turns up at a Kalgoorlie brothel and asks the Madam if she's got anything different on offer. 'As a matter of fact, I have,' says the Madam. 'You'll remember that the circus was through here a few weeks ago? Well they sacked the contortionist. So I've given her a job.'

The bloke is enthralled at the possibilities. Once inside the shabby little room, he watches with fascination as the contortionist ties herself into something approaching a Gordian Knot. Whereupon he starts circling her, staring, scratching his head.

'What's wrong, love?' asks the woman in a somewhat muffled voice.

'Look, would you mind farting,' he says, 'just to give me a hint?'

Sheila and Bruce have not been practising safe sex. While Bruce never takes his socks off, he was disinclined to wear a condom. Now the poor girl discovers that she's pregnant and says, 'If you don't marry me, I'm going to jump off Sydney Harbour Bridge.' Bruce's reply is a fond slap on the back. 'You're not only a great root, you're also a good sport!'

'Am I the first girl you ever made love to?'

'You might be. Were you around the back of Rushcutters Bay Stadium at the Everley Brothers' concert in 1960?'

While visiting Sydney a French girl found herself out of money just as her visa expired. Unable to afford passage back to France, she accepted a proposition from a friendly sailor. 'My ship is sailing tonight. I'll smuggle you aboard, hide you down in the hold and provide you with a mattress, blankets and food. All it will cost you is a little love.'

The girl consented and late that night the sailor sneaked her on board. Twice each day he smuggled a few sandwiches below decks and took his pleasure. The days turned into weeks and the weeks might have turned into months if the captain hadn't noticed something going on. He sprang the sailor bonking the girl and said, 'Miss, I feel it's only fair to tell you that this is the Manly Ferry.'

Coming home unexpected, the junior executive finds his wife in bed with a naked bloke. He's about to shoot him when his wife says, 'Don't! Who do you think bought us that condo in Surfers, the BMW, the first-class tickets to London?'

'Are you the bloke?' asks the husband. 'Then get your clothes on. Do you want to catch a cold?'

Nigel and Cedric felt a bit limp, so to cheer themselves up they thought they'd stroll down to Luna Park.

'I'm going to go on the chair-a-planes,' said Nigel.

'Are you sure, Nigel?' said Cedric. 'You're ever so brave.'

So Nigel went on the chair-a-plane. Round and around he went until the chain broke on his seat, sending him hurtling through the air for about 300 metres until he slammed into a brick wall. Cedric ran over to the crumpled heap at the base of the wall and cried, 'Are you hurt, Nigel?'

A dazed Nigel opened his eyes and said, 'Am I hurt? I should say I'm hurt. I went around six times and you never waved once.'

An arrogant red rooster was giving chase to a fluttery little hen. To escape him, she scrambled to the highway and was promptly run over by a truck. Two old maids on a nearby porch witnessed the accident. 'You see,' said one, with an approving nod, 'she'd rather die.'

A girl invited a country boy to her flat for a drink where she introduced him to the ins and outs of carnality. He stayed the night and in the morning she said, 'How about some money?'

'Oh, no thanks. You've been too kind already.'

An old couple arrived at the doctor's surgery with a strange request. 'We want you to watch us making love,' said the man. Puzzled, he obliged. When it was all over he said, 'Well, that was pretty good, particularly considering your age.' And he charged them the standard fee for the consultation.

This happened for week after week. They'd make an appointment, bonk away and pay the bill. The doctor was unable to find anything wrong with the way they screwed and finally asked, 'What exactly are you trying to find out?'

'Nothing,' said the old bloke. 'She's married, so we can't go to her house. I'm married, so we can't go to mine. They charge you $100 at a decent hotel and even a crappy motel charges $30. So we come here for $18 and get $12 back from Medicare.'

Ginger docked at Circular Quay after a frustrating three-month voyage. Unfortunately he'd lost most of his pay playing poker on board ship, so when he eventually found a lady of the night all he could offer her was 50 cents and a pair of plimsolls. She refused with disdain. He wandered around Kings Cross in search of a more accommodating girl, but was refused time and time again. Eventually he found a more sympathetic lady who told him that although she could not possibly accept his offer herself, he could always try Megan down the road. But she warned him not to expect much as she was very unresponsive and would probably just lie there passively.

He eventually found Megan and as times were hard she reluctantly agreed to accept the 50 cents and the pair of plimsolls for her services, but told him not to expect any kind of response from her. Ginger began the amorous act and after a few minutes was pleased to find an arm coming around his back. This was followed shortly after by a leg curling around his rear. Ginger, who had always fancied himself as a bit of a Romeo, gasped, 'I knew you wouldn't be able to resist my charms.'

'Don't worry about me, love,' answered Megan, 'I'm just trying on the plimsolls.'

When's a good time to fake an orgasm?

When a rottweiler's fucking your leg.

There are four kinds of orgasm. Positive, Negative, Religious and Fake. The positive goes, 'Yes, yes, yes, yes!' The negative, 'No, no, no, no!' The religious, 'Oh God, God, God, God!' And the fake, '. . ., . . ., . . ., . . .!' (Fill in the name of your lover in the blank spaces.)

How do you tell if a Mosman woman is having an orgasm?

She puts down her cigarette.

Some time ago a young couple were wed in a small country town. After the wedding they set off for their new home on a pony and trap. The journey went pleasantly enough, and they chatted together enjoying each other's company. After a short while the pony stumbled, but only enough to slightly disturb the newlyweds. The husband said, 'That's one,' and the new bride thought nothing of it. A little later the pony stumbled again which caused the husband to let out a stream of abuse, adding, 'That's twice.'

By now the bride was a little disturbed, but she said nothing, wishing to retain the post-wedding ambience. Unfortunately the pony stumbled yet again which caused the groom to lose his temper. He shouted, 'That's three times!' reined in the pony, jumped off the trap, took out a rifle and shot the pony. The bride was astonished. She ran up to her husband, beat him on his chest and abused him mightily. He pushed her aside and said, 'That's once.'

A young newlywed couple arrived in a rustic hotel in the Victorian high country. The proprietor checked them into the establishment and noticed that the young woman was a matchless beauty. He thought to himself, 'If that bloke is worth his salt he won't surface till dinnertime.'

At about 6 a.m. next day, the proprietor saw the young husband walk through the foyer and out the front door, loaded up with fishing equipment. He thought to himself, 'That's odd, I know what I'd rather be doing.' The husband didn't return until well after dinner that night.

This ritual went on for a few days, with the young bride staying mostly in the hotel room, and the young husband spending all his days fishing. It was too much for the proprietor, he had to know what was going on. So one morning, not long after dawn, he collared the young fellow as he made his way through the foyer. He asked the young man, 'Why do you go fishing all day and leave such a beautiful wife by herself in your room? If I was married to such a woman, I don't think I'd be interested in bloody fishing!'

The young man replied in a whisper, 'My wife has gonorrhoea, so we don't indulge in that sort of thing.'

The proprietor, taken aback by this revelation, was silent for a while then said, 'There are other, um, possibilities, you realise?'

'Yes, I know,' whispered the young man, 'but she also has haemorrhoids and that makes it difficult, you understand . . .' Surprised as he was, the proprietor pressed on, 'But there are further alternatives you must know of!'

The young man whispered in reply, 'Yes, yes I know, but she also has herpes and that makes it somewhat risky.'

The proprietor was stunned and asked the young man, 'With all these complaints and diseases, why the hell did you marry the woman?'

To this the young man replied, 'She also has worms and I love fishing.'

A man and his wife were about to spend their wedding night in a country pub. When the woman had gone upstairs, the bloke asked the barman for a glass of beer, a pot of green paint and a hammer. The barman obliged, but couldn't help asking, 'Look, we've had a lot of strange requests over the years, but never one like this. What's it all about?' To which the man replied, 'I ordered the beer because I like beer. When I get to my room, I'll go into the bathroom and paint my dick green. And if my wife says she's never seen one that colour before, I'm going to thump her with the hammer.'

One of Australia's battleships, containing 300 men, ran aground. Only one sailor survived. He found himself lying on the sands of a deserted island where, fortunately, there was an abundance of fresh water and tropical fruits. As he grew stronger he grew more and more amorous. But the only creature that might provide solace was a very belligerent wild sow. But even when he trapped her, he found that he couldn't possibly keep her still long enough to have his way with her. Flattery didn't work, nor did tying her down. The pig just wouldn't come across. Months passed and his frustrations intensified. The sow would not surrender her honour.

Then, one day, he saw another human being washed up on the beach. It was Elle Macpherson, almost dead from exhaustion and exposure. He dragged her up to his hut, revived her, and spent the next week administering fresh fruit and water until she was feeling much better. Quite her old self. She explained that she'd been on a photographic assignment, posing for her calendar, when the luxury yacht had hit the same reef as the battleship.

'Now I will do anything you desire,' she said. 'You have saved my life and I will be glad to reward you in any way.'

'Well, Elle,' he said, 'there's one thing. Do you think you could hold that fucking pig still?'

In an anatomy class, a young woman is called upon to name the three most important parts of the male body. 'First,' she stammered, 'there's the brain. Second,' she continued, 'there's the heart. The third thing ... the third thing ...' She looked hopelessly confused. 'The third thing ... I've had it on my fingertips ... I've had it on the tip of my tongue ... I've had it drilled into me a thousand times ... but I just can't remember it.'

After trying unsuccessfully for years to have a baby, a young couple went to see their doctor. After examining them both and finding nothing wrong, he suggested they do it 'like the cats do it.'

'Like the cats do it?' asked the husband. And then, with a smile, said, 'Oh, I see what you mean.'

A week later the doctor saw the young man walking down the street with a black band on his left arm. 'Who died?' he asked. 'My wife,' replied the young man. 'You see, we took your advice, but she fell off the roof.'

The various ages and stages of sex:

First, you have bathroom sex where you root in the shower or the bath.

Then you have kitchen sex where you root on the sink or the kitchen table.

Then there's bedroom sex where all your rooting is confined to the bedroom.

Finally, you have corridor sex where you see your wife in the hallway in the morning and say, 'Go and get fucked!'

A bloke approaches a girl and says, 'What about a fuck?'

'No!' she answered indignantly.

'Well how about lying down while I have one?'

At the height of the recession we had to have, a husband is desperate to save money. He tells his wife to learn to cook better. 'That'll save on restaurants.' She must learn to iron his shirts 'to save on the ironing lady'. She'll need to clean the house properly, 'to save on the cleaning lady'.

And she said, 'Why don't you learn to fuck properly, so we can get rid of the gardener?'

A little boy jumps up from the breakfast table and heads for the door. Mum says, 'Where are you going in such a hurry?'

'I'm going to the massage parlour, Mum.'

The mother grabs his arm. 'You won't leave this house until you stop this nonsense. Tell me where *are* you going?'

'Orright, Mum. I'm going to the park to play footy with the kids and Dad can go and get his own hat.'

A man met his ex-wife at a party and after a few drinks asked her if she would spend the night with him 'just for old times sake'.

'Over my dead body,' she said.

'That's right,' he replied, 'let's not change a thing!'

A middle-aged couple was deeply asleep when, about 3 a.m., the doorbell rang. The wife said, 'Percy, go downstairs and answer the door.'

Percy staggered downstairs and said, 'Who's there?'

The voice on the other side said, 'The Boston strangler.'

Percy walked back upstairs and said, 'It's for you, darling.'

Three young fellows from Brisbane were really close mates. They all went to Brisbane State High School, did their apprenticeships together at Evans Deakin and played League for Easts. They met their girlfriends one weekend at the Gold Coast and eventually decided on a joint wedding ceremony and honeymoon at Brampton Island, where they had adjoining units. After checking-in, they went to their units to change for a swim. When the first bloke's wife undressed she revealed herself a bit on the undernourished side. 'Gawd,' cried her husband, 'haven't you got small tits – I didn't realise you were so skinny!'

'What a rotten thing to say,' she cried, 'and on our wedding day, too. Leave me alone. Get out!' So he went out onto the patio and had a smoke.

In the second unit, the wife also undressed, but she was a bit on the generous side. 'Bloody hell,' cried hubby, 'I didn't realise you were fat. You kept that lot covered all right.'

'You beast,' she screamed, 'what a thing to say on our wedding day. Get out!' Husband number 2 joined number 1 on the patio. Shortly, they were joined by number 3. 'Ah,' cried the first two together, 'you must have put your foot in it!'

'No, I didn't,' said number 3. 'But I could have.'

After the first night in a honeymoon hotel the husband went downstairs to the restaurant to order breakfast.

'Egg, bacon and sausages for me, and lettuce for my wife,' he told the waiter.

'Isn't lettuce a rather unusual breakfast choice, sir?' said the waiter.

'Yes,' replied the husband, 'but I want to see if she eats like a rabbit as well.'

The Admiral took his daughter aside on her wedding eve and said gruffly, 'Mavis, I've never advised you on sex since your mother died, but I feel that as you're marrying a sailor I must say just one thing. Let him do anything he likes, but if ever he asks you to do it "the other way" don't let him.' Even though the daughter did not know what he meant, she promised to follow his advice.

The couple were married and had a blissfully happy sex life for six months. But all this time

Mavis had 'the other way' in the back of her mind. One evening she blurted out, 'Please Jack, let's do it the other way tonight.'

Her husband looked at her incredulously. 'What,' he said, 'and risk having babies!'

There was to be a bush wedding and the groom, just a simple country lad, was nervous about having to make a speech, so the vicar gave him a few tips to set him on the right track. The young man's mother had always made sure there was a nice cup of freshly percolated coffee for him whenever he came in from his work on the farm, so she decided to give him a special little coffee percolator so he'd always be able to have the coffee the way he liked it.

When it came the groom's turn to make his speech, he started off just the way the vicar had instructed him – 'I want to thank youse all for comin' along to me weddin' and I want to thank Betty's Mum and Dad for having such a lovely daughter who's now me wife and I specially want to thank me Mum for the perky little copulator she gave me.'

After thirty years of marriage an Italian woman addressed her husband one evening. 'For thirty years I've done everything you expected and asked of me without complaint. Now after thirty years together I wish to ask two things of you so that I may be even happier in my old age.'

'What are they?' asked the husband.

'My love, always you picka your nose,' replied the wife, 'and I wish you would not do that.'

'And the other thing?' enquired the husband.

'Whenever we have sex, always you are on the top and I would really like to be on the top of you sometimes.'

'Well, my dear,' said the husband, 'I have tried, as you have, to make our marriage good, and foremost in my mind I have kept the words of your father when we were betrothed. He said only two things to me. First, he said, "Now you marry my daughter make sure you always keep your nose clean". And second, he said, "And don't fuck up".'

'Yoo hoo, darling, I'm home,' called the man on his return from work. He entered the bedroom and saw a man and a woman just uncoupling. In a vicious voice he demanded, 'What's *she* doing here?'

Bruce returned home late, after boozing with his mates. The house was in darkness. He undressed in the lounge and, as he slipped into bed, remembered that he'd been neglecting his wife of late. Later, he went to the bathroom to clean his teeth and was astonished to find his wife in the bathtub reading a book.

'What the hell are you doing here?' he says.

'What's wrong with relaxing in the bath?'

'Nothing. But who the hell is that in our bed?'

'I told you that my mother was coming to stay!'

At this, Bruce slammed the door, went back to the bedroom and screamed at the recumbent figure, 'Why the hell didn't you tell me it was you!'

'How could I, Bruce, when we haven't been on speaking terms for years.'

What does an Aussie call matching luggage?

Two carrier bags from an offlicence.

What is the definition of an Aussie virgin?

A lamb who outpaces the shepherd.

How do you get an Aussie onto the roof?

Tell him the drinks are on the house.

What's an Aussie intellectual?

Someone who can understand the plot in 'Neighbours'.

What's the difference between an Aussie and a Qantas jet?

The jet stops whining when it gets to England.

Why do Aussies wear short trousers?

To keep their brains cool.

Why do Aussies put XXXX on a can of beer?

They can't spell 'beer'.

What's an Aussie man's idea of foreplay?

Digging his wife in the ribs and saying, 'You awake? Okay, brace yourself'.

Why did the Aussie haemophiliac die?

He tried acupuncture as a cure.

Why do Aussie men give their penises names?

It's because they don't want 95 per cent of their decisions made by a stranger.

What do you call the useless piece of skin on the end of a penis?

A man.

Why are Aussie men like toilets?

They're either engaged or full of shit.

What do you call 100 Aussie men standing in a paddock?

A vacant lot.

Why do Aussie men suffer from premature ejaculation?

Because they can't wait to get to the pub to tell their mates about it.

How do you get an Aussie man to do sit-ups?

Put the remote control between his toes.

What is an Aussie man's idea of a seven-course dinner?

A hot dog and a six pack.

What is the difference between Aussie men and government bonds?

Bonds mature.

Why don't Aussie men get piles?

Because they are perfect arseholes.

Why do Aussies have clear-top lunch boxes?

So they can tell if they're going to work or coming home.

Why wasn't Jesus Christ born in Australia?

Because they couldn't find three wise men and a virgin.

Why does a woman need an arsehole?

Well someone has to put out the garbage.

How many men does it take to put the loo seat down?

None! No men on earth know how it's done.

Why does it take three women with pre-menstrual tension to change a light globe?

Because it just *does*, all right?!!!'

How many men does it take to change a light globe?

One, and nine to pin the medal on his chest.

How many women does it take to change a light globe?

One, plus two to form a collective, and three to make an application for funding.

What do you call ten blondes standing ear to ear?

A wind tunnel.

How do blondes' brain cells die?

Alone.

What is the blonde's mating call?

I think I'm drunk.

Where would you find a blonde the day his ship comes in?

At the airport.

What did the blonde say to Humphrey B. Bear?
Speak to me! Speak to me!

Why do blondes drive BMWs?

Because they can't spell Porsche.

How do you know when a blonde's been using a dishwasher?

When the drain's clogged with paper plates.

What's the difference between a blonde and a shopping trolley?

A shopping trolley has a mind of its own.

What do an intelligent blonde and the Yeti have in common?

No one has seen either of them.

Why do blondes take the pill?

To find out what day it is.

Why did the blonde cross the road?

Who cares? She should have been chained to the bed.

How do you confuse blondes?

Give them a box of M&Ms and ask them to arrange them in alphabetical order.

How do you confuse blondes?

Give them a box of Jaffas and tell them to leave the red ones until last.

How do you confuse blondes?

Sit them in a round room and tell them to find the corner.

Why don't blondes like pickles?

Because they can't fit their heads in the jar.

A blonde and a brunette were walking in a park and the brunette said, 'Oh, a dead bird!' The blonde looked up and said, 'Where? Where?'

How do you kill blondes?
Put spikes in their shoulder pads.

What's a brunette's mating call?
Has that dumb blonde gone yet?

How does a blonde turn on the light after having sex?
She opens the car door.

What's the difference between a blonde and the *Titanic*?
We know how many went down on the *Titanic*.

How do you know when a blonde's been doing a crossword?
Because all the squares are coloured in.

Why was the blonde so pleased when she finished the puzzle in six months?
Because the cover said three to five years.

What do you call six blondes standing in a circle?
A dope ring.

How do you drown a blonde?
You put a mirror on the bottom of the pool.

What do you call a blonde with half a brain?
Gifted.

How do you make a blonde laugh on Monday morning?
Tell her a joke Friday night.

How many blondes does it take to make a chocolate chip cookie?
Thirteen. One to mix the dough, and twelve to peel the Smarties.

How do you give a blonde a brain transplant?
Blow through her ear.

Why do blondes have TGIF printed on their shoes?
So they know their Toes Go In First.

Why do blondes have fur on the hems of their dresses?
To keep their necks warm.

Why do blondes carry ID cards?
To remind them who they are.

How can you tell when a blonde has been using your computer?
There's white-out on the screen.

What do blondes and cowpats have in common?
The older they get the easier they are to pick up.

What does a blonde call a bottle of black hair dye?
Artificial intelligence.

What's the best part of being married to a blonde?
You can park in the handicapped parking space.

What's the first thing a blonde does in the morning?
Gets dressed and goes home.

What do you call a brunette standing between two blondes?
An interpreter.

Why don't blondes order quiche?
Because they can't pronounce it.

How do you know when a blonde's been shoplifting?
Her bag is full of free samples.

How can you tell when a ransom note's been sent by a blonde?
Because of the stamped, self-addressed envelope.

How do you make a blonde's eyes sparkle?
Shine a torch in her ears.

What do blondes wear behind their ears to attract men?
Their ankles.

What do blondes and turtles have in common?
Once they're on their back they are screwed.

What do peroxide blondes and a 747 have in common?
Both have big black boxes.

Why don't blondes like vibrators?
Because they chip their teeth.

What do a blonde and a computer have in common?
You don't know their true value until they go down.

Why did the blonde climb over the glass wall?
To see what was on the other side.

How does a blonde spell blonde?
B-L-oh it doesn't matter anyway.

How does a blonde like her eggs?
Fertilised.

Why can't blondes pass a driving test?
They keep jumping in the back seat at red lights.

How many blondes does it take to change a lightbulb?
Three. One to find a ladder, one to find the bulb and one to find a man to do the work.

How does a blonde kill a fish?
  She drowns it.

What did the blonde say when she found out she was pregnant?
  I hope it's not mine.

Why are all dumb-blonde jokes one-liners?
  So men can understand them.

THE BODY IN QUESTION

Three newcomers, a Yank, a Pom and an Irishman, blow into an outback pub and settle down for a quiet ale. They can't take their eyes off a huge bloke with no ears who is sitting across the bar. The publican comes around and warns them not to stare at the bloke as he gets 'real stroppy. He'll come round and barrel you in a minute!' But the Yank has another look at him. Sure enough, round he comes, grabs the Yank around the throat and belts him against the wall.

'What are you lookin' at, stupid?' said the bloke with no ears.

'Why, pardner,' the Yank drawls, 'I was just admiring your hair. You always want to look after that hair or you'll end up wearing a toupee like myself.' And he dips his wig.

Earless drops him and says, 'Sorry, mate,' blushing as he returns to his corner.

They go back to their beers, until the Pom steals a glance over his middy and sure enough around the bar comes Earless. He collars the Pom and whacks him against the wall. 'What are you lookin' at, stupid?'

'Why, old chap, I was just admiring your teeth! You always want to look after those teeth or you'll end up wearing dentures like myself,' he said, demonstrating them with a click.

'Sorry, sport,' said the earless one. He put him back down and straightened him up.

They returned to leisurely sipping on their grog until the Irishman had to have one last look at the space behind the mutton chops. As sure as eggs, around the bar he came. Earless grabbed the Irishman by the shirt, smacked him against the wall and said, 'What are you lookin' at, stupid?'

'Matey, I couldn't help but admire your eyes! You've got beautiful eyes! You always want to look after your eyes or you'll end up wearing spectacles like myself.' And he squinted beguilingly through the lens. 'And that'd be no good because you've got no ears to hang them on.'

One of Alan Jones' players at Balmain has an eye gouged out in a scrum. Inspired by his coach's peptalks he refuses to give up and has a glass eye fitted. But he finds it both socially and professionally limiting. He puts his name down for an eye transplant, but there's a lack of donors. One night, going home from training, his glass eye fails to detect a bloke trying to pass his car on a motorbike. At that very second he decides to change lanes and sends the motorbike flying.

It's late at night and nobody's around and it's clear to the rugby player that the cyclist is dead. He can tell this because both his eyes are wide open and they're pretty good eyes. So he cuts one out with his Swiss Army knife so he can rush to his transplant surgeon and have it popped in his socket. And he replaces the cyclist's missing eye with his glass one.

Everything's fine for a few weeks – his new eye is working wonderfully. But he starts to worry about the cyclist. Perhaps, after all, he wasn't dead. So one arvo he calls into the local pub and asks about the accident.

'Yes, the bloke was dead okay,' says the barman, 'but it's still very mysterious.'

The rugby player feels a chill of fear. 'Mysterious?'

'Yeah, how the hell did he manage to ride his bike all the way down from Surfers Paradise with two glass eyes?'

A man who has had one leg amputated receives an invitation to a fancy dress party. A suitable disguise will take some imagination, he realises, so he goes to a costume hire shop for assistance. The young woman at the counter assures him she has the ideal outfit, and from the storeroom she brings out a velvet coat, tricorn hat, an eye patch and a stuffed parrot. 'There you are, Long John Silver.'

'No, no, no,' despairs the man, 'I'm meant to be in *disguise*. Everyone will recognise me if I wear this.'

The assistant frowns. 'Well, I don't know. Let me have another look.' A minute later she returns with a large sheet. 'Here, I'll cut two eye holes in this and you can go as a ghost. Everything covered.'

'Oh, fabulous,' says the man sarcastically. 'What an imaginative idea.'

The assistant has one more try. Reaching under the counter she whips out a large tin of golden syrup and plonks it on the counter. 'Right, pour this over yourself, stick your wooden leg up your arse and go as a toffee apple!'

Australian troops taken prisoner of war during the Malayan campaign found that they could use bamboo in many ways – as a building material, as a diet supplement, and even as a substitute for toilet paper.

On one occasion troops were paraded to have their rear ends examined by the medic looking for signs of typhoid. While this was in progress, one of their mates was returning to the ranks after visiting the toilet. Noticing that a piece of leaf was still sticking to the tail of the new arrival, a digger broke into uncontrollable laughter. 'Look at that. Just goes to show that that bloody bamboo will grow anywhere!'

The breakdown of the State School dunny obliged the Father at the neighbouring parish school to extend appropriate hospitality. Soon a disgusted Sister was with him to complain about the appalling behaviour of the Protestant boys engaged, it appears, in a competition as to who could urinate the highest. 'What did you do then, Sister?' enquired the Father.

'I hit the roof!'

'Well done, Sister.'

A crim stands before the court on a charge of theft. He was caught standing outside Myer with a handful of expensive necklaces. The window in front of him was part of Myer's and it had been smashed in. A brick was found at the crim's feet. Anyway, he chose to represent himself in court. He argued to the judge that it was not he who committed the crime but rather his left arm. After all, it was his arm that threw the brick and then grabbed the necklaces.

The judge thinks to himself, 'Well, I'll fix this smarty', and proceeds to announce his verdict. He tells the crim that he's decided that he has been persuaded by such an original and eloquent defence and that he has found his left arm guilty, and hereby sentences it to six years' hard labour! The crim smiles, thanks His Honour, twists off his false arm, and hands it to the judge before skipping out of court.

The old bushie staggers across the Simpson Desert, lost and alone but for his faithful dog, Blue. He hasn't eaten for days and his water ran out this morning and, collapsing, he reaches out to pat his loyal friend. Voice breaking with emotion, he says, 'I'm sorry, mate. I've really stuffed it this time, but I'm afraid it's you or me and, well, what I'm trying to say is, I'm going to have to shoot you and eat you, mate.'

Later that night, the old bushie finishes gnawing on his last bone and chucks it on the little pile by the fire. He sits there awhile, wistfully eyeing the flickering flames and then his eyes wander to the little pile of bones and then back to the flames. And he sighs and sadly says to himself, 'Gee, I wish Blue was here. He'd have really loved them bones.'

The old farmer from north Queensland visited the Big Smoke for the first time since WWII. When he came back he told his mates that he'd had his eyes opened and that among other things, he'd bought himself one of those new plastic toilet brushes and was eager to try it.

A few days later his mates saw him in town and asked him how the new bush was working. The old guy replied, 'It does a real good job, but shit it hurts.'

A big young Irish jackeroo from Wellmoringle comes into town for the first time in twenty-two months, makes a beeline for the chemist shop, confronts the pretty young thing behind the counter and makes his requirements known. She goes through a variety of styles and he finally settles on the one he wants.

'How much is that one?'

She says, '92 cents plus tax.'

'Oh, bugger the tacks,' he says, 'I'll wire it on.'

Wally loved Wendy, so he decided to prove it by having her name tattooed on his penis for her birthday. After dinner, he showed it to her in all its glory. WENDY, tattooed along the length of it.

Wendy thought it was beaut. Even when it was detumescent and all you could see was WY.

Later on, Wally was in a public loo when he noticed that the bloke peeing beside him also had WY tattooed on his dick. Wally was at once suspicious and curious. 'Is your girlfriend's name Wendy?'

'No,' said the other bloke, 'I've never had a sheila called Wendy. Why?'

'Well, it's your tattoo,' said Wally as he rather shyly revealed his own.

'Great,' said the bloke. 'Very impressive.'

'You can only see WY,' said Wally, 'but when I get an erection it says WENDY. What does yours say?'

'Well, it's a bit of a mouthful. It says WELCOME TO WOOLLOOMOOLOO AND HAVE A NICE DAY.'

The scene is a country dance. Sitting under a window, the classic wallflower. She has no make-up, wears glasses, has her hair in a bun and very skinny legs. All the other girls are dancing except her. A bloke arrives late and sees that she's the only one available, so asks her for the fox trot. It's not long before she's in his car and they're on their way to his flat. 'I won't waste any time with this sheila,' he thinks to himself. So as soon as they arrive he grabs her hand, opens his fly and places his generative member on her palm. 'Now,' he says, 'that's a penis!'

'Oh,' she says, 'is it? It looks the same as a prick, only smaller.'

What is the difference between white onions, brown onions and a 30 centimetre dick?

None. They all make your eyes water.

The young farmhand was a simple peasant who knew nothing about the facts of life. One day he spotted the dairymaid bending over to milk the cows as her dress rode up. He felt an erection, but did not understand what was happening. Frightened, he ran to show his boss.

'It's perfectly natural, lad, it happens to us all.'

'Well, I don't like it, it frightens me.'

The farmer sighed. 'Okay lad, if it worries you that much get rid of it. Next time it happens grab a couple of handfuls of cow dung and rub 'em on. It'll soon go down.'

The next time it happened the boy rushed into the barn, dropped his trousers and picked up the dung. The maid walked in, saw the erection and her eyes lit up. 'What you doin' then?'

'I'm gonna rub the dung on my cock to make it go down.'

She dropped her knickers, laid in the hay. 'That'd be a terrible waste. Put it up here.'

So he did. Both handfuls.

A male customer approached the counter of the new Body Parts shop, the latest in anatomical technology. 'Would you have any spare penises?' he asked.

'Certainly, sir,' replied the assistant and produced one from under the counter.

'Very nice,' remarked the customer. 'Would you have one a bit bigger?'

'How about this?' suggested the assistant, producing a fair sized member.

'Yes, it is pretty good,' agreed the customer. 'I hate to be a nuisance, but would you have a bigger one, preferably uncircumcised?'

'Feast your eyes on this then,' said the assistant, triumphantly laying out on the counter a huge cock.

'Fantastic!' the customer enthused. 'Exactly the size I'm after. Now, have you got one in white?'

A Regional Development Conference in Sydney was concluded by a banquet at which all the dignitaries made the usual platitudinous speeches. At a table most distant from the podium was a young officer from the Department of Foreign Affairs and Trade. By the time they reached him the food was cold and the wine warm. He was thoroughly pissed off until he noticed an attractive young woman from the New Zealand delegation opposite him. 'Hmmm,' he thought, 'I've never had anything to do with a Kiwi bird. I wonder if we can manage a bit of trans-Tasman cooperation.'

So he knocked a knife onto the floor and, in retrieving it, caressed the girl's ankle. When he sat up, she gave him a little smile. 'Ah,' he said to himself, 'encouraging,' and knocked a fork onto the floor. Retrieving it, he ran his hand up her calf and was rewarded with a broad grin.

'Excellent,' he cried to himself, and down went a spoon. This time, he ran his hand right up under her long gown and massaged the back of her knee. When he sat up, the girl was writing on a scrap of paper. 'Great,' he thought, 'it's on tonight, no worries.' The girl passed the paper across to him and he opened it.

'Evince no surprise when you reach my balls – Evans, ASIO.'

There was an 80-year-old wheat cocky who married a stunningly beautiful 23-year-old blonde. After a month, his mate asked him how married life was. 'Oh, it's terrible, it's terrible,' he says.

'What do you mean?' says his mate.

'Well, I just can't keep my hands off her,' was the reply.

A month later he saw the cocky again and asked him how married life was now. 'Oh it's terrible, it's terrible. I just can't keep my hands off her.'

Two months later he saw him again and asked, 'How's married life now?'

'Fantastic,' came the reply.

'What do you mean?' said his mate. 'What happened?'

To this the cocky replied, 'Well, I sacked all me hands, and bought meself a Combine Harvester!'

Old Danny had been a regular at the old local pub for as long as anyone could remember, and took a poor view of the place being renovated. When the work was completed old Danny frowned his disapproval.

'I suppose it's all right,' he grumbled, 'but I liked things the way they were. Even the old spittoon in the corner has gone. I'm gonna miss that.'

'Yeah,' said the publican, 'you always did.'

Two Welsh miners were working in a shaft in the Hunter Valley. On their way home after a hard day's shift, they fell into conversation with a couple of girls from a local farm. Each finished up escorting a girl in a separate direction. The next day the miners met and one said, 'How did you make out last night?'

'Great, couldn't have been better – what about you?'

'Likewise. Only I got into a hell of a row with the missus.'

'How come?'

'Well, I was having a wash in the tub when my missus noticed my tossle was all clean.'

His mate said, 'You bloody fool – why didn't you do like me? I gave mine a couple of slaps with me cap.'

An eight-year-old child asks Mummy about the origin of babies. Deciding she is now too old for stories of storks or cabbages, mother decides to explain the procreative functions of penis and vagina.

'And when Daddy does that to Mummy, you get a baby.'

'But Mummy,' says the child, 'last night when I came into your bedroom, you had Daddy's penis in your mouth? What do you get that way?'

'Diamonds.'

What's the difference between a clitoris and a pub?

Nine out of ten Aussie blokes know where to find a pub.

Russ Hinze, the immensely fat Queensland Cabinet Minister, was on a fact-finding mission in North Queensland with his minders. They stopped for lunch at a remote café and were surprised to find turtle soup on the menu. After the owner verified that it was fresh turtle soup, Russ said, 'I haven't had that for years.' Off went the owner and while the party had a pre-lunch drink they could hear from the kitchen a continual and vigorous 'chop-chop' sound followd by an increasingly passionate string of invective. Eventually one of the minders went to investigate the delay and found the owner trying to decapitate a live turtle with a cleaver whenever the head appeared. But every time, the turtle was too fast. The minder said to the owner, 'When I say NOW you can get him!' He moved to the rear of the turtle and rammed his finger into the rear apperture of the carapace, upon which the turtle's head appeared, wearing a look of amazement and indignation. And the owner had no difficulty in chopping it off.

Impressed with the efficiency and simplicity of the strategy, the owner asked, 'Where did you learn that trick, mate?' to which the minder replied, 'Oh, that's easy. How do you think we get Russ's tie on each morning?'

A golfer made a terrific drive which everyone complimented. He said, 'Oh, I don't suppose it's too bad for a bloke with a wooden leg.' With that he unscrewed the leg to prove his point. At the next tee he drove even further and again he was complimented. 'Oh, not too bad for a bloke with a wooden arm.' He rolled up his sleeve and unscrewed his arm. At the next, he drove a real beauty straight down the fairway about 400 metres. Again he was complimented, and he said, 'Oh, it's not too bad for a fellow with a wooden heart.' He invited one of the ladies to go behind a bush with him to show her. He was gone for about twenty minutes and one of the others thought they should find out why they were away so long. And there they found the bloke screwing his heart out.

Why does a man have a hole in the end of his penis?

To get a bit of air to his brain.

HISTORY AND THE YARTS

During the French Revolution, a tumbril brings an Englishman, an American and an Irishman to the guillotine and the executioner steps forward, shushes the jeering crowd and sneers at the doomed men. 'So, which of you miserable wretches weel be zee first to die or shall I pick whichever one takes my fancy to face zee blade of doom?' The Englishman steps forward and says, 'No need to be like that, chappie, I'll happily face your blade of doom.'

'Hah!' crows the executioner. 'But how weel you face zee blade of doom? Face up, like a proud Frenchman, or face down like zee snivelling, cowardly English dog you are.'

'Put like that, chappie,' says the Englishman, 'face up it is.'

And so he takes his place at the guillotine, facing the glinting, razor-sharp blade, and the grinning executioner says, '*Au revoir*, miserable English pig-doggie,' pulls the handle and the blade goes whoosh, thunk! And stops a millimetre from the Englishman's neck. '*Sacre bleu*!' cries the executioner, 'it ees a sign from God, you are free to go.' And so the Englishman is freed.

The executioner approaches the American and the Irishman.

'So, who ees eet to bee? Do I drag one of you up here, crying and peesing in your pants, or . . .'

'Ah, shuddup,' says the Yank, shouldering aside the Irishman. 'Let's get this show on the road.'

'*Mais oui*,' says the executioner. 'But how shall you face zee blade of doom. Face down like the miserable snivelling coward you are . . .'

'Face up, and I repeat, shuddup!' says the Yank and he lays down and with an '*Au revoir*, American pig-doggie,' the executioner pulls the handle and, whoosh, thunk! The razor-sharp blade of doom stops a millimetre from the American's throat. '*Sacre bleu*, another act of God! You are free to go,' says the executioner.

Then he turns to the Irishman, but before he can get out a word, the Irishman says, 'If you don't mind, I'd prefer you to keep a civil tongue in your head and in answer to your questions, I'm coming of my own free will and I'll be facing the blade of doom, thank you very much.'

'Hah,' cries the executioner, and when the Irishman is in place, he says, '*Au revoir*, Irish pig-doggie,' but just as he is about to pull the handle, the Irishman stops him.

'Wait a minute!' he calls out, casting an appraising eye up at the guillotine, 'I think I be seeing your problem . . .'

All the Merry Men, and Maid Marion, gathered around Robin Hood's deathbed, waiting for the inevitable end. Manfully, heroically, Robin struggled up and said, 'Friar Tuck, fetch me my long bow. I will fire an arrow out the window and, wherever it lands, that's where you will bury me.'

Deeply moved, they placed the bow and arrow in his trembling fingers, propped him up and faced him towards Sherwood Forest. And with an immense effort, Robin aimed and fired. And so it came to pass that they buried him on top of the wardrobe.

Red Riding Hood is tripping merrily through the forest. Out jumps the big bad wolf, who grabs her and with fangs salivating says, 'Aha, Red Riding Hood. I'm going to gobble you up . . . gobble, gobble, gobble!' To which Red Riding Hood responds, 'Gobble gobble gobble, that's all they think about around here. Doesn't anybody fuck anymore?'

Once upon a time there dwelt, in Fairy Land, a particularly beauteous young man. He was kind of heart and fair of face and form. But, woe and lack-a-day, he also felt accursed, because he had, protruding from his navel, a silver screw. Verily, he could conceal it by adjustment of doublet and hose, yet it did sorely trouble him. So that each day he would go into the deep dark woods and sit in a glade, staring sadly at the silver screw.

Then one day a crone came through the woods carrying a bundle of faggots. The kindly youth adjusted his clothing to conceal his shame and said to her, 'Old crone, those faggots are too heavy for you to carry. Let me lift thy burden.'

The crone was grateful and took him through the woods to her gingerbread cottage where she revealed that she was, in fact, a witch. 'But you have been so kind to me that I will grant you a boon.'

The youth didn't need to consider the boon for a moment. 'Please, please, rid me of this silver screw in my navel.'

The crone bade him go to a distant mountain and to climb to a rocky ledge. There he was to exhort the heavens using a magic spell that she provided. The youth followed her instructions and, struggling through the cruel and stinging woods, came to the ledge. There he began to exhort the heavens, using the crone's magic spell. Suddenly, the blue skies vanished and dark sombre clouds appeared. A great wind sprang up and he heard a sound like angels singing. And from the black clouds came a great shaft of light that focused on him. And down that shaft of light came a giant golden screwdriver.

As the singing reached a crescendo, the screwdriver reached the silver screw, fitting into the groove on its head. The giant golden screwdriver turned once, twice, thrice, then retreated up the shaft of light which, in turn, disappeared. As did the dark boiling clouds and celestial chorus.

The young man looked down at the silver screw and tentatively touched it with trembling fingers. Yes, it was loose! So he turned the screw once, twice, thrice!

And his bum fell off.

Roy Rogers was aseat Trigger as they wended their way home after a most satisfying day at work tending the boundary fences on Roy's large spread. About a mile from the homestead Roy noticed a trail of dust rising from the trail that led from home to the main gate. As he approached, he saw that it was a large squad of cavalry soldiers led by Major Ted. As he came up to the column of troops Major Ted called, 'Whoa!' and addressed the famous cowboy.

'Good evening, Mr Rogers,' he said.

'Good evening, Major,' replied Roy Rogers.

'Are yo' heading home, sir?' asked the Major.

'I am indeed, yessir, I'm looking forward to a real meal.'

'Just before you go, Mr Rogers, there are a few things you should know.'

'Like what, Major?'

'Well, sir, the Indians have been on the rampage over at your homestead.'

'What's happened?'

'There's not much left I'm afraid, Mr Rogers,

they scalped your five children and appear to have raped the girls beforehand. They also raped your wife and mother before killing them. All the cattle are gone and they put an arrow through your dog Pal. Most of the village is burned to the ground and they put poison in your water supply.'

'Christ, I better get over there and see what I can do.'

'Mr Rogers . . .?'

'Yes, Major?'

'Just before you go. Hows about a little song for the boys?'

The Lone Ranger was finally captured by his enemies, the Comanches. As a tribute to his valour, they offered him one last wish. Our hero whistled his loyal and highly intelligent horse Silver, whispering something in his ear. The horse wheeled around and disappeared in a cloud of dust. A few minutes later Silver reappeared with a beautiful, naked and heavy-breasted girl on his back.

She approached the valiant Lone One, and pushed her pussy in his face. But for perhaps the first time in his life the Lone Ranger showed not the slightest interest. Instead he whistled Silver once more. The horse came promptly. The Lone Ranger hooked a finger in Silver's nostril and yelled in his ear, 'I said 'posse' you dumb horse.'

A would-be gunslinger is walking down a street in Texas one afternoon when he hears the music of a honky-tonk piano coming from the local saloon. He decides that it's now or never, and bursts through the swinging doors, stands legs astride, hat pulled down and arms akimbo. No one seems to take much notice as he looks around the room, spots the piano player with a cigar sticking out of his mouth and a lighted candle on each side of the piano. The gunslinger draws a gun, twirls it three times, shoots out the flame of the left-hand candle, and returns the gun to its holster.

Everyone sighs, looks agape and lulls into silence. All except the piano player who just keeps on playing. The gunslinger repeats the performance and shoots out the right-hand candle. Exactly the same response from everyone, but the piano player keeps on playing. So the gunslinger draws both guns, twirls them three times and shoots the cigar out of the piano player's mouth. And the piano player just keeps on playing.

Discouraged, the gunslinger goes to the bar and asks for a drink. The barman pours a drink and comments on the fine piece of shooting. He asks if the gunslinger would mind a bit of advice as he is obviously hankering to become a gunslinger.

'No, not at all,' replies the gunslinger.

'Well,' says the barman, 'firstly, I'd file the sight off the end of the barrel and smooth it right down. You don't need that as you shoot from the hip and it only hinders a fast draw. Then I'd file off the trigger guard and again smooth it right down. You don't need that either, as you could get your finger caught in it one day and it could cost you your life.'

The gunslinger thanks him for his advice and asks if there's anything else he should do.

'Yes,' replies the barman, 'lastly I'd cover both guns in Vaseline.'

'Vaseline?' queries the gunslinger, 'wouldn't that make it slippery?'

'That's the whole idea,' explains the barman, 'because when Wyatt Earp over there finishes playing the piano, he's going to come over here and shove those guns right up your arse!'

A publisher was fishing in the Atlantic, when he caught a rather unusual salmon. 'Please let me go,' begged the fish, and because it was small he threw it back. Later, when fishing again, he caught the same salmon and once more it begged to be released. 'No,' said the publisher, 'no way.'

'Oh,' replied the fish, 'not even if I tell you that I write poetry?'

'What about?' said the publisher, impressed despite himself.

'Oh, the sea and the *Titanic*. I spend a lot of time swimming around the wreck. My name is Rusty and if you let me off the hook, you can publish my first book.'

'Of course,' said the publisher, 'we'll call it Rusty Salmon's *Titanic Verses*.'

Did you hear about the blind man who was given a silver nutmeg grater for Christmas?

Said it was the most violent thing he'd ever read.

Oscar Wilde was reclining, as was his wont, in velour smoking jacket, carnation in button hole, vellum-bound volume of poetry in hand, in his undergraduate rooms, when he heard a great clatter on the stairs below and a door burst open to reveal eight hearty and perspiring rugger players manifestly bent on disturbing his repose.

Wilde rose to his feet and surveyed the scene in a dignified but slightly nervous manner. 'I say, chaps,' he said, 'I may be inverted, but I'm not insatiable.'

What's an innuendo?

An Italian suppository.

How many surrealists does it take to change a light bulb?

Fish.

Just imagine, for a moment, if there were no hypothetical situations.

The Bendigo Players have had a pretty good season. They got good reviews in the *Courier* for their production of *The Fantasticks* and sold out their three-night season of Terence Rattigan's *The Deep Blue Sea*. Their production of *Dimboola* also went pretty well. So they decided to end the year in a blaze of glory with a production of *Hamlet*. Unfortunately the bloke they chose to play the Prince of Denmark was not inordinately talented and kept muffing line after line and missing his cues. Moreover he spoke so badly that he could barely be heard by the audience which began to heckle and boo more and more loudly. Finally the actor strode to the front of the stage and yelled, 'Don't blame me, I didn't write this crap!'

Robert Newton and Wilfred Lawson, both great drinkers, were appearing in an Old Vic Shakespearean season and had to be hauled out of the pub to go on stage. Newton appeared first, and staggered around until a voice in the audience called, 'Hey, you're pissed!' Newton stopped, turned to the audience and said, 'You think I'm pissed? Wait till the Duke of Buckingham comes on.'

Bloke in the bar turns to the guy next to him and says, 'Can I buy you a beer?', and the other bloke replies, 'Look, I'll be perfectly frank with you so we won't waste any of our precious time. See, I'm a genius. And if you buy me a beer you'll want to talk, and what could you say that would interest me, a dead-set genius with an IQ of 196?' And the bloke says, 'An IQ of 196! This is incredible. I'm a genius too, with an IQ of 195 – we can talk! Bartender, two beers.' And so they settle down to discussing quantum physics and the great theories of the cosmos.

Down the bar a bit, a bloke nudges his neighbour and says, 'How about these two? I'm not stupid, in fact, I have an above average IQ of 127 but I wouldn't have a clue what these geniuses are talking about. Quantum what? Theories of where? It's way over my head.' And his neighbour says, 'You have an IQ of 127! I'm above average, too. My IQ is 126 – we can talk! Bartender, two beers.' And so they settle down to discussing feminism's impact on the Australian film industry and the safety features of Volvos.

Further down the bar, a bloke nudges his neighbour and says, 'Check this out, would you? Whatever those genuises are talking about, it's complete gobbledegook to me, and I'm not ashamed to admit that whatever a feminism is, I don't think I need one because I'm a complete moron. I mean all this stuff is way over my head.' And his neighbour says, 'What's your IQ?' The bloke replies, 'I'm stupid, okay. I've got an IQ of 63. You wanna make something of it?' And his neighbour says, 'This is great! I'm a complete moron, too. My IQ is 65 – we can talk! Bartender, two beers. So, been to any auditions lately . . .'

(By a simple adaptation of the punch line, this joke can be made to refer to a variety of professions, e.g. 'Written any good ads lately?')

A man went into a Paddo antique shop and said he'd just found two items in the loft of his old house. And he produced an old fiddle and an even older painting, both in a very tatty condition. He asked the dealer to give them a wipe over and suggest a value for them. The dealer asked the owner to return in a few days. When he did so, the dealer confessed that the examination had turned into one of those good news/bad news stories. So the customer asked for the good news first.

The dealer then said that what he had found was that the items were a Stradivarius and a Rembrandt, which had so amazed him that he had got them authenticated by a valuer of his acquaintance, a man who did regular assessments for Sotheby's.

'What then is the bad news?' asked the customer.

'Well, you see sir, Stradivarius never really made it as a painter . . .'

A young man was collecting money around Wagga for the Murrumbidgee and Murray River Valley Drum and Fife Marching Band. He walked up a long path to a cottage and knocked. An old lady answered the door. 'Madam,' he said, 'I am taking up a collection for the Murrumbidgee and Murray River Valley Drum and Fife Marching Band and I thought you'd like to contribute.'

'What's that you say?' said the old dear, cupping her hands to her ear.

The young man raised his voice. 'Madam,' he shouted, 'I am collecting money for the Murrumbidgee and Murray River Valley Drum and Fife Marching Band and I thought you'd like to contribute.'

'You'll have to speak up,' yelled the old lady.

The young man took a deep breath and roared out: 'MADAM, I AM TAKING UP A COLLECTION FOR THE MURRUMBIDGEE AND MURRAY RIVER VALLEY DRUM AND FIFE MARCHING BAND AND I THOUGHT YOU MIGHT LIKE TO CONTRIBUTE.'

'I still can't get it,' yelled the old girl, her hands cupped to both ears. The young man gave up and started to walk down the path. As he did so the old lady called out, 'Don't forget to shut the gate.'

'Oh, bugger the gate,' said the young man, all but under his breath.

'And bugger the Murrumbidgee and Murray River Valley Drum and Fife Marching Band,' yelled the old girl.

Two men were before the court charged with sodomy. In the course of evidence it was revealed that the man enacting the female role was a trumpet player in the Ashfield Town Band. When he heard this, the Judge immediately said, 'Case dismissed.'

The Prosecutor got to his feet and said, 'But your Honour, this is a proven case.'

'Case dismissed,' repeated the Judge.

'But your Honour,' shouted the Prosecutor, to be interrupted by the Judge who said, 'Have you ever heard the Ashfield Town Band play?'

'No,' confessed the Prosecutor.

'Well, I have,' said the Judge, 'and you can take it from me, they all want fucking.'

On the Mundi Mundi Plains, just north-west of Broken Hill, is a small town called Silverton. The story is told of the old miner who spent most of his time telling stories to tourists in return for a free beer at the local pub. One day, he threw an old sugar bag on the bar, opened up the tied end, and out stomped a large goanna. He bet the tourists that the goanna could play the piano. The goanna jumped off the bar, went over to the piano and started to play. The tourists were amazed.

After a few free beers, the old miner rushed outside to his beaten up FJ ute and started to rummage around in the back. One of the tourists asked him what he was looking for.

'I've got a bloody black snake that can sing in here somewhere.'

The word got around the tourist buses quickly, and everybody stood in the tiny bar. The old miner came in with another sugar bag and emptied it on the bar. Out slithered a long black snake. 'The bugger can sing!' said the old miner. The tourist dollars lined the bar in bets. The old miner was worried. He had only bet for free beers. He picked up the snake and draped it over the piano, the goanna began to play and the snake burst out into song. The tourists all cheered, the old miner picked up the hundreds of dollars in bets. He started to walk out the door when he broke out in uncontrollable laughter.

'I fooled you mob. The bloody snake can't sing. You see, the flamin' goanna's a ventriloquist!'

A man walked into a rough dockside pub in Port Melbourne and bought a pot of beer. Placing the beer on the table, he went across the room to speak to a friend and returned to his seat to find a monkey astride his glass cooling his testicles in the beer. He went over to the landlord to complain but the landlord said, 'The monkey belongs to the pianist, go and tell him.'

Aggrieved, the man went over to the pianist and said, 'Do you know your monkey's testicles are in my beer?'

Looking through his alcoholic haze, the pianist said, 'I don't, mate, but hum a couple of bars and I'll soon pick it up.'

TRAVEL TALES

An Aussie bloke is touring the world and he's in Spain, in a little coffee bar, drinking coffee, funnily enough. On the wall alongside him is a huge bull's head on a wooden plaque. Up close it's enormous. Massive horns, black silky hair, awesome!

The Aussie turns to the bartender and says, 'What's the story behind the bull's head? Excuse me mate . . . you . . . Yeah, it's you I'm talking to. What's the story behind the bull's head. Interesting yarn, is it? Around the bull's head? El Bull's Head? El Head-o de Bullula . . .?'

The bartender has gone very pale. His hand clutching the coffee cup has the shakes and the knuckles are blueish-white.

'Please, Senor,' he says, 'do not espeak to me of thees bull, for thees bull has keelled my brothir.'

The Australian feller, very sensitive to changes in mood, as most Australians are, says, 'Aw, sorry about that. Well, I've only just heard. Your brother was a bullfighter, was 'e, your brother? Bullfighter was 'e? Bullfighter, your brother, was 'e?'

'No,' says the bartender. 'He was sitting there one night and head fell on him.'

Two Australians, with zinc on their noses, were inspecting St Peter's in Rome. 'Gee, look at them Michael Angelo transfers!'

'Not transfers, mate, friezes. Michael Angelo friezes.'

'Well what about them muriels then?'

'Murals, mate, murals.'

At this moment an Italian priest opened the shutter of the confessional and offered to give them a guided tour.

'That's all right sport, you finish your shit in comfort.'

Bluey and Curly, two old Aussie diggers, won the lottery and decided to go on a world tour. In London they go to the Carlton for dinner. After a while Bluey says to Curly, 'I've got to go!' so they whistle up the head waiter and ask, 'Where's the little house, mate?' The head waiter said, 'Little house? Do you mean the lavatory, sir? Across the room, through the archway, across the passage, through the door, down two steps and there you are.' Bluey thanks him and sets off – across the room, through the archway, across the passage, through the door, falls ten metres down the lift shaft, picks himself up, dusts himself off and says, 'Bugger the second step, I'm gonna do it here.'

A businessman rushed into the station and just managed to catch the Brisbane to Rockhampton express. On taking his seat he asked the conductor what time the train reached Gladstone.

'There's no stop in Gladstone, Wednesdays,' replied the conductor.

'What!' exclaimed the businessman.

'There's no stop in Gladstone, Wednesdays.'

'But it's imperative. I have an important meeting there.'

The conductor is adamant. 'This is the weekly express and there's no stop in Gladstone, Wednesdays.'

After much argument a compromise was reached. The conductor agreed to ask the driver to slow down to 60 kilometres an hour as the train went through Gladstone. He would then hold the businessman out of the carriage window, the businessman could get his legs running in thin air as fast as he could and when the conductor thought his leg speed was sufficient he would lower him down onto the platform.

So when the train reached Gladstone this plan was put into action and the businessman hit the platform running at full lick. He ran the full length of the platform, hoping he could stop himself before the end. Just as the last carriage of the train was passing him by, his collar was grabbed by the strong arm of a shearer who heaved him back on board through an open window.

'You were lucky there, mate,' said the shearer, 'there's no stop in Gladstone, Wednesdays.'

A social worker, two children, a lawyer, and a Christian Brother were passengers on an aeroplane when suddenly the door to the cockpit opened and there was the pilot, one parachute strapped on his back and another in his hand.

The pilot says, 'The plane is going to crash, I can't do anything and there are only two parachutes. One is mine and you'll have to decide about the other one.' And he leaps out of the plane. The passengers are terrified. They start sweating and wringing their hands.

The social worker says, 'Perhaps we could strap the children together in the parachute.'

The lawyer screams, 'Fuck the children . . .'

And the Christian Brother says, 'Do you think we have time?'

Two birds were sitting on the roof of an aircraft hangar when an air force jet flew over them, just clearing the hangar roof.

One bird said to the other, 'Shit, he was going fast.'

And the other bird said, 'So would you if your bum was on fire.'

Two typical Australians, wearing blue singlets and thongs, decide to take a trip overseas. Barry and Gary arrive in Rome and are soon caught up in all things Italian – the food, the music, the women. They go into an Italian bar one night and ask the waiter what Italians drink. The waiter informs them that it's usually wine. 'But some people, for example, the Pope, drink other types of liquor.'

'What does the Pope drink?' asks Barry.

'The Pope drinks crème de menthe,' replies the waiter.

'That'll do us,' says Barry and Gary, 'we'll have two pots of this crème de menthe stuff then. '

The next day Barry and Gary wake up very hungover and very ill. Barry says to Gary as they lie near death on the hotel floor, 'If the Pope drinks that stuff all the bloody time no wonder they have to carry the poor bugger around.'

It was the start of the wet season and the English tourist stopped his car at the edge of a stream flowing across the road he was travelling. 'I say, my man, shall I be able to ford this stream?'

'Yeah, mate,' said the cocky, 'she'll be right.'

The Pom drove into the water and sank like a stone. When he spluttered to the surface he shouted, 'I thought you said it was safe to cross!'

'Can't understand it, mate,' said the cocky, 'that water only came halfway up our ducks!'

An Australian tourist was booking into a pub in Killarney.

'Will you have a room with a bath or a shower?' asked the receptionist.

The Aussie, considering his budget, asked what was the difference.

'Well,' said the receptionist, 'with a shower you stand up.'

From the diary of a young girl on her first cruise in the Pacific.

August 14: What a beautiful sunset as we are leaving Sydney Harbour.

August 15: The sea is beautiful and calm. I am slightly bored.

August 16: I met the captain.

August 17: The captain asked me for dinner.

August 18: When I refused the captain's

advances, he threatened to scuttle the ship.

August 19: I saved 2600 passengers and crew.

What's the difference between an English backpacker and a German backpacker?

About 200 metres.

RELIGIOUSLY OBSERVED

Some Brides of Christ were visiting the Taronga Park Zoo. They were all ooohing and aaahing as they gazed down at a huge gorilla. He was gently chewing a banana and reflectively eyeing the crowd. One of the demure young lasses of the cloth reached out a slim arm and beckoned this magnificent beast in a friendly gesture. The wind stirred ever so slightly and blew the hem of the nun's habit up the pit wall and, in a flash, the gorilla leapt the narrow moat, ran up the pit wall, wrenched the habit, beckoning arm and young nun into a screaming bundle under his long, strong arm – and bounded into his bamboo thicket with a look in his eye.

Some considerable time later, the zoo's gamekeepers were able to recover the young and incoherent nun from the grip of the gorilla. She was rushed to hospital and treated for a variety of bodily and mental wounds, which served to put her in a silent and reclusive mood for months.

At last the Mother Superior of the convent could stand it no longer and remonstrated with the numbed nun to the effect that she should put the unpleasantness behind her and get on with His works. She had certainly had a dreadful experience but was fully recovered physically and only through doing Good Works would her mind get well again.

However the young nun just broke down and cried. 'But he never calls, he never writes . . .'

A rabbi and a Roman Catholic priest were alone in a railway carriage. After a while the Catholic priest leaned forward and said to the rabbi, 'I understand in your religion you're not allowed to eat pork.'

'That is correct,' said the rabbi.

'Well, just between you and me, have you ever tasted pork?'

'As a matter of fact, I have.'

After a pause the rabbi said, 'I understand in your religion you're not allowed to have sexual intercourse.'

'That's correct.'

'Well, just between you and me, have you ever had sexual intercourse?'

'As a matter of fact, I have.'

The old Jewish rabbi slapped him on the knee and said, 'It's a damned sight better than pork!'

An Australian hellfire preacher wanted to impress his congregation. He arranged for a boy to get above the pulpit in the loft, instructing him to light a piece of paper and let it flutter down when he reached the great climax of his sermon. 'When I shout "send fire from Heaven" light the paper and let it flutter down.' The great day came and the thunderous sermon was given. The preacher shouted, 'Send fire from Heaven,' but nothing happened. He shouted again, 'Send fire from Heaven'. Still nothing happened. He shouted again and again and again. Finally the voice of the boy could be heard. 'I can't ... the cat's pissed on the matches.'

During the brief, distinguished reign of Pope John XXIII, a young priest riding his bike in New York was stopped at the traffic lights and saw Christ walking across the pedestrian crossing. Excited by the sight, he rode feverishly to the cathedral and reported the incident to the Monseigneur. The Monseigneur said, 'This is too big for me to handle – you'll have to speak to the Cardinal.'

The Cardinal was then informed of the incident and said, 'This is too big for me to handle – I shall have to ring Rome.' So the Cardinal got out the green phone, dialled Vat 69 and spoke to the Pope. He said to the Holy Father, 'We have a dreadful problem in New York. Christ is here and he's coming to the cathedral. What are we going to do?' There was no reply from the Pope, just heavy breathing.

The Cardinal then said, 'Your Holiness, you'll have to advise us. He will be here at the cathedral in a few minutes.'

There was another long silence at the end of the line. Finally the Pope said, 'You betta lookka very bizzi . . .'

A priest and a minister travelling in a plane sat next to each other. After take off, the hostess asked the priest whether he desired a drink. He replied, 'Scotch and soda, please'. She asked the minister whether he desired the same. 'No thanks,' he said, 'I'd rather commit adultery than drink alcohol.' The priest turned to the hostess and said, 'May I change my order? I didn't know that I had such a choice.'

Two nuns drove to the supermarket in their red Mini Minor to do the weekly shopping. Unable to find a parking spot, one rushed inside the supermarket while the other kept looking. After completing the shopping, the first nun returned to the parking area and asked a man standing nearby whether he'd seen 'a nun in a red Mini?' His reply was, 'Not since I signed the pledge.'

In a country hotel in Queensland the vicar was lunching with his bishop who was undertaking a pastoral tour. The waitress approached and turned to the vicar. 'What will you have, Les?' The bishop raised his eyebrows, mildly surprised at the familiarity. Then it was his turn. 'And what will little Robin redbreast have?'

Jesus was hanging on the cross at Calvary when he saw Peter walking by and yelled out to him. 'Hey, Pete, mate, come up here for a minute. I've got something to tell you!' So Peter started going up the hill, but was intercepted by a guard who cut off his arms. He staggered around from the blow and then heard Jesus calling him again.

'Hey, Peter. Come up here. I've got something to tell you!' So Peter tried again, but this time he got his legs cut off.

'Come on, Peter, it's really important,' cried Jesus. So Peter rolled himself to the top of the hill and gasped, 'Okay, what is it?'

'I can see your house from here!' said Jesus.

Did you hear the one about the nun who was working in the condom factory and thought she was making sleeping bags for mice?

After an exciting sermon, one of the Reverend Nile's parishioners remained seated in an otherwise empty pew, still thrilling to the great man's tirade against the gay and lesbian mardi gras. He noticed that the Reverend had left his sermon on the pulpit. Intrigued, he couldn't help but take a peek. More interesting than the text, which he'd already heard, were the marginal jottings, 'Argument weak here – shout very loudly.'

There was a sizeable graffiti on the wall of Central Railway Station in Sydney. JESUS LIVES! Below it, in smaller lettering, someone had put the question, 'Does this mean we don't get an Easter holiday?'

All the cardinals gather in the Sistine Chapel to elect a new Pope. An assassin plants a bomb and all are killed instantly. So the eighty of them arrive at the Pearly Gates *en masse*. As they're strolling in, Peter stops them and says, 'Where do you think you're going?'

'We have come to collect our eternal reward,' they chorus, 'we are princes of the church.'

'Well, nobody gets straight in without answering this question. Have you committed adultery?'

Suddenly the cardinals look very sheepish and

confused. Then, one by one, they shuffle outside the gates leaving only a single cardinal within.

'Okay, okay,' says Peter to the seventy-nine cardinals. 'Away you go to Purgatory for twelve months. And take that deaf bastard with you.'

It was suggested to a staid and somewhat absent-minded Bishop that he attend a sermon by one of the younger prelates who was attracting surprisingly large crowds with new-style sermons. The Bishop was particularly taken with one of the prelate's anecdotes, 'Some of the happiest hours of my life were spent in the arms of another man's wife. I'm referring, of course, to my mother.'

The bishop decided to borrow this for one of his own sermons a few weeks later. He began, 'Some of the happiest hours of my life were spent in the arms of another man's wife.' Whereupon his face went blank and he said, 'And do you know, I can't for the life of me remember who she was!'

Old Fred worked in the same sawmill for thirty-seven years and on every day of those thirty-seven years he stole a piece of wood. Over the years this amounted to quite a lot of wood. In fact he was able to build himself a house, a shed and even a small place for his daughter when she married. On his retirement the firm threw a big party for Fred, putting on food and a keg and all the trimmings. The Managing Director attended and presented Fred with a gold watch, saying that he'd been such a valued and trusted employee.

Afterwards, Fred moped about the house in a depressed state. When asked by his wife what was wrong, he replied, 'I just can't live with my conscience. There I was being made a fuss of by all those people and they didn't know I'd been pinching wood every day for thirty-seven years.'

'Look,' she said, 'go to confession. It doesn't matter that you haven't been to church since you were a kid. It will ease your conscience.'

Reluctantly Fred trotted off to confession and saw Father Murphy. He said, 'Bless me, Father, for I have sinned. I worked for this firm for thirty-seven years and every day of that thirty-seven years I stole some wood from them. I can't live with myslf. How can I make amends?'

Father Murphy thought for a moment and said, 'Well, Fred, this is a pretty serious matter, so for your penance I want you to make a novena.'

Fred looked at him quizzically and replied, 'I'm not sure what you mean, Father ... but if you've got the plans ... I've got the timber!'

The small outback town had grown a bit and become more scattered so that the local clergy – a Salvation Army captain, a Roman Catholic priest and a Jewish rabbi – were having a hard time keeping each other from stealing their respective flocks. A hasty meeting of the local branch of the Council of Churches was called and, after a good deal of haggling, it was finally agreed they would contribute, equally, to the purchase of a second-hand motor car.

The great day finally arrived and down the main street swung the Army band with the old black A-model rolling behind. At the Post Office the priest stepped out and, midst clouds of incense, sprinkled the ancient chariot with holy water. The rabbi was dumbfounded! What could he do to better these symbolic acts of proprietorship? He racked his brain.

At last inspiration! Down to the beloved acquisition he swept, waving the Star of David and, drawing a pair of tinsnips from the folds of his gown, whipped two inches off the exhaust pipe!

Father O'Flaherty, who was known to like an occasional flutter on the horses, was given a certainty for Saturday by one of his parishioners. But he was told that he had to back it on the course because, if they lost their price, they'd pull it. He thanked the parishioner profusely and began looking forward to Saturday when he remembered that he had scheduled confessions. 'Bloody hell, I can't cancel them,' he cursed. Then he realised he had Michael, a novitiate priest in training with him.

So he approached Michael and said, 'How about doing confessions for me on Saturday.' Michael was shocked. 'I can't do that, Father, I haven't received the sacrament.'

'It's all right, Michael, no one will know and I'll pay you twenty dollars.'

'Twenty dollars is tempting but I wouldn't know what to say, what penances to give,' said Michael.

'It's easy,' said Father O'Flaherty, 'come and look inside the confessional.' He showed Michael inside the priest's side of the confessional and there on the wall was an alphabetical list of sins and their recommended penance. 'See how easy it is,' he said. So Michael agreed to do it.

Confession time arrived on Saturday and the first sinner entered the confessional, 'Bless me Father, for I have sinned ... I have been guilty of telling lies.' Michael ran his finger down the list – A, B, C ... L – Lies – and saw the relevant penance – three Hail Marys, which he gave, and the follow-up blessing. 'Well,' he thought, 'that wasn't too hard,' and began to relax.

In came the next sinner. Same routine, the penance was found and given, and the sinner departed. Then a third sinner entered. 'Bless me Father, for I have sinned ... I have been guilty of having oral sex.' Michael ran his finger down the list – came to O – but there was nothing about oral sex. He began to get agitated and broke out in a bit of a sweat. Just then he looked out the window of the confessional and saw an altar boy walking past. 'Pssst,' he called. The altar boy came over.

'What does Father O'Flaherty give for oral sex?' he asked.

'Oh, usually a can of Coke and a Mars bar.'

A naive young Catholic priest, returning from his rounds, had to walk back through Kings Cross. As he stopped at a corner to cross, one of the ladies of the night approached him and asked, '$200 for a naughty, Father?' Not knowing quite what to make of this, he continued on his way. The same thing happened to him several more times, each time a different girl but asking the same amount. Eventually he arrived back at the seminary and sought an audience with the Mother Superior. 'Mother Superior, what's a naughty?'

'Look, it's $200 – the same as up the Cross. Take it or leave it!'

For many centuries, at Christmas, most of the world's religious leaders paid a visit to the Pope at the Vatican. Each visitor would give a token gift to the Pope, which the Pope blessed and then, unopened, gave back to the giver. For years the Popes had wondered what the Jewish rabbi would have given to the head of the Catholic Church. To settle the question, a recent Pope organised for one of his bishops to intercept the proffered gift, quickly open it and have a look inside, and then hand it back to the Pope.

So the rabbi duly presented his gift to the Pope, wishing His Holiness a happy Christmas. The bishop quickly took the gift behind the throne, opened it and saw what was inside. Then just as quickly he handed it back to the Pope who passed it back to the rabbi with a blessing and his thanks. The Pope could hardly wait to hear what the bishop had found in the 'gift'. Finally the bishop told the Pope what he'd found – a bill for the Last Supper!

A novice went to a monastery where the monks were only allowed to speak two words a year, and those to the abbot. At the end of each year they were given an audience and said their two words. Naturally they were expected to be something along the lines of 'Jesus loves' or some other eternal verity. However at the end of his first year the novice offered, 'Bed hard' and at the end of the second year, 'Food bad' and at the end of the third year his two words were, 'I quit'.

'I'm not surprised,' said the abbot, 'you've done nothing but whinge ever since you came here.'

Two missionaries in the depths of the New Guinea highlands are working hard to convert the local tribe to Christianity. One Sunday, the chief organises a big feast to which the missionaries are invited. As soon as they arrive, they are stripped and bundled into a large cooking pot, already bubbling with vegetables and fragrant herbs. The chief smiles in anticipation. Suddenly, one of his sons rushes forward and spears one of the missionaries.

'Why did you do that?' frowns the chief.

'He was eating all the potatoes.'

When the Queen has a baby, a 21-gun salute is fired.

When a nun has a baby, they fire the dirty old canon.

A nun is in the shower when there's a loud banging at the convent door. All the other nuns are out the back, in the garden.

'Who is it?' she calls out.

'I'm the blind man from the village,' is the reply.

So she runs downstairs in the nude and opens the door.

'Great knockers,' says the visitor. 'Where do you want the blinds?'

Each week the Mother Superior at the convent had a novice drive into town in the Ford to do the shopping. And each week the girl, on her return, would complain that she'd been stopped by police. 'I really don't want to go into town any more,' she implored the Mother Superior. 'Can't you get somebody else to do the shopping?'

'This is really very strange,' said the Mother Superior. 'Are you driving too fast? Are you going through red lights?'

'No, no,' said the novice. 'But no matter how carefully I drive they stop me.'

The Mother Superior decided to accompany the novice on the next trip, to see what was going wrong. She did her best to keep out of sight in the back seat. The novice was driving very, very carefully towards the shopping centre, but lo and behold there was the familiar flashing of blue lights and the sound of sirens. The police car stopped in front of the convent's Ford, and a couple of cops got out. As they walked towards the novice they began unzipping themselves.

'You see, Mother,' said the young girl, 'it's the same every week. Here goes with the bloody breathaliser.'

An old man decided to write a letter to God:

Dear God,

I am nearing the end of my life. The doctors tell me I am dying of cancer and have only a few months to live. In fact, as You know, throughout my entire life I've had nothing but bad luck. But no matter what You have inflicted on me, I have never lost my faith in You.

In return for this loyalty I ask just one thing of You. Please prove Your existence to me by sending $100 in cash, and I will die a happy man.

Yours insignificantly,

An Old Man.

The letter arrived at the local post office where the employees noticed it was addressed To God: Heaven. They all knew the old man and, after reading the letter with tears in their eyes, took pity on him and had a whip around. Ninety dollars was raised and posted to him. The old man was overjoyed and immediately wrote a 'thank you' letter to God. The post office employees received the letter and all gathered around to read it.

Dear God,

I thank You with all my heart for taking time from Your busy schedule and answering my request . . . I am now a happy man.

Yours (in the very near future),

An Old Man.

P.S. I only received $90 of the $100 I asked for. I bet those thieving bastards down at the post office pinched the rest.

When their credibility was at a low ebb, Jimmy and Tammy Bakker decided that a revelation of some sort, a miracle perhaps, was needed to restore their flagging ratings. Somehow, Jimmy managed to contact Jesus. He explained their predicament and asked for divine help.

'Tell you what,' suggested Jesus, 'gather all the faithful and the doubters to the shores of Lake Superior and I'll do my walking-on-water routine. It slayed 'em at Galilee.'

'Fantastic idea,' agreed Jimmy, and sped off to make the arrangements.

On the appointed day a huge crowd – everyone is interested in a second coming – gathered at the lake. Mr Whippy vans and hot dog stands were all over the show. Then, to a deafening cheer, Jesus appeared in pristine white robes. A breathless hush fell over the throng as with theatrical deliberation, arms raised, He stepped slowly onto the lake and walked into the sunset. As the sun sank slowly in the west, Jesus sank slowly into the lake, step by step. Immediately there were enraged cries of 'Fraud!', 'Cheating bastards' and 'Give us our money back.' When the pandemonium subsided, Jimmy was not unnaturally aggrieved. 'Jesus,' he said with some emphasis, 'you've ruined me. I'll never live this down. What the hell happened?'

Jesus was as puzzled as He was wet. 'I can't understand it,' He lamented. 'It went great before.'

Suddenly, the penny dropped. 'Of course!' He cried. 'How could I be so stupid? When I first did this trick I didn't have holes in my feet!'

During a visit to Australia, the Seven Dwarves attended Sunday Mass in Melbourne. They were seated together in one pew, with Grumpy on the aisle. As the service proceeded, the dwarves were talking together, when the dwarf on the seat farthest from the aisle nudged his neighbour with his elbow and whispered in his ear. The message went along to Grumpy, who got up and walked down the aisle to the Mother Superior of the local religious order.

'Mother Superior,' Grumpy asked, 'are there any dwarf nuns in Melbourne?'

'No, Grumpy,' the Mother Superior replied, 'there are no dwarf nuns in Melbourne.'

Grumpy thanked the Mother Superior and returned to his pew, whispering the reply on his return to the dwarf next to him, who passed it onto his neighbour, and so on. When the message reached the end of the pew, the dwarf there thought for a moment and whispered a message to his neighbour, who passed it on, and down the line it went to Grumpy, who got up and walked to the Mother Superior again.

'Mother Superior, excuse me, but are there any dwarf nuns in Victoria?'

'No, Grumpy,' the Mother Superior replied, 'there are no dwarf nuns in Victoria.'

Back in his seat, Grumpy whispered the reply to his neighbour, it travelled along the row, then back came another message, and Grumpy returned to the Mother Superior.

'I'm very sorry to disturb you,' he said, 'but could you please tell me if there are any dwarf nuns in Australia?'

A little peeved by now, the Mother Superior turned to her questioner. 'Grumpy,' she said, 'there are no dwarf nuns in Melbourne, Victoria, Australia, or anywhere else in the world.' Grumpy walked slowly back to the Seven Dwarves' pew, took his seat and passed on the message to his neighbour, as before. It travelled along the row, and there was a brief silence. Then all six of his companions broke into a shrill chorus: 'Grumpy fucked a penguin, Grumpy fucked a penguin . . .'

The scene is Tibet, a few years before the Chinese takeover. A devout young Buddhist wants to be a monk and applies to the leading monastery. He's granted an interview by an ancient lama who says they're willing to give him a try. However, he must try and observe the highest standards of chastity. 'But we understand that, in the beginning, it's very, very difficult. Whatever you do, do not climb over the wall and go down into the town and have anything to do with loose women. We've been in this business a very, very, long time and we make alternative arrangements for the novices. If you must have sex, simply use the yak provided. But if you do, remember to take him a present.'

After a few weeks, the young man feels overwhelming sexual urges but finds the thought of the yak unappetising. So he climbs over the wall and goes into the town. On his return, he is hauled up before the lama. 'This must not happen again! If you feel sexual desire, use the yak. But remember to take it a present.'

A few weeks pass and, once again, the young man is overwhelmed by lust. Once again he ignores the availability of the yak, climbs over the wall and has truck with a lady of easy virtue in the brothel below the monastery. Yet again he is carpeted by the old lama. 'You have had your last warning, my son. Should you disobey me on another occasion, you will be shown the door. And this will have very serious implications for future reincarnation.'

So the very next night the young man feels a quickening of desire and decides to try the yak. He joins the end of a longish queue of novices and monks, each of whom is carrying a beautifully wrapped gift. Finally it is his turn to mount the yak. The yak looks at him and says, 'Where's my present?'

'I didn't bring one,' stammered the young man.

'Typical, typical,' snarled the yak. 'Another case of "fuck you, yak, I'm all right!"'

Every morning the monks filed silently into the great hall. The abbot stood at the front of the hall, watching over them. When the monks were all present, the abbot chanted, 'Good morning,' and the monks reverently replied in unison, 'Good morning.' Prayers then commenced. This went on day after day, year in, year out. A rather spirited monk, small in stature but with a mischievous glint in his eye, decided a change was necessary. One morning, when everything appeared to be following its time-honoured pattern, the abbot chanted, 'Good morning,' and the reply of 'Good morning' was given by all the monks except the mischievous one who said 'Good evening'. The abbot immediately responded tunefully, showing an unexpected familiarity with South Pacific, 'Someone chanted evening.'

A small weatherboard church in North Queensland needed repainting. Tenders were called and naturally the lowest was accepted. The two blokes whose tender was successful realised that they'd under-estimated the cost of the job. But as they were using a water-based paint they managed to cover the church by thinning it down.

'Once it's dry,' they said, 'the congregation will never know the difference!'

When it was completed they stepped back to admire their work, just as a sharp tropical downpour started, leaving a streaky mess on the woodwork.

'Oh, God!' they yelled, 'what are we gonna do now?'

There was a flash of lightning and a voice from the clouds thundered: 'REPAINT! YOU THINNERS!'

Two clergymen, of different racial backgrounds, were arguing whether God was black or white. The argument was getting quite heated when some of their parishioners suggested they hold a combined prayer meeting and ask God in the form of a supplication. 'Tell us, oh God, if your holy presence could be considered black or white!'

There was a pause and then a great voice from the sky filled the church, 'I AM WHAT I AM!'

'Told you so,' said the white preacher.

'What do you mean? How do you get that out of what he said?'

'Well, if he were black he'd have said "I is what I is!"'

A MEDICAL CONDITION

An old bloke, over 90, was brought into Alice Springs for a medical. It was a regular, yearly trip, made by his daughter and her husband from their cattle property about 100 kilometres out of Alice, and the old bloke was getting a bit forgetful. Their regular doctor got him to strip and they went through all the tests. Tap tap, cough, take a deep breath, stick your tongue out, all the usual stuff. The old bloke was all sunburned on his face and hands but the rest of him was blueish white, semi-transparent. You could have held him up to the window if you'd wanted to check the state of his organs.

'Well, Mr Quinn,' said the doctor, 'you are in remarkable physical condition for a man of your age. There's just one more test. But you probably remember the routine from last time.'

The old man said, with a shaky voice, 'how do you mean "routine"?'

'Well, you'll remember that we went through all these tests last year.'

'I've never seen you before in my life,' was his quivering response.

'I assure you you have. But no matter.' The doctor pointed to a shelf containing an array of different shaped beakers and said, 'It just remains for you to fill one of those bottles with a sample of your urine.'

'What?' says the old fella, pointing with a shaking hand across the room. 'From *here*?'

An old man was sitting on the curb outside the pub, sobbing helplessly. A cop asked him what was wrong. 'I'm 75 years old,' he cried, 'and I've got a 25-year-old wife at home who's beautiful, randy, and madly in love with me.'

'So what's the problem?' asked the cop.

'I can't remember my address.'

A doctor had the unenviable task of informing a patient that he had only a few minutes to live. The patient said, 'Isn't there anything you can do for me?'

To which the doctor replied, 'Well, I could boil you an egg.'

A young artist had just had his first exhibition at the Roslyn Oxley Galleries and asked if anyone had shown any interest in his canvasses, vividly expressive of inner torment. 'Well, I've got good news and bad news,' said Ms Oxley. 'The good news is that someone has enquired about your paintings, wondering how much they'd appreciate in value if you died. And he bought all of them.'

'And the bad news?'

'He's your doctor.'

A mother took her 16-year-old to see the doctor because his penis was still the same size as a 10-year-old's. The doctor prescribed plenty of hot buttered toast for breakfast as an aid to normal growth. At breakfast the next morning, the boy was confronted with a huge mound of hot buttered toast. But as he reached for it, his mother slapped his hand away. 'Leave your father's breakfast alone.'

A doctor ended an examination of a pregnant woman and asked, 'Do you smoke after intercourse?'

'Dunno,' she said, 'never looked.'

A young woman is fearful of having a baby because her husband is such an over-achiever on the John Singleton criteria of Australian masculinity, with particular reference to his obsessions with booze and football. So oafish is his behaviour that, when she finds herself great with child, she considers having an abortion. But a friend in Right to Life persuades her to have the child, suggesting that she stroke her tummy whenever possible whilst murmuring, 'Be polite, be polite.' Oddly, the baby never arrives and finally the woman dies at the grand old age of 90. When doctors perform an autopsy, they find two little old men sitting inside her saying, 'After you.' 'No, after you.'

An old miner came into town from the sticks to see a doctor and was greeted at the reception desk by a sweet young thing. She asked his name and address and enquired what it was that ailed him. The miner said, 'I've got a sore cock.' The SYT was shocked and rushed into the doctor to complain. When the miner was admitted, the doctor rebuked him. 'You mustn't use coarse language like that to my receptionist, she's not used to it. If you're asked what's wrong with you in circumstances like this, say that you've got a sore ear or something of that sort.'

Two weeks later the miner returned for further treatment and was again asked to hint at his ailment. The miner said, 'I've got a sore ear.' The SYT asked, 'What's the matter with it?'

'I can't piss out of it,' said the miner.

A bloke went to see his doctor. 'Doctor, I've got a problem. I've got a square dick.'

'Baloney,' said the doctor, 'never seen that in all my years. Whip it out, sport, and let me have a look.' The doctor turned it in between his thumb and forefinger like a piece of limp celery.

'Boy, it's square all right. How did you do that?'

'Putting a crate in the back of the one tonner and my mate dropped his side. Talk about hurt! So I took it to the workshop and tried to squeeze it back into shape in the vice. But the bastard ended up square!'

'Hmmm,' the doctor washed his hands in the basin in the corner of his surgery and started writing out a form on his clipboard.

'What are you doing, doc? Writing me out a script?' His voice was crippled with worry.

'No, I'm giving you three days off work to try and pull yourself round.'

An Australian businessman was in Hong Kong for a few weeks and, after each day's meeting, he'd sneak off to a brothel or a girlie bar. After a few days he began to worry about the appearance of his dick. It was a very strange colour. So he went to an English doctor who specialised in expatriate business executives. 'Oh dear, oh dear,' said the doctor, 'how very sad. That's a classic case of Hong Kong Dong. I'm afraid there's no alternative but to amputate.'

The businessman was appalled and insisted on a second opinion. So he went to a Chinese doctor who specialised in acupuncture and herbal medicine. 'What do you think, doc?' said the terrified Australian. 'The other two doctors I went to see say it's Hong Kong Dong and I'll have to have it amputated.' The Chinese doctor gave him a beatific smile and shook his head. 'Not to worry. Not necessally.'

'You mean you don't have to amputate?'

'No, with Hong Kong Dong it will drop off on its own in just a few days time.'

A bloke went to the doctor to get his sick note signed. The doctor reached into his breast pocket and pulled out a rectal thermometer. 'Damn!' he exclaimed, 'some bum's walked off with my pen again.'

A famous movie star was having a medical by a noted gynaecologist. As he poked and prodded he muttered, 'Ever had a check up there?'

And she replied, 'No dollink, only a Pole and a few Hungarians.'

Two Indian doctors were standing beside the sister's station in a British hospital. One said to the other, 'I don't know whether it's spelt WHOMB or WHOOMB.' The sister stood up and said, 'I couldn't help overhearing you doctor, but it's spelt WOMB.'

'Young woman,' said the doctor, 'I don't think you've ever seen a water buffalo, let alone heard it pass wind under water.'

Did you hear about the girl who swallowed a razor blade? It not only gave her a tonsillectomy, an appendectomy and a hysterectomy, it circumcised her husband, gave the Bishop a hare lip, took two fingers off the hand of a casual acquaintance – and it still had five good shaves left in it.

A Telecom linesman somewhere way out in the outback of Queensland was given a long-haired 'hippy' youth as his assistant. While the linesman was up a pole doing what linesman do, the assistant lay in the long grass at the base of the pole. Suddenly, the assistant screamed out, 'I've been bitten by a snake.'

The linesman quickly connected a portable telephone to a pair of lines and dialled the nearest hospital and reported the incident. After a bit of three-way conversation to establish the identity of the snake, the doctor at the hospital gave detailed instructions on the necessary treatment. 'Put a tourniquet around the limb on the side nearer the heart, make two cuts with a razor blade through the bite marks and suck out the poison.' When he had finished, the linesman asked, 'What will happen if I don't do all that?'

'He'll be dead in half an hour,' replied the doctor.

'What did he say?' asked the assistant.

'You're going to die,' replied the linesman.

A doctor, who had his rooms on the top floor of a Manhattan skyscraper, used to drop into the cocktail lounge on the ground floor on his way home at exactly 5 p.m. every afternoon. Richard, the bar attendant, would always have his favourite drink, an almond daiquiri, which is an ordinary daiquiri with almond nuts sprinkled on top, waiting for him. One afternoon Richard was preparing the doctor's drink and found he was out of almond nuts and so substituted hickory nuts. The doctor arrived, sipped his drink and said, 'Is this an almond daiquiri, Dick?'

Richard replied, 'No, it's a hickory daiquiri, Doc.'

During a divorce case in Adelaide, many years ago, the woman complainant, who was not represented by legal counsel, told the judge that she knew her husband had committed adultery.

'How do you know?' the judge asked.

The woman replied that her husband had contracted Venetian disease.

The judge queried, 'And what is Venetian disease, may I ask?'

The woman looked flustered, but counsel for the defendant stood up and said, 'I think she means a case of gondoliers, Your Honour.'

A doctor made a house call to a dilapidated building on the outskirts of the city to visit a Mrs Jones. There seemed to be a horde of children of all ages and colours and he asked Mrs Jones if they were all hers.

'Yes,' she said.

'Why didn't you go on the pill?' asked the doctor.

'I couldn't afford the pill, all I had was Smarties.'

A patient visited a doctor and said, 'I've been graped.'

'You mean you've been raped,' said the doctor.

'No,' said the woman, 'there were six of them.'

Three surgeons were discussing operations.

First surgeon: 'I like operating on Germans, they are superbly built inside, all pipes are vertical and muscles diagonal, and thus very easy to put together again after cutting.'

Second surgeon: 'I like operating on the Japanese, they are transistorised inside, all their pipes are coloured – so easy to join afterwards. Red to Red, Green to Green, and Blue to Blue.'

Third surgeon: 'I like operating on politicians because they only have two moving parts – their mouth and their arse, and those parts are interchangeable.'

'You've been diagnosed as having syphilis and two highly infectious Asian skin complaints,' said the doctor. 'You'll receive special treatment and a diet of pizza and pancakes.'

'Thanks for the special treatment,' said the patient, 'but why the pizza and pancakes?'

'They're the only foods that can be shoved under the door.'

A young man visits his local doctor and says, 'I don't know what's wrong with me, doctor, but I can't concentrate and life isn't fun anymore.'

'Do you drink?' asks the doctor.

'No,' replies the young man.

'Look,' says the doctor, 'have a couple of wines or whatever you like each evening before your meal. That'll make you feel more relaxed. Do you smoke?'

'No,' says the patient.

'It won't hurt you in small amounts. Have a couple of fags with your drinks – it helps to calm people. Do you have any contact with young ladies – you know, do you ever go to bed with one?'

'Very seldom, doctor.'

'Well, try a little harder. I can assure you that intercourse a couple of times or more a week is good for young men. Try these things and see me in a fortnight.'

The fortnight passes and the patient returns to the doctor's consulting rooms.

'How are you?' asks the doctor.

'A lot better, thank you, doctor.'

The doctor asks if he is having a few drinks each night.

'Yes, doctor, I now have a nice cellar of good wines. It's doing me good,' replies the patient.

'And what about cigarettes?'

'Well, yes, I smoke a pipe now and it is most relaxing.'

Then the doctor says, 'I don't want to be too personal, but what about sex?'

'Well, doctor, I can't arrange it more than twice a week – you know, it's a bit difficult when one is the parish priest in a small country town!'

An 85-year-old has had a triple bypass. He comes back to the doctor saying that his wife is afraid of having sexual intercourse, for fear that it might do him in. The doctor reassures the old chap that he's in fine fettle, that sex cannot possibly hurt him. Delighted, the patient asks the doctor to put it in writing. The doctor happily agrees and scribbles furiously for a few moments. He's then asked to read it aloud.

'Dear Mrs Smith, your husband is in remarkable physical condition. He now has a heart as strong as an Olympic athlete. I wouldn't be at all surprised if he couldn't make love three or four times in a single evening. Yours sincerely . . .'

The old man is delighted, but he asks for a slight amendment.

'Could you please cross out Mrs Smith and make it To Whom It May Concern?'

The gynaecologist completed his examination. 'I'm sorry, miss, but the removal of that vibrator is going to involve a very delicate operation.'

'I'm not sure I can afford it, doc,' sighed the girl. 'Why don't you just replace the batteries?'

A man went to a doctor to have his eyes tested.

'Put your left hand over your right eye and read the top line of the chart,' said the doctor. The man put his right hand over his left eye.

'No, put your LEFT hand over your RIGHT eye and just read the top line of the chart,' said the doctor. The man put his left hand over his left eye.

'No,' said the doctor, 'put your LEFT HAND over your RIGHT EYE and just read the letters on the top line of the bloody chart.' The man put his right hand over his right eye.

'Oh, for Chrissake,' said the doctor and he grabbed a cardboard box, cut a small hole where the man's left eye would be and fitted the box over the man's head.

'Now read me the top line of that chart,' he said.

There was a muffled soft sobbing sound coming from inside the cardboard box.

'Oh, my God,' said the doctor, 'what's wrong now?'

'Well, what I really wanted,' said the man, 'was a pair of those little *round* glasses like John Lennon.'

Two psychiatrists, Dick and Harry, meet twenty years after graduation. Dick says he feels burned out and depressed and is thinking of early retirement.

Harry: 'Let's see. I've got three questions which I try out on my patients to see what shape they're in. Why don't I run them past you, and see how bad it really is.'

Dick: 'All right.'

Harry: 'First, what does a man do standing up, a woman do sitting down, and a dog on three legs?'

Dick: 'That's easy . . . shake hands.'

Harry: 'Right. Second question. What does a dog do in your backyard which, when you step in it, causes you to utter an expletive?'

Dick: 'That's obvious . . . digs a hole.'

Harry: 'That's right too. Finally, where do women have the curliest hair?'

Dick: 'I know. In Fiji.'

Harry: 'Right. Look, there's nothing whatever wrong with you. But you should hear the bizarre answers I get from some of my patients.'

A psychiatrist was concerned that too many of his professional clients seemed incapable of making a decision. To demonstrate this inability he devised a simple experiment. His first patient was a civil engineer. When asked what 2 plus 2 made, the engineer fumbled in his pocket, operated the slide rule and, after some manipulation, looked up in a puzzled way and said, '3.98. No, that doesn't seem right, I'll try again.' Becoming more and more agitated, he thought it might be 4.01.

The next client was a physician of some distinction, and he was posed the same question. What he said was, 'I think it's probably 4, but it could possibly be something else. Perhaps we'd better refer the matter to a specialist.' The lawyer client, who was next, thought that in general it would be considered 4, but that they should have counsel's opinion.

The psychiatrist's last patient was an accountant who, when asked the question 'What does 2 and 2 make?' looked him straight in the eye and said, 'What do you want it to make?'

There are two shrinks, one young and one old, with offices across the hall from each other. Every morning they meet in the lift, both looking pretty good. At the end of the day, when they meet leaving the building, the young shrink looks whacked whilst the older bloke looks on top of the world. One day the young shrink couldn't stand it any longer and said to the old shrink, 'I give up. How do you put up with it? I hear these terrible yarns from my patients all day and just get depressed. What's your secret?'

The old shrink looked at the young shrink and simply said, 'I never listen.'

A gentleman developed a most unfortunate habit. Each Sunday he couldn't resist taking a coin out of the collection plate when it came around. Naturally the parson remonstrated with him and he replied that he found the urge irresistible. 'It worries me, but no matter how much I try I cannot resist taking the money out. It really has me worried.' The parson suggested some psychiatric advice to which the gentleman agreed, also agreeing to stay away from church until he was cured. Six months later, the parson was pleased to see him back in the congregation. But when the time came for the collection, the parson watched in horror as the man, smiling happily, took a handful of coins from the plate. 'I thought you weren't coming back until you were cured,' he said.

'That's right,' said the man, 'I am cured – it doesn't worry me at all now.'

Two psychiatrists pass in a corridor. 'Good morning,' said the first. The second walked on wondering, 'I wonder what he meant by that?'

Neurotics build castles in the air.
Psychotics live in them.
Psychiatrists collect the rent.

The psychiatrist spoke in calm, reassuring tones to his worried looking patient. 'What we're going to do now is . . . I'll draw something on this piece of paper, and I want you to tell me what it means to you. Okay?' Taking his pen, the psychiatrist drew a single, short line on the paper. 'What is that?' he asked.

'That's a clergyman masturbating,' replied the patient, after several seconds.

'All right, now what's this?' said the shrink as he drew two short parallel lines on the paper.

'Those are two lesbian nuns having sex.'

'Well,' said the psychiatrist, as he drew three short parallel lines on the paper. 'What do you see now?'

'Filthy bastards!' exclaimed the patient, staring at the last drawing. 'That's two priests with a nun between them, and they're both having sex with her.'

Looking directly at his patient, the psychiatrist slowly replaced his pen on the desk. 'It's a good thing that you've come to see me. You are badly in need of treatment.'

'I'm in need of treatment?' shouted his patient. 'That's a bloody beauty! You're the one who's going around drawing filthy pictures!'

A psychiatrist was visiting a mental institution and whilst on his rounds noticed one of the inmates stabbing a large watermelon viciously with a knife. He asked him what he was up to. The patient replied that when he left the institution he was going to become a butcher and so was practising on the watermelon. The psychiatrist said this was excellent therapy and encouraged him to continue.

The next patient was making mud pies and explained he was going to be a baker when he got out. Once more, the psychiatrist was pleased and encouraged him to continue 'the good work'. When he got to the next patient, he was surprised to see that he had his prick jammed into a packet of biscuits.

'What are you doing?' he asked.

'Well, I'm never going to get out of here because I'm fucking crackers.'

Why is psychoanalysis a lot quicker for a man than for a woman?

When it's time to go back to his childhood he's already there.

What's a specimen?

An Italian astronaut.

A patient recently came into a psychiatrist's office and told him he had a major problem. When the doctor asked him what the problem was, the man said, 'Well, some mornings I wake up and think I'm a teepee. Other mornings I wake up and think I'm a wigwam.' The psychiatrist responded immediately, 'I know exactly what your problem is.'

'Well, doc, what is it?'

'You're too tense.'

Why don't pygmies use tampons?

They'd trip over the string.

During the war there was a reluctant hero who wanted to fail his medical. He limped in and stated that one leg was shorter than the other. He was passed A1. 'What do you mean, A1? One leg is shorter than the other!'

'That's all right,' said the medical officer, 'where you're going the ground's uneven.'

The sergeant asked a new recruit for his name, to which he replied 'Mack.' The sergeant said, 'I must have the full name.' The recruit replied, 'That is my name.' The sergeant then pointed out that everyone had a Christian name and a surname. To which the recruit replied, 'I was christened John Thomas McDangle originally, but I'm now known simply as Mack.' The sergeant was curious.

'Well, I left school at 16 and, because I was extremely bright, was admitted to medical school. I qualified before I was 21, thus becoming John Thomas McDangle, MD. But I was considered too young to practise medicine, and so decided to do further study. I chose theology. On completion of these studies I became John Thomas McDangle, MD, DD. Then, unfortunately, I got into trouble with a lady of ill repute and got VD. So the medical board removed my MD, the church removed my DD, the VD removed my John Thomas – nothing left to dangle, so just call me Mack.'

GOING, GOING, GONE

Three octogenarians were discussing the plight of the aged. One said, 'I think the worst thing is to lose your hearing. I'm passionately fond of music, but I'm so deaf I can hardly hear a note any more.'

The second said, 'I think it's dreadful to lose your sight. I'm passionately fond of art, but I'm so blind that I can no longer see the paintings in the gallery.'

The third said, 'That's nothing compared to my affliction. On my 80th birthday I married a beautiful young wife of 24. Every morning I wake up and there she is lying beside me. I say to her, "Kylie, let's make love" and she says, "But my darling, we just made love ten minutes ago, before you dropped off again". The worst thing that can happen is to lose your memory.'

A young reporter was interviewing Maggie Mulligan, a spinster lady who had just reached her 100th birthday. 'To what do you attribute your extremely good health?' he asked her.

'Well,' she said thoughtfully, 'I have always eaten moderately and worked hard. I don't drink or smoke, and I keep good hours.'

'Have you ever been bedridden?' he asked.

'Of course,' replied the old lady, 'but don't put that in the paper.'

Kicking and struggling all the way, Dad is carted off to what Dame Edna describes as a 'high security twilight home'. But on his first morning, things take a decided turn for the better. He wakes up to discover that, for the first time in years, he's got a great, thumping erection. On hearing the nurse approach, he covers his proud secret with the sheet. But she's too experienced not to notice and, whipping back the sheet, smiles approvingly.

'Now, isn't that marvellous! And what a pity if it was wasted.' Whereupon she gives the old chap a 'polish'.

'Now, off you go and have a shower,' she says brightly, as she sets off to see the next resident.

The old bloke is in a dormitory block with a shared bathroom and joins several other old codgers for his ablutions. And he's still feeling very, very pleased with himself when he drops the soap and is immediately sodomised by another octogenarian with an erection. That afternoon his son comes to see how Dad's settling in and he describes both sexual encounters, the pleasant surprise and the unwelcome incident. The son says, 'This proves this place is wonderful for the libido.'

'Yes,' says the old codger. 'But I only get an erection once every six months and I'm always falling over.'

An old couple go to the doctor for the husband to have a check up. After a preliminary check the doctor says he wants to do some more tests. He asks for a specimen of urine, a specimen of semen, a blood sample and a faeces sample. The old man, who is hard of hearing, asks his wife, 'What did he say?' She replies, 'He wants to see your underpants!'

Three senior citizens were sitting around talking about their memories. The first said, 'I really have problems. I find myself standing in front of the refrigerator. I don't know whether I just put something in or if I came to get something out.'

The second said, 'I find myself at the foot of the stairs. I don't know if I just came down or if I want to go upstairs.'

The third said, 'I will have to knock on wood

because I do not have these problems.' He gave the table top a vigorous rap. A few seconds later he said, 'Will someone go and see who is at the door?'

There's a new condom on the market. It's designed for men over 60 years old. It's called softwear.

Bill and Daphne have been residents at the Twilight Rest nursing home for some years, during which time they have come to an 'arrangement'. They watch the news and several of their favourite programs together in a discreet corner of the television room each evening. And Daphne gives Bill a 'polish' at the same time.

One evening Daphne comes to join Bill and finds her seat on the couch occupied by another woman. 'Bill, how could you!' she cries. 'You hardly know Bernice, and she's *older* than me! Must be 90 if she's a day!'

Bill smiles, and says sheepishly, 'Yes, but she's got Parkinson's.'

What's grey and hangs out your underpants?
Your grandma.

An old bloke was dying and his four sons, three of whom were priests, and the youngest, Joe, a 'no-hoper' from the bush, were gathered around the bed. In a weak voice the old man said, 'I have a confession to make. Your mother and I were never married.' He then expired. There was a shocked silence eventually broken by Joe, who said, 'Well, I don't know about you three bastards, but I'm going up to the pub for a schooner.'

A young sailor was sitting at The Gap, Sydney's well-known suicide spot. He was telling himself to end it all when a voice said, 'Don't throw yourself off the Gap. I'm a good fairy and I can grant you any three wishes you want.'

Looking around he saw an old crone behind a rock. 'Oh yeah,' said the sailor, 'and what do I have to do to earn these three wishes? Nothing's for nothing in this cruel world.'

'All you have to do is make love to me,' said the crone.

The sailor did this and shortly afterwards, while the old crone brushed her hair, he asked, 'When do I get my three wishes?'

She replied with another question, 'How old are you, sonny?'

'I'm 29,' he said, 'why do you ask?'

And she said, 'Aren't you a bit old to believe in fairies?'

A woman is reading the *Age* on a Melbourne train. She is so astonished by a story on life expectancy that she turns to the stranger beside her and says, 'Do you know that every time I breathe, somebody dies?'

'Fascinating,' he answered, 'ever tried mouthwash?'

How do you tell when a Double Bay woman's husband has just died?

She's the one wearing the black tennis skirt.

Two blokes were talking on the footpath of a small country town, when a funeral cortège went past.

'Who died?' said Bill.

Tom replied, 'The bloke in the back, lying down.'

Two old blokes used to go into the pub every pension day. One day only one came. The publican opened the conversation.

'G'day Bob, how yer goin'? Where's Fred?'

'He got burned last week.'

'Sorry to hear about that. Still, I suppose he'll be back on deck soon.'

'Nah, I don't think so. They don't muck around in them crematoriums.'

When a man died his wife put the usual death notice in the paper, but added that he died of gonorrhoea. No sooner were the papers delivered than a good friend of the family phoned and complained bitterly, 'You know very well that he died of diarrhoea, not gonorrhoea.'

Replied the widow, 'I nursed him night and day so of course I knew he died of diarrhoea. But I thought it would be better for posterity to remember him as a great lover rather than the big shit he always was.'

In Heaven, the police are English, the chefs are French, the industrialists are German, the managers are Swiss, and the lovers are Italian.

In Hell, the chefs are English, the police are

German, the managers are French, the industrialists are Italian and the lovers are Swiss.

A Frenchman, an Englishman and a German all knocked at the same time at the Heavenly Gates. Before admitting them, St Peter asked them to fill out an admission application. The first question asked, 'Have you been unfaithful?' The Frenchman had been unfaithful sixty times. St Peter had a hard look at him and said, 'Well, I suppose we can let you in under these circumstances. But all you'll be able to drive is a battered Volkswagen.'

The Englishman had only cheated twenty times and was given a Peugeot, whilst the German, who had remained completely faithful to his wife, who had never harboured any lustful thoughts, was rewarded with a Rolls Royce.

A few weeks later the three happened to pull up at the same time at a celestial intersection. Both the Frenchman and the Englishman were as happy as larks, but the German had obviously been crying.

When they askd him what was wrong he replied, 'Well, my wife passed me three days ago – and she was on roller skates.'

Lord Olivier arrived in Heaven. 'Who are you?' asked St Peter. 'I'm Laurence Olivier, the world's greatest actor, poet and playwright,' came the reply.

'Well,' said St Peter, 'let's look at the Great Register.' He opened the book and started thumbing through, 'Olivier ... Fred, Olivier ... Jim, Olivier ... Laurence ... Yes! Here we are! Well, your instructions are to follow that pathway over there until you come to a vine-covered English cottage in which you'll find Lord Byron and William Shakespeare.'

'Right,' said Lord Olivier, and set off. Pretty soon he found the cottage and knocked on the door.

'Come in,' said a voice, 'and identify yourself.' Lord Olivier entered. 'I'm Laurence Olivier, the world's greatest actor, poet and playwright.'

'Aha,' replied Byron, 'I'd heard about the actor and playwright bit – but the world's greatest poet! Indeed, Shakespeare and I would contest that point.'

'Indeed we would,' agreed Shakespeare. 'So why not a small rhyming competition to settle the argument once and for all?'

'I agree,' said Olivier.

'Me too,' said Byron, 'but what shall we rhyme about?'

'How about a bow-legged man standing by a river?' suggested Shakespeare.

'Okay with me,' said Olivier, 'I'll go first.

'Down where the mighty river flowed
There stood a man whose legs were bowed.'

'Very good,' said Byron, 'but methinks far too simple. Try this!

'Where the river to the sea comes out
Stands there a man with legs about.'

'Excellent, Byron,' said Shakespeare, 'but I'm sure I can do better than both those . . . listen!

'Sooth, what manner of man is this
Whose balls hang in parenthesis?'

Just then Banjo Paterson happened to be walking past their window. He stuck his head in and said,

'Well! I've copped some lurks and seen some rackets.
But a bastard, with his balls in brackets?'

A Pope and a lawyer arrived at St Peter's Gate at exactly the same time. The Pope was assigned a modest condo in a gloomy courtyard, whilst the lawyer was given a gleaming mansion overlooking a splendid golf course. 'How can this be?' the lawyer asked St Peter. 'The Father of Christendom gets only a lousy condo and I've been given this joint!'

To which St Peter replied, 'Well, we've thirty-nine Popes here, but you're the first lawyer!'

A young, bedraggled nymphet wandered around the slopes of Mt Olympus at dawn, after an all-night orgy. She was confronted by the imposing, obviously still excited figure of Thor. 'Good morning, my little beauty,' said the deity. 'I'm Thor.'

To which the nymphet replied, 'You're Thor! I'm tho thor I can't even pith!'

St Peter was talking to the Virgin Mary. 'And what's it like being mother of the world's most talked-about prophet?' The Virgin replied, 'Well, actually we were hoping he'd become a doctor.'

There was a carload of nuns (you know the way they always pack about twenty into a Camira) tearing along the highway when they came barrelling around a corner, hit a Mack truck and ended up at the Pearly Gates. 'You can't come in, girls, unless you're pure. We just happen to have a big bowl of holy water here, in case any part of you happens to be impure,' said St Peter, rubbing his hands together.

The first nun bowled up, washed her hands. 'Come on in sister, you're pure.'

The next nun stepped up, stripped off, started splashing under her armpits, across her bosoms and between her legs. 'Gawd, I hope she doesn't pee in there,' said the next nun in line, 'I've got to gargle that!'

St Peter was taking his weekly walk around Heaven checking that all the inmates were happy and contented. He came upon a group of little mice. 'Hello little mice,' said St Peter, 'are you happy here in Heaven?'

'Oh yes, St Peter, we love Heaven. The weather is just lovely, the flowers are beautiful and the sound of the angels singing is wonderful. We just love the sound of the angels singing.'

St Peter said, 'That's just great, little mice. If there's anything I can do to make it even better for you, just let me know.'

'Well,' said the little mice, thinking hard, 'there is something you can do for us. Heaven has such long corridors and we have such little legs that sometimes we get tired walking around. Could we have roller skates?'

'Certainly you can have roller skates,' said St Peter, 'as good as done.'

Next week St Peter was taking his weekly walk around Heaven checking on the inmates and he came upon the cats. 'Hello cats,' said Peter, 'are you happy here in Heaven?'

'Oh yes, St Peter, we love Heaven. The weather is just lovely, the flowers are beautiful and the sound of the angels singing is wonderful. We just love the sound of the angels singing.'

St Peter said, 'That's great, cats. If there's anything I can do to make Heaven even better for you, just let me know.'

'Well, St Peter, we don't think there is anything more you can do for us. Since last week, when you introduced Meals-on-Wheels, life has been just about perfect.'

An old man knocked at the gates of Heaven. 'Yes,' said an angel with a clipboard, 'What can we do for you?'

'I'm looking for my son,' said the old man, 'I'm a carpenter, and it has been a long time since my son and I worked together side by side in my workshop. I was told that I would find him here. They say he has a very important position.'

'Well,' replied the angel, consulting his clipboard, 'we have a few carpenters' sons here, and one or two are rather high up. Does your son have any distinguishing features?' The old man thought for a while. 'Only the holes in his hands,' he eventually whispered.

At that the angel smiled. 'Now I know who you mean. Come with me. We'll find him in the administration area, but I must warn you that he is very busy, and he may simply not remember you. After all,' he said checking his clipboard again, 'you weren't his *real* father, were you?'

The old man sadly shook his head, and they moved on. But as they neared the central high area, a cry went up from one of the great chairs, and a figure rushed towards them.

'Father!'

'Pinocchio!!'

A sailor in the Sydney to Hobart race was washed overboard. After days of being tossed around in the ocean he came to and found himself lying on a golden beach, fringed with palms. Standing over him was a beautiful young woman.

'Gawd, this must be Heaven,' he exclaimed, 'I never thought I'd make it.'

'No, it isn't,' said the girl, 'it's just an island off the trade routes. You must be hungry and thirsty after your ordeal. Let me get you something to eat. You can have anything you like.'

'Come on, this must be Heaven,' said the sailor, but the girl reassured him. 'All right,' he said unconvinced, 'I'll have a pepper steak, rare, with French fries and a side salad and a bottle of champagne.'

'Right,' said the girl, 'give me ten minutes.'

The sailor was still muttering 'this must be Heaven' when she returned with his meal on a silver tray. Hardly able to believe his luck, the sailor devoured his meal and lay back on the sand. The girl lay beside him and threw a leg across him.

'Now that you've eaten and rested, perhaps you'd like to play around with me,' she said.

'Now I know it must be Heaven,' he cried, sitting bolt upright. 'Don't tell me you've got a bloody golf course here as well!'

A new widow attended a séance and was pleased to make contact with her late husband.

'Are you happy, dear?' she whispered, tearfully.

'Very happy,' he replied.

A bit put out at this, she asked, 'What is it like in heaven, then?'

'I don't know, dear – I'm in a lovely field of green grass with a whole herd of beautiful little cows.'

'My poor darling, you must be lonely there without me,' wept the widow.

'Not really,' he answered. 'I'm the only bull here.'

An Australian, a Scotsman and an Aborigine were in a car crash and were all killed. When they arrived at the Pearly Gates, St Peter met them and said, 'Sorry boys, we are full up. You will have to go down below.'

The Australian started to argue saying it was too hot, and he whipped out a $20 note waving it under St Peter's nose and said, 'Will *this* get me in?' St Peter snatched it from his fingers and said, 'It won't get you in *here* but it will get you back where you came from.'

The Aussie agreed. With that he 'came to' and was surrounded by ambulance men. One said, 'Blimey mate, you are lucky. You were clinically dead for half an hour. You're a bloody miracle. What happened?' So the Australian told him how he had given St Peter $20 but still couldn't get into Heaven and had been sent back.

The ambulance man said, 'Well, that's okay for you, but what about these poor devils lying here. They're as dead as dodos.'

'Well,' said the Aussie, 'when I left them up there the Scotsman was trying to beat St Peter down to $5 and the Aborigine was trying to convince him the government would pay for him.'

A poodle in Darwin died and went to Heaven. At the pearly gates he was refused entry by St Peter. 'Why?' asked the dog.

'Because you haven't got a tail. You will have to go back to Earth and get your tail.'

The dog returned to his owner and told him of his plight. 'Well, I can't help you but if you go to the vet who now runs our local supermarket he might be able to help you.'

So the dog trotted down to the local supermarket and, sure enough, there was the vet behind the counter. The vet immediately recognised the dog and asked him what he could do for him. The dog told the vet of his problem. But the vet shook his head and said, 'I am sorry, Rex, but we don't re-tail spirits on Sundays in Darwin.'

And the Last Laugh . . .

It's during the Depression when, late one evening in a country town, an old swaggie knocks on a lonely door. He hears footsteps approaching and it opens, revealing a man with his collar back-to-front. The swaggie says, 'Oh, I'm terribly sorry to disturb you, Father.'

'I'm not a Father,' says the bloke, 'I'm a Church of England clergyman.'

'Whatever, I'll be on my way.'

'No, no. Come on, and tell me what I can do for you.'

Unused to religion, the swaggie's a bit shy. 'I don't want to come in. I'm going around seein' if I can get a meal in return for an odd job or two. I cut wood and stuff like that.'

The clergyman says, 'You are more than

welcome. Sadly, I've just finished cutting our wood. However, if you'd care to stack it at the back of the house I'd be most pleased. And, of course, I'd give you a meal in exchange.'

So the swaggie stacks the wood, washes his hands and stands on the verandah at the back of the house. The clergyman insists that he enters, sitting him down at the kitchen table.

There's not much conversation during the meal. At the end of dinner, the swaggie says, 'Thanks Father, I'll be on my way.'

'No, no relax. Be comfortable. You can sleep out on the verandah tonight if you like.'

'Thanks very much, but I've got to be getting along.'

'Well then, before you go, let me pour you a cup of tea.'

The swaggie pours some into his saucer, blows on the surface and drinks it down. Meanwhile the clergyman has opened his *Bible* and is having a good read.

The swaggie looks at him curiously and says, 'Must be a good book.'

The clergyman lifts his eyes and says, 'As a matter of fact, it's *the* good book.'

'Oh, yes. What's it about?'

'Surely you know what the *Bible* is about?'

'Well, I've *heard* of the *Bible*.'

'You've never read it?'

The swaggie's a bit embarrassed. 'Well, you see, I can't read.'

'That's nothing to be ashamed of, my man. That's why there are people like me involved in the church. We're able to read the word of God and pass it on to our less fortunate brethren.'

'Yeah, well what's it about?'

'Well, it's about quite a number of things. All sorts of stories. Stories of the flood, of our Saviour. This particular part that I'm reading now is about an extremely powerful man of God. A man called Samson who came from a little town called Jerusalem. And he had a woman called Delilah. And these particular verses describe him joining Delilah in the fields whilst she was grinding the corn. Suddenly they were descended upon by 5000 Philistines. Samson called on God, picked up the jaw bone of an ass, slew 3000 of them and completely routed the rest.'

The swaggie looks at the minister in astonishment. 'And would this be a true story?'

'Of course it's true. It's the word of God.'

'He must have been a pretty strong sort of bloke.'

'Oh, an extremely powerful man. As a matter of fact, he was capable of tearing down temples with his bare hands. Simply by pushing over the pillars.'

'Fair dinkum?'

'How could it be anything else. It is, as I've emphasised, the word of God.'

'Yeah, I see.'

The following evening, late, the swaggie's looking for somewhere to camp and sees, in the middle distance, the glow of a campfire. He wanders up. Tentatively, observing the protocol of the bush, trying not to come too close. Beside the campfire is an old rabbiter, brewing up a bunny stew in his 4-gallon kero tin. He sees the swaggie in the shadows and says, 'G'day. Come and get warm and help yourself to the stew.'

The swaggie hops into the bunny stew very appreciatively and the rabbiter says, 'What do you know?'

'Oh, nothing much. Oh, yeah, I did hear something. Terrible story. About this bloke called Simpson. Simpson from Jerilderie. A real bastard. He's going around ripping up the telephone poles. It turns out he was out in the paddock one day giving his girlfriend Delicious a grind in the corn, when all of a sudden 5000 Filipino bastards appeared. So he picks up the arse-bone of a cow, slays 3000 and completely roots the rest. Turned out to be a bit of a poofter.'

INDEX

Aborigine(s)
  and guesswork 68
  and the law 69
  life expectancy of 66
  tracking skills of 65–6
  and whitewash 66–7
actors
  IQ of 387–8
adultery
  in preference to alcohol 408
  rewards of 332
aeroplanes
  for the birds 398–9
airline
  discounts 124
alcohol
  worm-free 319
arm
  false 363
arseholes
  bottle-opening 330
  butchers' 308
  a matter of taste 311–12
art appreciation 431
ASIO
  cross dressers 368–9
astronaut(s) 286, 287, 288
  Italian 447
Australian male(s)
  identifying characteristics 346–8
babies
  and parental intellect 43
backpackers 401
bamboo
  as bum wiper 362
band
  unmusical 390
banking etiquette 288, 289
bar brawls
  domestic 325
  weapons for 102
barmaids
  and soliciting 43
bastards 157
  by birth 455
bedridden
  meaning of 452
beer
  quality control of 69
  root 39
  as tool of seduction 322
betting
  on midgets 230
bicycles
  as criminal elements 69
birdshit 184
Bishop, Bronwyn 242
black eyes
  and bum steers 154
blind man
  and nude nun 417
blondes

on everything 349–55
blowflies
curried 315
eating habits of 306
boomerangs
stationary 71
bore water
pigging out on 311
Boston strangler 342
bowling balls
and mistaken identity 70–1
breasts
as work assets 297
breathaliser(s) 279
for nuns 418
bricklaying
in the Sahara 290–1
brothel(s)
and coloured lights 92
and French tradition 38–9
and genetic inheritance 118–19
as soup kitchen 111
brown nosing 123
bull fighting
in cafés 395–6
bulls
cross-eyed 187–8
and erections 50
for heifers 188
bush logic 104–5
butlers
and cross dressing 150
and custard 151
and farting 156

camping
and Irish mosquitoes 103
cancer
terminal 144
cannibals
and missionary stew 417
canon
dirty old 417
caravan
detached 281–2
cardinals
adulterous 410–11
carpentry
and Irish literature 89–90
castles in the air
renting 445
Catholics
and raffles 36
cat(s)
home burial for 190
Irish impersonations of 95–6
milk saucer for 188–9
named George 189–90
woofing 189
cattle duffers
and courtesy 52
cattle duffing 280–1
cemeteries
grave responsibilities 97
and headstones 100
chair-a-plane
smash up 332–3
chambermaid
Japanese 306
chicken(s)
see also roosters
three-legged 54–5
chicken farmers
novice 294
chicken soup
Jewish penicillin 117
childhood
men's return to 447
Chinese
grocers 72
military protocol 72–3
on the moon 135–6
Christ
and the Easter holiday 410
and leaky feet 420
in New York 407–8
view from the Cross 409
Christian Brothers
time for children 398
Christianity
conversion to 130
cigarettes
see also smoking
pissed on 54
circumcision 129
of exhaust pipe 412–13
Clinton, Hillary
mechanical skill 244
and puppies 243
clitoris
how to find 371
coal dust

on the penis 370
coconuts
and cow's milk 52
combine harvester
to keep the hands off 369
Communion 167
conception 166
condom(s)
for daffodils 300–1
to duck the issue 193
as sleeping bags 409
softwear 454
waterproof 105
wired up 365
confession
as bragging 130
confessional
as dunny 396
convicts
Jewish 113–14
corgis
groin-loving 199–200
Corinthians
letters to the 320–1
cornflakes
and discipline 169
corpse(s)
gutted 213
courtesy
extreme in pregnancy 432
cow dung
as cold shower 367
cows
seduction of 276
crap
the morals of 238
crematoriums
up in smoke 457
cricket
as a rain dance 285–6
crocodile shoes
how to catch 190–1
cruises
safety procedure 400–1
cucumbers
in preference to men 306–7
currency exchange
and fluctuation 112–13
custard
shark-infested 312
Dad 'n' Dave 31–46
daiquiri
hickory 436–7
dangle
bits which 448
deafness
selective 389
death
by doctor's orders 107
by holiday 101
death notice(s)
flattering 457
Jewish 116
deathbed scenes 119–20
definitions
legal 280
deodorant 329
diaphragms
gold 131
diesel fitters
head jobs for 301–2
dingoes
control of 191
floral tributes to 207
meals 207
and self-examination 33
divorce
not in front of the children 270
dog(s)
and intelligence tests 60–1
man's best meal 364
meowing 192
movie buff 192
names of 167–8
through windows 149
vicious 94
dog food
habit-forming 309–10
dominoes
Kerry Packer's 90
droughts
and sexual favours 51
drowning
in beer 321
drugs
Irish painkillers 96
drunkenness
on stage 386
duck shooting
for the dogs 101
dunnies

and implosion 34, 41–2
locks on 159–60

ear(s)
as handles 80
lend me your 359–60
to piss out of 432–3
Earp, Wyatt
on keyboards 383–4
education
benefits of 173
eggs
disadvantages of 307
and orifices 45
electric chair
shocking death 147–8
elephants
bottled 193
eggs 37
Elliott, John
crocodile food 313
employment figures 106
emus 194, 195
engineers
and broom handling 293
and surveying 293
English
food 76
horse sense 76–7
husbands 76
introduction 151–2
IQ 74, 75
stockmen 75
erections
and the bull treatment 50
and fishing 42
and five bells 37–8
and personal growth 37
explosions
and dunnies 34, 41–2
eye(s)
glass 360–1
test 441–2

fairies
belief in 455–6
family court
divorce settlements 269
fancy dress
toffee apple 361–2
farmers
and family roots 51
and lotteries 50
and metrication 51–2
farting 155–6
and horses 202
and the Queen 156–7
in pantihose 156
in turn 152
water buffalo 435
fencing
barbwire 223
fish
out of water 195
fishermen
Irish 87
fishing
and erections 42
flashers
football 141
flat food 439
flux
and plicks 113
Fokker
transported insult 84
football(ers/s)
and fumbling Swans 211–12
gridiron 87–8
and mallee roots 213
foreplay
Tasmanian 140
friends
influential 228–30
frog(s)
in blenders 312
talking 195–6
wide-mouthed 196–7
funeral(s) 456
and false teeth 97
golfing 213–14
and grooming 108–9
notices 99

galley slaves
working conditions of 294–5
gambling
on piles 224–6
on testicular weight 226–7
goanna(s)
and haulage skills 62
as ventriloquist 390–1
God

images of 166
not black or white 425
and the Post Office 418–19
goldfish
mucking around 195
golf
between holes 215
at St Andrew's 214–15
golf balls
in holes 215–16
and suction 223
golf course
for playing around 464–5
golfer(s)
adulterous 217–18
celibate 217
equipment 218–19
grip 219–20
novice 214
wooden-hearted 372–3
golfing
robots 220–2
gorilla(s)
mating with Poms 197–8
suits 200
graffiti
Italian delicacy 310
grandma 455
Greiner, Nick
bad press 244
tattooed 244–5
greyhound buses 110
guided tours
passed hotels 326
guillotine
Irishman on the 377–8
guinea pigs
stuck up 197
gynaecologist
just checking 435

halitosis
and life expectancy 456
ham
for rabbis 115
Hamlet
with the Bendigo Players 386
hands
off 157
hangovers
and memory loss 96
Hart, Gary
hands off 248
Hawke, Bob
and C words 252–3
and God 246–7
and lying 248
and the ultimate sacrifice 247
headmaster 172
and peanuts 177
heart bypass
and sex 440–1
Heaven
sending fire from 407
heifers
and mispronunciation 51
heir apparent 206
Hewson, John
negatively geared 248
Hill, David
as God 250
and oral gratification 249–50
Hinze, Russ
tied up 371–2
Hitler, Adolf
no more Mr Nice Guy 248–9
holidays
in disguise 71
homosexuality
in the Army 148
honeymooners
like rabbits 343
mealtimes 313
physical dimensions of 342–3
horse(s)
cricketing 201–2
races 231, 232
Hussein, Saddam
and the magic mirror 250–1

initiation ceremonies
and alcohol 82–3
innuendo
as suppository 385
insurance
false claims 115
insurance companies
amalgamation of 295–6
insurance fraud
Irish 86
intercourse
see also individual entries

alcohol-induced 77–8
in an arresting position 278–9
better than pork 406
bi-sexual 345
and cars 127–8
catty 339–40
with clean nose 345
with contortionist 330–1
corridor 340
at the doctor's 333–4
with dry biscuits 446
and the English 73
free 333
with gardeners 341
navvy style 343–4
in plimsolls 334–5
positions 131
and shearers 46
sheepish 132, 133
and smoking 431
with speechless mother-in-law 346
with your ex 341
introduction service
Irish 111
IQ levels
and brain surgery 103–4
and immigration 101
IQ tests
and thongs 98
IRA
and heads for heights 89
Irish
birthmarks 91
cleaning lady 91
language 102
phonetic spelling 90–1
prison law 91
sporting prowess 96
translation of German 92
Italians
and monkeys 83

Jesus Christ
Irish murder case 99
Jewish
American princesses 131
appearance 115–16
business sense 123
grandmothers 114
mothers 114–15
job descriptions
in Heaven and Hell 457–8
jokes
by numbers 155
JPs
drunk 270–1
judges
character sketches of 273–6
jury
Irish 112
duty, late for 272–3
system, challenges to 92

kangaroo balls
on toast 305
Keating, Paul
as God 251
mistaken for pig 255–6
as raffle prize 252
as reconstituted fart 251–2
rented cemetery plot 254
sleeping alone 253–4
and the vegetables 254–5
kissing hand 72–3
Kissinger, Henry
as marriage broker 256–7
kleptomania 444
koala
tea 59–60

language
spoken in Hell 126–7
Last Supper
bill for 415–16
Lawrence, D.H.
quoted 147
lawyers
and the Devil 265–6
in Heaven 263–5, 460
and hot air 266–8
and rats 268
and sharks 268–9
legs
uneven 448
levitation
and sex 153–4
Liberal MPs
and blown deposits 239
lift shaft
fall into 396–7
light bulb
surreal change 385

lions
  eating tealadies 204
  and tame sex 205, 206
litigation
  Jewish 117
Lone Ranger
  fetch a posse 382
lotteries 80–2
lottery win
  and God 118

MacPherson, Elle
  and economics 292
  shipwrecked 338–9
manhole cover
  change for a 322–3
martinis
  in the desert 323–4
massage parlour
  lost hat 341
mastication
  of underwear 136
masturbation
  and bank managers 289
mathematics 121–2
Melbourne Cup 231–2
memory
  loss of 430, 451, 453–4
  selective 331
mermaids
  fishing for compliments 158–9
mice
  as meals-on-wheels 462–3
migration
  reverse 74
milkmen
  sleeping with 175–6
monastery
  chanting 423–4
  two-word order 416
monkey(s)
  in space 287–8
  with testicles in beer 391–2
mourning
  in tennis blacks 456

Napoleon 257
nativity play 171
navel(s)
  as plugs 165
  screw, to attach bum 379–81
Nazis
  discourteous 121
nephews
  naming of 84
New Zealanders
  IQ of 132, 133
Nile, Reverend
  sermon notes 410
Nullarbor
  bridge over 101
nuns
  bathing the impure 461–2
  and brothers 121
  and gorillas 405–6
  in Minis 408
  naughty 415
nutmeg grater
  blind violence 385
nymphomaniacs
  striving to please 296

olives
  jar of martini 310
Onassis
  and marriage 137
onions
  and penis size 366
optometrists
  Irish 109
oral sex
  and diamonds 371
  religious payment for 413–15
orgasm
  before death 329
  faked 335
  and moaning 125–6
  in Mosman 335

Packer, Kerry
  and dominoes 90
paint, water-based 424
parachutes
  and backpacks 237
  Irish 110
  and lawyers 266
Parkinson's
  for hand jobs 454
parrots
  in clerical collars 185–6
  frozen 183–4
  immoral 107

and peckers 186–7
shipwrecked 184–5
Paterson, Banjo
poetic genius of 459–60
Pearly Gates
doing deals at 465–6
penguin(s)
as dwarf nuns 421–2
entertaining 203
habits 202–3
identifying features 202
penis(es)
air holes 373
colour co-ordinated 367–8
forgettable 339
green 338
Hong Kong Dong 434
and hot buttered toast 431
how to identify 366
as perky little copulator 344
size of 174
square 433
pianos
and sex 176–7
pigeon post 93–4
pigs
see also policemen
on bikes 56–7
and cricket 68
and servicing 45–6
three-legged 55–6
Pinocchio
as Son of God 463–4
piss off 322
pizza
Irish-size 102–3
poker
for dogs 192–3
police batons 285
police force
Irish recruits 99
policemen
see also pigs
political one-liners 241
politicians
as bananas 235
brains 242
and chaos 238–9
children's view of 236
dead 226
and doorknocking 241
and Easter bunnies 246
as fools 235
sheepish New Zealand 240–1
poodles
retailing 466–7
pools
in depth 277–8
Pope, the
and crème de menthe 399
('s) wife 124–5
porpoises
immoral 203–4
Porsches
and erections 35–6
hand-painted 290
and penis size 193–4
and towropes 282
postmen
retirement benefits 128–9
pregnancy 109
beauty of 174
dressing for 324
as joint responsibility 44
threat of 331
priapism
and worms 35
priest(s)
sex life of 439–40
prison brutality
and role playing 276–7
prostitutes
inexperienced 131
and political babies 239–40
psychiatrists
dirty drawings 445–6
guarded courtesy 445
listening skills 443–4
questions 442, 443
tense 447
punt
as rhyming slang 111
put down
the ultimate 271

Quasimodo 78–9
Quayle, Dan
IQ of 257
mistaken identity 245–6
Queenslanders
IQ of 134–5
quiz shows

Irish 90

rabbits
as bum wipers 183
and English habits 41
rabbit trappers
and entrails 49–50
racists 141–4
radar speed traps 179
rape
by a bunch 438
and forgery 289
Scottish 140
wharfie-style 299
razor blade
swallowed 435
Reagan, Ronald
abused in the snow 258
Red Cross
donations to 129
Red Riding Hood
gobble, gobble, gobble 379
reincarnation
as a dog's turd 67
relations
habits of 74–5
religious conversion
Irish 100
reputation
acquisition of 86
rescue mission 94–5
retirement village(s)
sexual services in 452–3
Richardson, Graham
and Keating's trousers 255
rissoles
camel shit 314
robin redbreast
the bishop 409
Robin Hood
and the wardrobe 379
Rogers Roy
just a song 381–2
roller skates
for adultery 458
roosters
see also chickens
rampant 57–9
and *rigor mortis* 172
rottweilers
and faked orgasm 335
and social workers 287
Russian
business sense 136
seduction 137

Sampson
from Jerilderie 468–71
sandwiches
raspberry jam 308
savoir faire
keeping it up 153
sciatica
and leg pulling 117
Scottish
lunch orders 137–8
scars 138–40
seance(s)
only bull 465
seduction
taken lying down 340
sermons
for another man's wife 411
service stations
and sex 134
sex
time for 170
shearers
and indecent members 46
and personal hygiene 47–8
and sheeps' names 47
sheep
as sex objects 53–4
shoe repairs
time taken 297–8
shopkeepers
Jewish 120
shopping
and sex 35
shop signs 120
shotgun wedding 336
shower
to stand up in 400
Smarties
as contraceptive 437–8
snake bite
outback cure 436
socks
smelly 93
speaker
gavel flinging 236
specimens

as insults 86–7
speech impediment
childish 165
and punting 223–4
and religious discrimination 88
speech-making
and sex 152
speed
and acid 166–7
speeding
Irish 97
and presumed adultery 278
spelling
bugger all 175
and horse piss 44–5
spinsters
and roosters 333
spittoons
hit and miss 370
spoonerisms
and sugar bowls 277
Stalin
and resurrection 135
statues
and pigeons 149–50
stockmen
in history 49
Stone, John
inarticulate scab 258–9
stowaway
on Manly Ferry 331–2
Stradivarius
the painter 388
Superman 242–3
swagmen
and publican 48
Sydney Harbour Bridge
overnight sensation 292

tall poppy syndrome 259–60
tampons
and freedom 85
and pygmies 447
Tarzan 285
dinner for 307–8
tattoos
penis 365–6
taxation department 119
taxidermists
and drovers 298
taxidermy
and the English 74
taxi drivers
and Irish passengers 105–6
tea
koala 59–60
telephones
to God 122
Texas ranchers 324
timber
theft of 411–12
Titanic verses
Rusty Salmon's 384
thermometer
rectal 434
thongs
as found items 69
Thor
and pithed 461
toilet(s)
see also dunnies
brush, as bum wiper 364
facilities 92
and refreshment 40
tomato(es)
sauce for Christmas 314
shortage of 83–4
Tomb
of the Unknown Warrior 120
train(s)
crashes 40–1
stop, Gladstone 397–8
tree fellers
Irish 106–7
trucks
mating 320
turpentine
as horse medicine 201
twins
as optical illusions 319–20

underpants
checking contents of 453
urinals
and arsenals 291–2
musical 161
urinating competitions 363
urine
analysis for beer 325
sample 429

Venetian disease 437

ventriloquists
and mistaken identity 108
vibrator
recharged 441
vice
captain 171
Vietnam
veteran 178–9
war 158
virgin(s)
Irish 110
sheepish 206–7
Virgin Mary
and mixed marriage 86
and son's career 461
vote
the right to 66

wardrobe
a boy named 177–8
water
drinking fire 313
level for ducks 399–400
wedding(s)
Jewish 115
nights and horsing around 34
Wellington boots 93
wharfies
on compo 299, 300
visitors' book 299
Wilde, Oscar
not insatiable 385
wishes
a chest of 170
worms
matrimonial 336–7

yak
I'm all right 422–3